AF182275

AUSTRALIA: ECONOMIC, POLITICAL AND SOCIAL ISSUES

AUSTRALIA: ECONOMIC, POLITICAL AND SOCIAL ISSUES

LACHLAN J. WILLIAMS AND
ETHAN N. LEE
EDITORS

Nova Science Publishers, Inc.
New York

For permission to use material from this book please contact us:
Telephone 631-231-7269; Fax 631-231-8175
Web Site: http://www.novapublishers.com

LIBRARY OF CONGRESS CATALOGING-IN-PUBLICATION DATA

Australia : economic, political & social issues / [edited by] Lachlan J. Williams and Ethan N. Lee.
p. cm.
ISBN 978-1-60456-856-1 (hbk.)
1. Australia--Social conditions. 2. Australia--Economic conditions. 3. Australia--Social policy. 4. Australia--Economic policy. I. Lee, Ethan N. II. Williams, Lachlan J.
HN843.5.A884 2008
306.0994--dc22

2008025940

Published by Nova Science Publishers, Inc. ; New York

CONTENTS

PREFACE

Australia's economic, political and societal issues have become major points of interest to countries all over the globe. This new book presents in-depth analysis of such issues such as foreign policy, political reform, and overall economic developments.

Chapter 1 - Some sociologists and higher education scholars view theory and empiricism as separate worlds, arguing that one has nothing to offer the other. This work proposes that the boundaries between theoretical conceptions and empirical realities have a transilient fluidity, that one domain informs the other. Hence this study explores connections between three theoretical conceptions of the university, Weber's bureaucracy, Ritzer's McUniversity and Clark's Entrepreneurial University and the leadership style of executives in Australian public universities. Information about executives' leadership style was gathered from case study interviews with seventeen executives from four Australian public universities. This work found that at each of the case study universities leaders' views of their university comprised elements of these three conceptions of the university, none of the three conceptions of the university were actualized in a 'pure' form. This work also identifies four different leadership styles used by these executives: entrepreneurial transformers, facilitators, bureaucrats and collegial leaders. It finds some connections between leaders' theoretical conceptions of the university and how they led their universities. However, the connections between theory and empiricism were complex, reflexive ones rather than unidirectional causes and effects.

Chapter 2 - Recent years have seen growing interest in research and development (R&D) in Australia. Unfortunately, little is know about the contributions of R&D to Australian economic performance. Even less is known about the contributions of university R&D. This paper examines the impact of both university and non-university R&D on output levels in Australia, using data for Australian states, for the period 1979 to 2003. Both Cobb-Douglas and Translog versions of the production function are estimated. The results indicate that while both types of R&D make important contributions to the generation of output, not all university R&D has a positive effect. Pure basic and applied university R&D both have had a positive effect on regional output. However, this is in sharp contrast to the impact of strategic basic and experimental R&D, which are shown to have a negative effect on output.

Chapter 3 – The paper is divided into four sections. The first section introduces the Queensland prison system that may provide a useful context for non-Australian readers. Recent trends in the Queensland prison population are examined in the second section. General trends are also examined in gender and race contexts, examining the composition of prison population. An extended examination of possible reasons for those trends comprises the third section of the paper before the final section, which argues for increased support in prison research. At the outset it must be emphasized that this paper is largely based on data from secondary sources such as the Queensland Corrective Services and the ABS. Relying extensively on secondary data is usually problematic, and, for example, different data sources may vary in their ways of operationalizing concepts and operational definitions may not be sufficiently specified (see Jupp, 1989; Riedel, 2000; May, 2001). Therefore, any conclusions drawn in this paper are tentative and require further investigation.

Chapter 4 - Why do political activists operating in similar polities experience different degrees of success in pursuit of the same strategy? What role do institutions play in shaping the success of activists strategies? This chapter considers these questions through a study of feminist activists engagement with the bureaucracy in three parliamentary democracies – Australia, Canada and the United Kingdom. It analyses why certain Australian feminists have had a relatively high degree of success with a 'femocrat' strategy, compared to counterparts in Canada and the UK. The chapter argues that internal institutional factors as well as the interaction between institutions and political parties best explain this outcome. The argument advanced in the chapter illustrates not only the importance of taking institutions seriously in explaining political activists' strategies, but also the need to pay careful attention to the differences between similar institutions across polities and variations in the political contexts in which they operate.

Chapter 5 - Over the past few decades the direction of Australia's exports has moved away quite rapidly from its traditional trading partners to embrace Asia as an important export destination. Within Asia, South Asia has become an increasingly important destination for Australia's exports, and within South Asia, India has been the largest market in the region over the past two decades. During 1997, India was Australia's 12th largest export market, up from 24th in 1977. Bilateral trade with India reached A\$2.33 billion in 1997 (with Australian exports valued at A\$1.69 billion and imports at A\$0.64 billion), an increase of 38.1 percent over the previous year. With few exceptions since 1977, the balance of trade has always been in Australia's favour. India is likely to be of special economic significance for Australia in the future, especially by serving as a market for Australia's exports, with the ability to supply its products at a comparative cost advantage to similar Indian products.

Chapter 6 - Broome occupies a tiny portion of coastline in the Kimberley region of far North Western Australia. From an aerial perspective, the town spreads seductively below, clusters of single story buildings partially hidden amongst vigorous leafy green. Broome lies vulnerably sandwiched between the deep milky aqua of salt-laden Roebuck Bay to the West and the encroaching creep of ochre desert to the East, where horizontal terrain stretches hundreds of kilometres and melts into hazy horizon. During the wet months, this inland desert country is abundant with flora and carries a tropical guise. A prehistoric river cuts through this desert, a raging, cleansing flood for some months of the year gouging gorges of awesome proportions. In the dry season, the Fitzroy River forms placid, dark pools. It eventually empties into the shallows of King Sound, near Derby, to the North of Broome. This river has sustained human existence far longer than the pearls, palm trees, exotic attractions, cattle stations and promise of desert adventure that draws tourists to the modern Kimberly region.

The Australian Aboriginal children featured in this chapter live in the inland desert region, several hundred kilometres East of Broome, within a tiny community eighty kilometres off the main highway. The area is undeniably beautiful, with a deep, glowing redness of sand reflected in layered hues of the surrounding rocky hills. Dominant colours change from soft, dusky pinks of morning to a deep glowing rust preceding a sub-tropical downpour, when the greens of wet season growth complement the sand. The guarding hills, crowned with balls of spinifex, feature distinctly even plateaus as if some mythical giant has passed over with a lawnmower. Temperatures range from oppressive, steamy hot during the wet season to warm sunny days and cool nights over the dry months. The children's home location will be referred to as "The Community".

The author's connection with The Community is from working there in his first year as a teacher a few years ago.

Blinded by early career enthusiasm and culture shock he spent too much time floundering with emerging teaching philosophy. Perhaps, the potential value of life-world knowledge was overshadowed by focus on curricular detail and striving for personal satisfaction as a teacher.

Chapter 7 – Many Australians struggle to articulate their identity in clear-cut terms. Nevertheless, they wear the badge of citizenship proudly and have a sense of belonging that seems unquestioned. They also display nationalism with great enthusiasm whenever the opportunity presents, such as at the 2000 Olympics held in Sydney or sporting events like cricket's World Cup. The difficulty in 'answering the question' of Australian citizenship seems to occur because of the continuing pioneering status of its population profile. There always seems to be a new frontier to negotiate. Since European settlement just over two hundred years ago the population has been continually re-profiling. The gradual shift from European dominance to embrace more aspects of its geographic positioning in the world has not diminished the 'old world' links so much as embellished them. The nation's people are still writing the script for Australian identity. Perhaps the difficulty of finding appropriate descriptors is best deflected by the personal qualities that are more clearly identifiable in Australian citizenship. Strongly embedded in the ideals of democracy, being an Australian in the twenty-first century brings expectations of a good life; a just life with access to high quality resources that protect personal freedoms and choice. The environment exists for these to happen. Learning to be an Australian citizen is about making the 'right' decisions.

Chapter 8 - Australian NGOs have in recent years attempted to engage with the aid effectiveness debate through joint research and publication of the NGO Effectiveness Framework. At the same time the wider aid world has begun to approach aid effectiveness more broadly, with an emerging agreement that aid effectiveness is the result of a complex set of processes and interrelationships. This is in line with the findings from the Australian research. In response to these emerging themes some Australian NGOs are now experimenting with alternative organizational forms and different ways of doing development in order to try to promote more effective aid. Some challenges remain however, including the questions of how to assess effectiveness from the perspective of the beneficiaries of aid, how to best measure effective aid and what reliable evidence we have about the effectiveness of one aid interventions over another? As NGOs in Australian continue to contract with the Australian Government and other donors for aid delivery they continue to have to find space to address these debates and to challenge the more restricted views of those donors.

Chapter 9 - The Commonwealth of Australia and the United States are very close allies. Australia shares similar cultural traditions and values with the United States and has been a treaty ally since the signing of the Australia-New Zealand-United States (ANZUS) Treaty in 1951. Australia made major contributions to the allied cause in both the first and second World Wars and has been a staunch ally of Britain and the United States in their conflicts.

Under the former Liberal government of John Howard, Australia invoked the ANZUS treaty to offer assistance to the United States after the attacks of September 11, 2001, in which 22 Australians died. Australia was one of the first countries to commit troops to U.S. military operations in Afghanistan and Iraq. In October 2002, a terrorist attack on Western tourists in Bali, Indonesia, killed more than 200 persons, including 88 Australians and seven Americans. A second terrorist bombing, which killed 23, including four Australians, was carried out in Bali in October 2005. The Australian Embassy in Jakarta, Indonesia, was also bombed by members of Jemaah Islamiya (JI) in September 2004.

Kevin Rudd, of the Labor Party, was elected prime minister on November 24, 2007. While Rudd has fulfilled an election promise to draw down Australian military forces in Iraq and has reversed Australia's position on climate change — by signing the Kyoto protocols — relations with the United States remain very close. Rudd has initiated a review of Australia's defense policy that is expected to reaffirm Australia's traditional view that the United States is a key source of stability in the Asia-Pacific region.

The previous Howard Government and the U.S. signed a bilateral Free Trade Agreement (FTA) and negotiated a Treaty on Defense Trade Cooperation that would require Senate ratification to come into force. Despite the strong strategic ties between the United States and Australia, there have been some signs that the growing economic importance of China to Australia may influence Australia's external posture on issues such as Taiwan. It is likely that Australia would not support a policy of containment of China if the United States sought this.

Australia plays a key role in promoting regional stability in Southeast Asia and the Southwest Pacific. Australia has led peace-keeping efforts in the Asia-Pacific region, including East Timor and the Solomon Islands, and has supported U.S. efforts and worked closely with key regional states in the war against terrorism in Southeast Asia. These actions demonstrate Australia's resolve to promote stability in Southeast Asia and the South Pacific. Australia has also worked closely with Indonesia to counter terrorism in Southeast Asia.

In: Australia: Economic, Political and Social Issues
Editors: Lachlan J. Williams and Ethan N. Lee
ISBN: 978-1-60456-856-1

Chapter 1

AUSTRALIAN UNIVERSITY LEADERS: AGENTS OF THE MCUNIVERSITY, ENTREPRENEURIAL TRANSFORMERS, OR BUREAUCRATS?

Deanna de Zilwa*

Sociology, School of Political Science,
Criminology and Sociology, University of Melbourne,
Victoria, 3010, Australia

ABSTRACT

Some sociologists and higher education scholars view theory and empiricism as separate worlds, arguing that one has nothing to offer the other. This work proposes that the boundaries between theoretical conceptions and empirical realities have a transilient fluidity, that one domain informs the other. Hence this study explores connections between three theoretical conceptions of the university, Weber's bureaucracy, Ritzer's McUniversity and Clark's Entrepreneurial University and the leadership style of executives in Australian public universities. Information about executives' leadership style was gathered from case study interviews with seventeen executives from four Australian public universities. This work found that at each of the case study universities leaders' views of their university comprised elements of these three conceptions of the university, none of the three conceptions of the university were actualized in a 'pure' form. This work also identifies four different leadership styles used by these executives: entrepreneurial transformers, facilitators, bureaucrats and collegial leaders. It finds some connections between leaders' theoretical conceptions of the university and how they led their universities. However, the connections between theory and empiricism were complex, reflexive ones rather than unidirectional causes and effects.

* Email: ddezilwa@unwired.com.au

Introduction

Australian public universities are currently subjected to a myriad of environmental pressures. Some pressures are economic: intensified levels of competition in global student, staff and research funding markets, declining levels of public funding and increasing operating costs from the massification of student cohorts (increasing numbers and diversity of students), rising salary and infrastructure costs and costs of compliance with accountability measures set by regulatory authorities. These economic pressures have a profound impact on the university as an organization posing significant challenges for universities and their academic units to adapt to this situation and on the social and cultural identity and values of academics (faculty). Other studies have explored these issues (de Zilwa, 2006; Harman, 2005; Marginson, 2006; Meek, 2002, 2003) so this study has a different focus. It explores how executives[1] in Australian universities deal with this situation.

This study has three objectives. First, it seeks to discover how Australian university leaders conceive their universities as organizations. Do these leaders view their university as a Weberian bureaucracy, as Ritzer's McUniversity, or as Clark's Entrepreneurial University (Clark, 2004; Ritzer, 1998, 2006; Roth and Wittich, 1978)? Second, how do these leaders conceive their role in leading and managing their universities? Third, is there any association between how leaders conceive their university and how they approach their leadership and management role? In précis this study's research methods entail answering its research questions by contrasting the three theoretical conceptions of the university with empirical data (interviews with Australian university leaders); a more detailed account of research methods follows.

This chapter has three parts. First the three conceptions of the university are introduced; this is done at some length for the benefit of readers who are unfamiliar with this work. These theories are not critiqued in this section of the chapter because this is not the task at hand, analysis occurs later. Second notes are provided about how the interviews with the university leaders were conducted. Third is the data analysis section of this study. This analysis contrasts empirical findings with theoretical perspectives evaluating the relevance and explanatory power of these theories in relation to the study's empirical findings. Finally conclusions and reflections on the study are made.

Three Conceptions of the University

The three conceptions of the university chosen for this study were selected because they are well known and provide diverse representations of the university. Each conception of the university reflects a particular political position, a worldview that privileges certain norms and values over others. This work does not offer a normative view; it does not endorse any of these conceptions of the university. Instead it seeks to discover whether Australian university leaders support any of these conceptions of the university and whether these leaders view their role as aligned with any of these conceptions of the university.

[1] Executives refers to vice-chancellors, deputy and pro-vice chancellors, directors and general managers, sometimes known as presidents in United States universities.

WEBER – THE UNIVERSITY AS A BUREAUCRACY

Weber's work spans an enormous gamut of empirical and theoretical topics in Sociology. Our primary interest is his work on bureaucracy, authority, and rationality. Weber observed that many public and private organizations are bureaucracies including political structures, the military, judiciary, banks, commercial firms, schools and universities. Indeed Weber argued that universities were typical bureaucracies. Therefore before examining some of Weber's specific comments on the university as a bureaucracy it is helpful to examine how Weber defined the characteristics of a bureaucracy and how he interpreted its advantages and disadvantages. As with many theorists Weber's work has been interpreted in vastly different ways by various scholars. Classical organizational theorists 'read' Weber as advocating the virtues of bureaucracy whereas some contemporary sociologists and organizational theorists (Edles and Applerouth, 2005 pp.181-182; Morgan, 2006 pp.17-18, 294, 371-372) argue that Weber viewed bureaucracies as dehumanizing organizations that denied people freedom, individuality and led to the homogenization of society. Because of this debate surrounding how Weber's work on bureaucracy should be interpreted this work uses Weber's actual texts rather than later commentaries on his work[2].

Weber's famous essay on bureaucracy was included in *Economy and Society*, a work published posthumously in 1925. Two authoritative translations of this work are (Henderson and Parsons, 1947; Roth and Wittich, 1978). Weber stated that a bureaucratic organization functions in the following manner:

> There is the principle of official *jurisdictional areas,* which are generally ordered by rules, that is by laws or administrative regulations.
>
> This means:
>
> (1) The regular activities required for the purposes of the bureaucratically governed structure are assigned as official duties.
>
> (2) The authority to give the commands required for the discharge of these duties is distributed in a stable way and is strictly delimited by rules concerning coercive means, physical, sacerdotal, or otherwise which may be placed at the disposal of the officials.
>
> (3) Methodical provision is made for the regular and continuous fulfillment of these duties and for the exercise of the corresponding rights; only persons who qualify under general rules are employed. ...
>
> 11. The principles of *office hierarchy* and of channels of appeal (*Instanzenzug*) stipulate a clearly established system of super- and subordination in which there is a supervision of the lower offices by the higher ones. ....
>
> 111. The management of the modern office is based upon written documents (the "files"), which are preserved in their original or draft form, and upon a staff of subaltern officials and scribes of all sorts. ...
>
> 1V. Office management, at least all specialized office management – and such management is distinctly modern – usually presupposes training in a field of specialization. ...
>
> V. When the office is fully developed, official activity demands the *full working capacity* of the official, irrespective of the fact that the length of his obligatory working hours in the bureau may be limited....

[2] I have used translations of Weber's texts because his original work was written in German and I do not read German.

> VI. The management of the office follows *general rules*, which are more or less stable, more or less exhaustive, and which can be learned. Knowledge of these rules represents a special technical expertise which the officials possess. It involves jurisprudence, administrative or business management.... (Roth and Wittich, 1978 pp.957-958).

Weber states that the bureaucratic office is a "vocation" that requires special training, is a full-time job, office holders are paid a salary but do not "own" the position which they occupy (Roth and Wittich, 1978 p.959). Weber notes that officials in bureaucracies are held in high esteem by others in their society because of their technical expertise (Roth and Wittich, 1978 p.960).

Weber's distinction between three ideal or pure types of authority[3] is integral to his conception of the bureaucratic organization. Weber identified three types of authority: rational-legal, traditional and charismatic. Rational-legal authority 'rests on a belief in the legality of enacted rules', traditional authority 'rests on an established belief in the sanctity of immemorial traditions and the legitimacy of those exercising authority under them', charismatic authority 'rests on devotion to the exceptional sanctity, heroism or exemplary character of an individual person, and of the normative patterns or order revealed or ordained by him' (Roth and Wittich, 1978 p.215). For Weber the bureaucratic organization was an exemplar of rational authority. According to Weber a monocratic bureaucracy (where power and authority is held by an individual) was a superior form of organization to a collegial form of organization (where power and authority is shared amongst a group) of people.

> Once fully established, bureaucracy is among those social structures which are the hardest to destroy. Bureaucracy is the means of transforming social action into rationally organized action. Therefore as an instrument of rationally organizing authority relations, bureaucracy was and is a power instrument of the first order for one who controls the bureaucratic apparatus. Under otherwise equal conditions, rationally organized and directed action (Gessellschaftshandeln) is superior to every kind of collective behavior (Massenhandeln) and also social action (Gemeinschaftshandeln) opposing it. Where administration has been completely bureaucratized, the resulting system of domination is practically indestructible (Roth and Wittich, 1978 p.987).

For Weber a bureaucratic organization was also an extremely efficient organization that was technically superior to other types of organization, its officials made informed, impartial decisions quickly.

> The decisive reason for the advance of bureaucratic organization has always been its purely *technical* superiority over any other form of organization. The fully developed bureaucratic apparatus compares with other organizations exactly as does the machine with the mechanical modes of production. Precision, speed, unambiguity, knowledge of the files, continuity, discretion, unity, strict subordination, reduction of friction and of material and personal costs – these are raised to the optimum point in the strictly bureaucratic administration, and especially in its monocratic form. As compared with all collegiate,

[3] Weber used the word herrschaft in the original text of *Economy and Society* to refer to why subordinates in an organization accept the authority of superiors. It is interesting to note that Parsons in his 1947 edition of *Economy and Society* translated herrschaft as legitimate authority , (Henderson and Parsons, 1947), p.297. Whereas in Roth's 1968 translation of *Economy and Society* Roth translates herrschaft as legitimate domination (Roth and Wittich, 1978), p.53 and p.212.

honorific, and avocational forms of administration, trained bureaucracy is superior on all these points. And as far as complicated tasks are concerned, paid bureaucratic work is not only more precise but, in the last analysis, it is often cheaper than even formally unremunerated honorific service (Roth and Wittich, 1978 pp.973-974).

Although Weber acknowledged the efficiency of a bureaucratic organization he also noted that a bureaucratic organization has a tendency of dehumanizing its officials and the people affected by its rules and decisions, he stated that bureaucracies operate 'without regard for persons':

> Bureaucracy develops the more perfectly, the more it is "dehumanized", the more completely it succeeds in eliminating from official business love, hatred, and all purely personal, irrational, and emotional elements which escape calculation. This is appraised as its special virtue by capitalism (Roth and Wittich, 1978 p.975).

Next some comments that Weber made about universities as bureaucracies are noted. Weber argued that universities play a key role in providing the training and specialized expertise for bureaucratic officials:

> Educational institutions on the European continent, especially the institutions of higher learning – the universities, as well as technical academies, business colleges, gymnasia, and other secondary schools –, are dominated and influenced by the need for the kind of "education" which is bred by the system of specialized examinations or tests of expertise (*Fachprufungswesen*) increasingly indispensable for modern bureaucracies (Roth and Wittich, 1978 p.999).

Especially pertinent to this work are Weber's comments that bureaucratic organizations such as universities tend to concentrate resources at the apex of their hierarchy, leading to a concentration of power and privileges:

> In the field of scientific research and instruction, the bureaucratization of the inevitable research institutes of the universities is also a function of the increasing demand for material means of operation. Liebig's laboratory at Giessen University was the first example of big enterprise in this field. Through the concentration of such means in the hands of the privileged head of the institute the mass of researchers and instructors are separated from their "means of production" in the same way as the workers are separated from theirs by the capitalist enterprises (Roth and Wittich, 1978 p.983).

Another example of the bureaucratization of the university for Weber related to the appointment of academics (faculty). Weber stated that "the freedom of science, scholarship and teaching" in a university certainly does not exist where appointment to a teaching post is made dependent on the possession –or simulation – of a point of view which is "acceptable in the highest circles" of church and state" (Shils, 1973 p.19). Weber remarked:

> Universities do not have it as their task to teach any outlook or standpoint which is either "hostile to the state" or "friendly to the state". They are not institutions for the inculcation of absolute or ultimate moral values. They analyse facts, their conditions, laws and interrelations; they analyse concepts, their logical presuppositions and content. They do not and they cannot

teach what should happen – since this is a matter of ultimate personal values and beliefs, a fundamental outlook, which cannot be "demonstrated" like a scientific proposition (Shils, 1973 p.21).

For Weber further evidence of the bureaucratization of universities is demonstrated by university leaders' desire to maximize the efficiency and productivity of academics' work. In a paper written in 1919, Weber mentions two signs of the bureaucratization of universities. First he notes that academics in United States Universities had "heavy" teaching loads (many hours of classes) and second that junior academics do not have tenure (contract staff could easily be dismissed or not have their contract renewed):

> In Germany the career of a scientist or scholar depends on his having private means, for it is extremely hazardous for a young scholar, who has no financial resources of his own, to expose himself to the conditions of an academic career... In the United States, on the contrary there, is a bureaucratic system in which the young man is paid from the very beginning – although moderately to be sure. Usually his salary barely corresponds to the wages of a not entirely unskilled labourer. Nevertheless, he begins with an apparently secure position, for he receives a definite salary. The rule is that like the German assistant, he may be dismissed, and he has to be ready for this should he fall short of expectations. However, this threat disappears if he packs the house" This threat of dismissal does not exist for the German Privatozent. Once he is appointed he remains permanently (Shils, 1973 pp.54-55).

> In America things are organized on a different principle. It is indeed in his earlier years that the assistant is heavily overburdened, precisely because he is *paid.* In a German department, for instance, a full professor will give a three hour course on Goethe and that is all – while the younger assistant is lucky if his assignment is 12 hours per week .... (Shils, 1973 p.55).

RITZER – THE MC UNIVERSITY

Ritzer a contemporary sociologist argues that the dominant paradigm of many modern societies is rationalization. For Ritzer, the fast food restaurant, Mc Donalds epitomizes this process of rationalization. Ritzer's Mc Donaldization thesis draws from Weber's concept of rationalization and his view that rationalized systems such as bureaucracies become "iron cages" restricting and controlling people (Weber, 1930). Ritzer initially outlined his McDonaldization thesis in an article published in 1983. Later he revised and extended this work (Ritzer, 1993, 1998, 2000, 2004, 2006). Ritzer stated:

> Mc Donaldization involves an increase in efficiency, predictability, calculability and control through the substitution of non-human for human technology. While undoubtedly bringing with it many positive developments, Mc Donaldization also involves a wide range of irrationalities, especially dehumanization and homogenization. It is these irrationalities of rationality (and associated problems) which represent the true heart of the McDonaldization thesis (Ritzer, 1998 p.vii).

Ritzer defines the four elements that he views as the primary means of attaining Mc Donaldization: efficiency, predictability, calculability and control in the following way.

Efficiency refers to the fastest means or optimum method of attaining a goal, 'for consumers, Mc Donalds offers the best available way to get from being hungry to being full' (Ritzer, 2004 p.12). Predictability refers to the assurance that a product or service will always be the same over time and in all places, that 'The Egg McMuffin in New York will be, for all intents and purposes, identical to those in Chicago and Los Angeles' (Ritzer, 2004 p.14). 'Calculability is an emphasis on the quantitative aspects of products sold (portion size, cost) and services offered (the time it takes to get the product). In McDonaldized systems, quantity has become equivalent to quality; a lot of something, or the quick delivery of it, means it must be good' (Ritzer, 2004 p.13). Control means programming and controlling peoples actions through non-human technology especially computers 'Mc Donalds has lines, limited menus, few options, customers do what management wants them to – eat quickly and leave' (Ritzer, 2004 p.15). The way McDonalds' employees perform tasks such as preparing hamburgers, cooking fries or pouring beverages is also regulated and controlled in work manuals and automatically by machines. Ritzer argues that the process of Mc Donaldization applies to many fields including universities, credit cards, Disney world, health care, travel, leisure and dieting (Ritzer, 2004 p.2; 2006). (Alfino, Caputo, and Wynward, 1998; Hartley, 1995; Hayes and Wynward, 2002; Parker and Jary, 1995) provide critiques of the McDonaldization thesis.

At the heart of Ritzer's conception of the McUniversity is the idea that the 'university can be conceived of as a means of educational consumption, one that allows students to consume educational services and eventually to obtain important "goods" – degrees and credentials' (Ritzer, 1998 p.151). According to Ritzer students and parents now have a consumerist orientation and expectations of universities, they want them to operate like their banks and fast food restaurants – to be conveniently located and to operate during convenient hours, they expect personnel to offer professional services, they want high quality products at low cost and are prepared to comparison shop for the best deal (Ritzer, 1998 p.152). Ritzer adds that in addition universities now operate with less government funding (Ritzer, 1998 p.154). According to Ritzer prestigious and wealthy universities such as Harvard and Oxford are largely able to ignore these pressures but most universities are forced to try to adapt to this situation (Ritzer, 1998 pp.152-153). Ritzer contends that this later group of universities have become McUniversities – these universities have borrowed ideas on how to attract and process more students/customers and reduce operating costs by emulating business practices developed by McDonalds, shopping malls and banks (Ritzer, 1998 pp.152-159).

Ritzer identifies several strategies employed by McUniversities to attract more students, generate more revenue and reduce operating costs including opening satellite or branch campuses overseas, increased reliance on computers for online teaching, student administration, access to information for research and assignments (Ritzer, 1998 pp.154-155). According to Ritzer McUniversities deliver modularized, standardized curriculum to reduce costs, cheaper teaching assistants deliver the curriculum whilst assessment costs are reduced by using multiple choice tests that are graded by computers (Ritzer, 1998 pp.157-158). He observes that McUniversities increase management's control over academics (faculty), they no longer devise courses, their performance in teaching and research is evaluated often using quantifiable measures to ensure efficiency and quality control (Hartley, 1995 pp.411-412). Ritzer also notes that McUniversities like many corporations are heavily engaged in downsizing – reducing staff numbers and streamlining processes to make them more efficient and to reduce operating costs (Ritzer, 1998 p.155). Other theorists refer to these sorts of changes implemented by universities as strategies and actions associated with 'new public management' or managerialism (Considine and Painter, 1997; Currie, 2004; Meek, 2003).

More recently Ritzer has called for universities to resist McDonaldization suggesting that in order to attract more students thereby increasing their revenue, universities should emulate the spectacular aspects of the cathedrals of consumption (mega malls, Disney World, Las Vegas) (Ritzer, 2002 p.20). Ritzer observes that the cathedrals of consumption create spectacles to enchant and attract customers such as the simulation of Venice in Las Vegas(Ritzer, 2002 p.21). He also suggests that the cathedrals of consumption use implosion of space and time – 'the elimination of boundaries between extant phenomena so that they collapse in on one another' to attract more customers (Ritzer, 2002 pp.21-22). Ritzer acknowledges that universities are subject to regulatory and financial constraints that restrict their capacity to use implosion to attract more students (Ritzer, 2002 p.22). He recommends that universities can attract and retain more students, generating more income if they make their 'quotidian' (core activities of teaching and learning) spectacular (Ritzer, 2002 p.22-28). Ritzer suggests several ways universities can do this: reinstate small tutorials so that students have direct contact with their professors, ensure that star professors teach undergraduate classes, customize the curriculum and make it unpredictable, focus on the quality of teaching and research not on quantity (Ritzer, 2002 pp.26-30). In Ritzer's view if universities take such 'spectacular' actions they will overcome the 'irrationality of rationality', the dehumanizing affects of McDonaldization.

Clark – The Entrepreneurial University

Clark trained as a sociologist yet much of his work has focused on higher education. Clark argued that from the 1990s universities many countries faced an imbalanced situation where 'the demands on universities outran their capacity to respond' (Clark, 1998b p.6). He identified four particular demands on universities. First, universities have to teach more students and more different types of students (Clark, 1998b p.6). Second, more employers demand more university graduates trained for highly specialized occupations at different degree levels, in addition graduates require retraining throughout their professional careers (Clark, 1998b p.6). Third, universities are now subjected to pressures from a diverse range of stakeholders and are accountable to these groups for funding received, governments expect universities to do more at lower unit cost, industry also wants to see healthy returns for its investments (Clark, 1998b p.6). Fourth, expanding areas of knowledge require more resources, new research centers – departments always want more funding, personnel, students and space (Clark, 1998b p.6). Clark argued that national governments made some efforts to deal with these pressures that universities faced by trying to introduce system wide differentiation between universities but this strategy had limited success (Clark, 1998b p.8). Clark argued that in the past universities had been too passive that they had displayed inertia in the face of these pressures. According to Clark universities should take a more active entrepreneurial and innovative approach to survive these pressures (Clark, 1998b p.8). Clark defined an entrepreneurial university as a university that:

> Actively seeks to innovative how it goes about its business. It seeks to work out a substantial shift in organizational character so as to arrive at a more promising posture for the

> future. Entrepreneurial universities seek to become "stand-up" universities that are significant actors on their own terms. Institutional entrepreneurship can be seen as both a process and outcome (Clark, 1998a p.4).

In the 1990s Clark conducted case studies of how five European universities transformed themselves to become entrepreneurial universities: University of Warwick (England), University of Twente (Netherlands), University of Strathclyde (Scotland), Chalmers University of Technology (Sweden) and the University of Joensuu (Finland). Clark reported his findings from this study in *Creating Entrepreneurial Universities* published in 1998. In this work Clark identified five pathways that these universities took to attain entrepreneurial transformation: a strengthened steering core, an expanded development periphery, a diversified funding base, a stimulated academic heartland; and an integrated entrepreneurial culture (Clark, 1998a p.5). Clark's definitions of these pathways for entrepreneurial transformation follow. A strengthened steering core refers to universities enhancing their management's capacity to respond more quickly and with greater flexibility and focus to changing environmental demands, to refashion and change its courses, organisational structure and mode of operating (Clark, 1998a p.5). Clark also identified stronger line authority (between rectors – deans – department heads) as a key facet of this strengthened steering capacity (Clark, 1998b p.8). An expanded development periphery refers to increasing numbers of organizational units outside the boundaries of traditional academic departments engaged in outreach activities such as knowledge transfer, developing industrial partnerships, intellectual property, continuing education, fundraising, alumni and marketing, interdisciplinary project oriented research centers working on applied, practical research problems (Clark, 1998a p.6). The diversified funding base refers to widening the sources of revenue from independent (non-government) sources such as industrial firms, local governments, philanthropic foundations, royalty income from intellectual property, earned income from campus services, student fees and alumni (Clark, 1998a pp.6-7). This independent income, Clark called it second and third stream income gave universities greater autonomy. It reduced their dependence on government funding – which was being significantly reduced and was accompanied by stringent rules anyway. The stimulated academic heartland refers to academic units (departments, schools and faculties) becoming entrepreneurial units 'reaching more strongly to the outside with new programs and relationships and promoting third stream income' (Clark, 1998a p.7). Clark added that successful entrepreneurial transformation was dependent upon staff from academic units accepting stronger lines of management authority, these staff should also participate in central steering groups (Clark, 1998a p.7). The integrated entrepreneurial culture refers to the blending of traditional collegial academic cultures and values held by academics from academic units with the new entrepreneurial culture and values (Clark, 1998a p.7). Clark identified the rigidity and path-dependence of traditional academic cultures as one of the most significant obstacles to successful entrepreneurial transformation, arguing that universities needed to develop the capacity to embrace change ((Clark, 1998a p.7).

Clark revisited his work on the entrepreneurial transformation of universities in 2004 when he published *Sustaining Change in Universities: Continuities in Case Studies and Concepts*. In this later work, Clark revisited the European universities in his 1998 study adding fourteen additional case study universities from Latin America, Africa, Australia and the United States[4]. His primary research question for this later study was to discover how universities sustained the process of entrepreneurial transformation. Clark argued that the case study universities sustained entrepreneurial transformation when they attained a 'steady state of change' (Clark, 2003 p.111; 2004 p.178). For Clark universities attain a 'steady state of change' when they have three forms of dynamism – the 'dynamism of reinforcing interaction': where all units and people within the university are change oriented, the 'dynamism of perpetual momentum': where there is cumulative incremental change and the 'dynamism of collegial volition': where academics are committed to proactive change and willing to take risks to be self-reliant (Clark, 2003 pp.110-115; 2004 pp.90-95). It is interesting to note that Clark observes that when universities embark upon processes of entrepreneurial transformation the 'bureaucracy grows. But it is based on a change orientation very different from the old rule-enforcing, state-mandated bureaucracy that gets left behind. The old bureaucracy looked to the prevention of error; the new bureaucracy looks to the stimulation of initiative' (Clark, 2003 pp.108-109). Finally it is important to mention Clark's observation that not all universities will undertake entrepreneurial transformation, for some levels of inertia are too strong, others are too wary of the risks associated with new ventures, some believe that government will eventually increase funding, and in others there is active resistance to entrepreneurialism (Clark, 2004 pp.170-171).

Research Methods

I wanted to conduct an empirical inquiry to investigate whether Australian university leaders subscribed to any of the three conceptions of the university and whether there was any association between the leaders' perceived leadership style and their conception of the university. I had the opportunity to explore these questions when I interviewed leaders from four Australian public universities as part of a project investigating how academic units in Australian public universities were adapting to changing operating environments. The universities were: Monash University, Queensland University of Technology, Murdoch University and The University of Sydney[5]. The interviews were conducted between 1999 – 2002.

These four universities are very different. They are located in different states of Australia; vary in age, resource capacity, research activity and strengths, course profile and reputation amongst stakeholders including potential domestic and international students, graduate employers, firms and government agencies seeking research partners. Useful insights about the different attributes of Australian universities are provided by Marginson's typology of Australian public universities (Marginson and Considine, 2000 pp.189-202). Marginson identified five types of Australian public universities:

---

[4] Clark did not conduct these later case studies himself he used data collected by other researchers.

[5] There are 39 Australian public universities. Australia's universities are almost all public. Only 5 of the 44 institutions that are eligible for funds under the *Higher Education Funding Act 1988* are private and four of these receive limited funds. In 1999 there were 86 registered private higher education institutions. They are typically single-purpose institutions such as colleges of theology and business institutes. Together they account for approximately 3 per cent of higher education students (DEST 2002).

1. *Sandstones*

- the oldest universities in each state,
- with superior economic resources,
- capacity to attract leading academics,
- strong networks with alumni, professions, international scholars
- strong discipline based academic cultures
- do not need to be entrepreneurial

2. *Redbricks*

- second university in capital city[6],
- less traditionally academic than sandstones,
- more corporate and modernist than sandstones,

3. *Gumtrees*

- founded between the late 1960s and 1975,
- modern and nationalistic, reflected in their native tree plantings,
- inter-disciplinary,
- democratic governance and informal management style,
- weaker links to alumni and professions,
- school leavers second, third or fourth choice,

4. *Unitechs*

- formed from institutes of technology,
- weaker discipline based cultures than in pre-1986 universities,
- strong graduate professional cultures,
- teach occupational skills, strong links to industry,
- move quickly into new markets,
- innovative curriculum – new media, communications, creative industries,
- committed to mass access for students regardless of age, or background
- corporate, market oriented culture,

5. *New universities*

- developed from merger of expansion of Colleges of Advanced Education
- post 1986 establishment,
- a heterogeneous sub-sector that may eventually fragment,
- some are regional, rural universities with branch campuses in metropolitan cities

Source: (Marginson and Considine, 2000 pp.189-202).

[6] This applies to Monash and the University of New South Wales but not to the Australian National University.

Monash University, classified as a Redbrick by Marginson was founded in 1958; it was the second university in the southern state of Victoria, after The University of Melbourne. Monash's original campus is at Clayton, an industrial suburb situated approximately twenty kilometers south of the central business district of Melbourne. Monash University enrolls more students than any other Australian public university, approximately 50,000 students (DEST, 2005). Monash University has undertaken considerable global expansion with campuses in South Africa, Malaysia and centres in Prato, Italy and London in addition to its six domestic campuses (Monash University, 2000). Queensland University of Technology (QUT) classified as a Unitech by Marginson was established when the Queensland Institute of Technology was redesignated as a university in 1989, the following year it was amalgamated with the Brisbane College of Advanced Education. QUT's main campus is situated at Garden's Point within walking distance of Brisbane's central business district, providing easy access for mature age students to attend classes after work. Brisbane is the capital city of the state of Queensland. Murdoch University classified as a gumtree by Marginson is one of five universities in the state of Western Australia. Murdoch University was established in 1973 however it did not enroll students until 1975. Murdoch University has three campuses, its main campus – South Street, is fifteen kilometers from Perth, the capital city of the state of Western Australia and eight kilometers from the port of Fremantle. In 1996 Murdoch University opened its third campus at Rockingham, forty-five kilometers from Perth. Rockingham is an industrial area with many people from low socio-economic groups. Prior to Murdoch University establishing a campus at Rockingham few people in this area had the opportunity of attaining higher education. The University of Sydney was established in 1850, it is the oldest public university in Australia. Marginson classifies The University of Sydney as a sandstone university; it is a wealthy and prestigious institution with strong networks with its alumni, the professions, government and industry.

Semi-structured face-to-face interviews were conducted with seventeen vice chancellors, deputy and pro-vice chancellors and directors of planning and resources from these four universities[7]. These university leaders were asked questions about their university's strengths and weaknesses, to identify factors in its environment that were influencing its operations, to identify its major competitors in local and global research and teaching markets and to describe how they perceived themselves as leaders, how they thought their staff perceived their leadership style and how their leadership style influenced their approach to managing change. The interviews were tape-recorded; the tapes were transcribed, coded and analyzed using the software package ATLAS ti. The analysis identified patterns and trends within the data, points of similarity and contrast between the leader's responses to questions. More specifically the data analysis sought answers to three questions. First, how did each participant perceive their university, was their perception of their university aligned with Weber's bureaucratic university, Ritzer's Mc University or Clark's Entrepreneurial University, or did these leaders hold totally different views about their university? Second, how did these executives perceive their role as leaders? Third was there any association between the way an executive viewed their university and their chosen leadership style and approach to managing change?

[7] Sixteen of these seventeen executives were male and all were aged over 50.

LIMITATIONS OF THE STUDY

It is important to acknowledge that this is an exploratory study. Therefore the study's findings are tentative pronouncements rather than definitive statements. This study focuses on the traits and skills of university leaders. However if one uses an alternative definition of leadership, if leadership is defined as a relationship between leaders and followers then it can be argued that leaders may perceive themselves as using one leadership style and followers may view their leadership style in a different way. Those who support this later definition may view this study as limited because it does not report followers' perceptions of their leaders. For insights on how employees in these universities viewed their leaders, see (de Zilwa, 2006).

A further limitation is that this study's findings' refer only to this specific empirical context. Whilst a consequence of globalization is that universities situated in different countries now display greater levels of homogeneity in some facets of their operations. It is self-evident that universities situated in different countries are subjected to different state resource and regulatory policy that create heterogeneity in their operations. Therefore a similar study conducted in a different empirical setting could yield markedly varied findings. Despite these caveats I hope that this preliminary work can serve as a useful foundation for further work.

DATA ANALYSIS

To recap Ritzer's McUniversity thesis suggests that how universities operate including how they undertake their core functions such as teaching students has been rationalized and standardized: that education is now just another commodity for mass consumption. Ritzer identifies a primary cause of the McDonaldization of universities as reduced government funding. Ritzer identifies a key outcome of the McDonaldization of universities as the diminution of the quality of teaching and research conducted by universities. Further the McUniversity thesis suggests that the raison d'etre of contemporary universities is purely economic. That they are fordist factories whose primary goal is to increase their revenue by increasing production throughput (teach more students more cheaply) and improve levels of operational efficiency (reduce costs). Thus Ritzer's conception of the McUniversity represents a strong critique of the norms, values and goals of the contemporary university. However university leaders play a significant role in developing and sustaining the enculturation of their university's norms, values and goals. Their leadership role entails acting as the 'spokesperson', or salesperson for their university's values, goals and strategic directions. University leaders are largely responsible for motivating, encouraging and supporting staff to attain these things. Yet even more significantly the claim that McDonaldization leads to the diminution in the quality of university 'outputs', of its teaching and research is problematic for universities currently pushed towards marektization. As an integral aspect of marketization is intensified levels of competition between universities for students, staff and research funding in local, regional and global markets. Given that a university's capacity to attract students, research investors and partners, to gain a competitive advantage over rival universities in its markets is influenced by its reputation, 'its brand image', then it would probably not be prudent for key spokespeople responsible for 'selling the brand' (university leaders) to acknowledge that the quality of its teaching and research had diminished. Therefore it seems unlikely that university leaders would support Ritzer's McUniversity thesis which critiques the norms, values, goals and outputs of the university. Hence it is not surprising that this study found that only three of the seventeen Australian university leaders interviewed for this study made statements that acknowledged that Australian universities were affected by the process of McDonaldization or that any Australian universities were McUniversities.

One of the vice chancellors[8] interviewed for this study who agreed with the McDonaldization thesis stated that reduced government funding had resulted in reduced quality of teaching and research, referring to this process as 'everybody colluding with the spiraling down'. This vice chancellor suggested that in the future an Australian public university may actually refuse to accept government funding arguing that the level of this funding is inadequate to provide an acceptable education for students:

> Although we don't complain about declining government money, we do complain about a government that basically under-funds the students that we deliver programs for, that's unforgivable. If they want to cut funding, fine, but they should still fund what they buy appropriately. There will come a time that a university will turn around and say we are terribly sorry but we can not in all consciousness take the money that you are offering in the contract that we have with you because we can not deliver a quality education on the money that you are willing to pay. At the moment everybody is colluding with the spiraling down, it has been going on for twenty years it did not happen last week. For the last twenty years in most developed countries the real student dollar per student provided by governments to pay for the education of their citizenry has gone down. Sooner or later an Australian university will just turn around and say to the government that the money you are paying to buy the students' education isn't enough and we will demean our reputation as an institution by taking your money (vice chancellor).

Even though this statement suggests that Australian universities are affected by McDonaldization it is interesting to note that the vice chancellor who suggested that 'everybody was colluding with the spiraling down' of Australian universities did not suggest that the quality of teaching and research and at his university had diminished, it was a generic statement referring to the Australian higher education system as a whole. In a somewhat oblique reference to the McDonaldization of universities another vice chancellor stated that 'we have got to be careful about fast food and slow food, we have got to be careful about fast education and slow education'. Another university leader acknowledged the McDonaldization of Australian universities, yet this leader used McDonaldization as a competitive tool, attempting to strengthen his university's reputation by attacking the quality of a rival university's teaching:

> You have the 'sandstone university'[9] which is old and elite, you have the 'university of technology' which perceives itself as being very industry focused and job oriented and XXXX

---

[8] The quotes provided in this study list the interviewee's position title but not their university to provide anonymity for the participants.

[9] University types have been inserted in the quotation in place of university names to protect anonymity.

> University which is frequently described as Kmart University. Except if you get a degree from there and you don't like it, you can't go and get your money back (pro-vice chancellor).

Only one of the leaders interviewed for this study described his university as a Weberian bureaucracy. This deputy vice-chancellor was asked how decisions about the university's strategic plan were made and his response reinforced important aspects of the Weberian conception of decision-making in a bureaucratic organization: a vertical hierarchical structure, an established chain of command, with each level having a designated function, and budgetary authority.

> The main practical way where that gets worked through is in discussions with the Vice Chancellor's group, particularly though in the Committee of Deans- which is the ten Deans and the Vice Chancellor's group that is probably in a sense the major priority setting group and where most big decisions stand or fall at the Committee of Deans. They are discussed at Academic Board, reviews coming in other ways but that is really the group, the Deans and the Vice Chancellor's group decide if something is going to happen and if they don't it doesn't by and large at the big strategy level (deputy vice-chancellor).

This deputy vice-chancellor was asked to explain how leaders at his university decided how to allocate resources to academic units when there were insufficient resources and hence intense competition between units for resources. His response reinforced his conception of his university as a Weberian bureaucracy. He mentioned another two key indicators of a traditional Weberian bureaucratic mode of decision-making - the formation of sub-committees and working parties to investigate issues and decisions being made according to codified policies and procedures, in an impartial apolitical fashion:

> The Committee of Deans receives submissions from different faculties and then decisions are made according to established policies, procedures and precedence. It is the Committee's job to keep vested interests in check. So within the Deans themselves load is very scarce now that DETYA has cut back. New programs are coming and wanting load, every now and again we have had a process where we have said 3000 or 200 or some number of places available bids come in to have a new program in Biomedical Ethics or a new program in Information Technology Networking or something or other we usually then form a working party from the Committee of Deans to look at the issue and write a report so that the Committee of Deans can make a recommendation to the Academic Board, sometimes the matter may need to be referred to the Vice Chancellors Group (deputy vice-chancellor).

Most of the leaders interviewed for this study (thirteen of the seventeen) stated that their universities were in a transitionary or uneven state with some parts (academic units, marketing and commercial units) displaying characteristics associated with entrepreneurialism – an external orientation, risk taking, diversified revenue streams, quick decisions made by executives) and other parts of their universities functioning as conventional bureaucratic organizations (central administration offices – such as student administration – internal orientation, focus on policies, procedures, precedence, decisions made by committees). It was interesting to note that this group of university leaders described the organizational units concerned with purely administrative functions as monocratic bureaucracies, whereas they identified some academic units in their university as collegial bureaucracies. Several university leaders said that the co-existence of these two organizational types 'the entrepreneurial university' and the 'bureaucratic/collegial university' was problematic, a point of great tension within their university. A general manager of resources articulated his views on the co-existence of the entrepreneurial university and the bureaucratic/collegial university:

> Well I think there are two groups here there are those that are more comfortable with yesterday. The life where the Commonwealth government provided 80 per cent of your money and didn't have to go out and earn your bread, your bread was always there and the only issue was how you digested it. Thankfully that group is in the minority at our university otherwise we would not be where we are today. Then we have the other group, the real go getter entrepreneurs out there. The biggest difficulty that I face is getting those that are looking back to the past to realize that they are responsible for their own future they have to be financially self-reliant (general manager resources).

A pro-vice chancellor at another university spoke about the difficulties that he encountered trying to get academics to move towards entrepreneurialism describing this process as 'herding cats'. Another pro-vice chancellor of resources mentioned that he was familiar with Burton Clark's work and that he 'had been to Warwick University three or four times to look at how they set up their earned income group' and that is why his university had decided to use OPTs (operational performance targets) to reward academic units that generated independent income. This pro vice-chancellor suggested that the bureaucratic aspects of his university impeded its efforts to become more entrepreneurial 'I think that we have been a bit slow in getting our act together with commercialization and entrepreneurship in a structured and supportive way. I think that we have too much policing of policies, this is anti-entrepreneurial and it is done by people who are supposed to be facilitating entrepreneurialism'.

This study's findings support Burton Clark's findings that not every university has the capacity to be entrepreneurial, or wants to be entrepreneurial. A pro-vice chancellor of resources who had previously worked in a commercial firm spoke about the resistance that he faced from some academic units and academics when he tried to implement some entrepreneurial initiatives to generate independent revenue (third stream revenue):

> When you come in from the private sector and you have a short term appointment you have got to do something pretty quickly. I brought forward to the university some big commercial things which I believed had a lot of up side to them. But it was a pretty hard slog for me. I had to tackle the cultures head on and it has been like banging your head against a brick wall. It has been very difficult to get some of the academics to embrace some of the changes in the Senate. They sabotage the Senate by vested interests (pro vice-chancellor resources).

One of the vice chancellors in this study stated that he wanted to encourage academic units and academics at his university to be entrepreneurial but that some academic units in Arts and Sciences lacked the capacity to be entrepreneurial adding that they needed to be cross-subsidized by those academic units that were capable of being entrepreneurial. According to this vice- chancellor one of the main impediments that some academics and academic units had constraining their capacity to be entrepreneurial was a low degree of comfort and acceptance of risk taking:

> If you always want to be on certainties you will never do anything, you will never cross the road. So if we are risk taking I say to University Council and I say to my staff occasionally at some point we are going to make a real boo boo and we will fall over and graze our knee but that is what taking risks is all about. And we don't want to recriminate on who made the decision we will just get out of it as best we can because we have to make many decisions without total information. So as long as the strike rate is okay, nine things out of ten succeed and one thing falls over disastrously well that is okay, that's life that's the penalty for risk taking. We are trying to be increasingly risk taking, investment and return, risk and reward that is the rhetoric (vice chancellor).

Here the vice chancellor's use of the phrase 'risk and reward that is the rhetoric' is noteworthy as it suggests an awareness that there may be dissonance between the espoused or theoretical conceptions of the entrepreneurial university and the reality that for some universities becoming an entrepreneurial university is not an easy task. In closing this discussion reporting findings about how the leaders interviewed for this study conceived their universities it is important to emphasize that a university leaders' preferred way of conceiving his university was not necessarily shared by other leaders, nor by staff in central administration units, nor by academic units. One of the consequences of this dissonance in views over what type of organization a university should aspire to become was that these three theoretical conceptions remained as ideal types in the Weberian sense they were not fully realized or actualized by the leaders in the case study universities. In this regard we can conclude that conceptual views of the university are largely aspired to rather than actually attained. Our next task is to explore how the university executives interviewed for this study viewed their role as leaders before concluding by investigating whether there was any association between leaders' conceptions of their university and how they conducted their roles as leaders and managers.

Defining leadership is not an easy task. Some theorists define leadership as a skill or ability, others as an action, others as an influencing relationship between leaders and followers, whilst some theorists question whether there even is such a thing as leadership (Barker, 1997; Lakomski, 2005). There is an equally spirited debate amongst theorists about whether leadership and management are dichotomous concepts (Drucker, 2001; Hooijberg, 1996; Kotter, 1999). Whilst it is important to acknowledge that these debates exist I will not enter into them here. Rather than arbitrarily selecting definitions of leadership and management from the plethora of options available this work presents data that depicts how the university leaders interviewed for this study defined leadership and management and described their style or approach as leaders and managers. When analyzing this data a clear theme emerged: the university executives described themselves as using one of four different leadership/management styles:

- Entrepreneurial transformers
- Facilitators
- Bureaucrats
- Collegial

Further it was possible to identify a number of characteristics or traits that were associated with the different styles of leadership (Avery, 2004; Bryman, 1996). This is a useful task because it provides insights into the different ways that the university executives understood what it meant to be a leader and manager. It will also help us to explore our last research question whether there is any link between leadership style and leaders' conception of the university. I found nine leaders in this study who described themselves as entrepreneurial transformers (ETs). They stated that they were risk-takers, innovative and creative thinkers, that they were flexible, not path-dependent. They described themselves as having a sense of urgency, they wanted to act quickly which in practice meant that they often bypassed the traditional decision-making forums such as committees, and processes such as consultation and consensus preferring executive decisions. These comments made by a vice chancellor articulate the traits of an ET:

> My job is to provide the framework and encouragement that enables academic units to be entrepreneurial. I facilitate transformation I do not enact it. I have got to set the tone, I have got to constantly reinforce the views in our strategic plan so people are confident to make decisions. I keep telling people to make decisions. Don't put a paper to a committee make a decision (vice chancellor).

This vice chancellor was asked what lessons he had learnt in his role as vice chancellor, he responded:

> Intestinal fortitude is one of the things that you need, you have got to get used to the fact that the buck stops with you and that all of the problems, the big ones, eventually all really come onto your desk and then everybody just sits back and says well. Ninety-nine per cent of the key decisions have to be yours. And there is absolutely no doubt about it those are the decisions that there is no right answer to. If there was a right answer that's easy, so its all about judgment, its about being confident in your judgment and the more you do it the more you realize that the world doesn't fall over. I mean I used to wake up in the middle of the night in cold sweats (vice chancellor).

ETs seemed to perceive themselves as charismatic leaders who motivated and inspired their staff to strive to become successful entrepreneurs. Yet it was also evident that ETs could display an authoritarian command and control management style, with little time, patience and tolerance to listen to alternative points of view, or to tolerate resistance from staff:

> I say to people quite openly in meetings. If you don't agree with the route that we are taking with the strategic directions that we are heading towards with our push to be entrepreneurial, there are plenty of other universities, find one that you are happy in (vice chancellor).

Another example of the ET style of leadership and management is this response from a deputy vice-chancellor from another university in the study when asked to describe how he viewed his role as a leader and manager he stated:

> This can be quite a conservative university and my job is to push, push, push. Every now and again the VC says no more, or stop that, or its too fast, or I don't want to go there but I have an incredibly strong relationship with him based on the fact that we actually don't agree

> with each other on almost anything but there can only be one boss and he gives me very wide discretion to do what I want in terms of running the place and that is great, it works well (deputy vice-chancellor).

I found four leaders who were Facilitators. Facilitators led through others. They did not perceive their role as the sole locus of power, authority and innovative ideas. Facilitators actively delegated decision-making responsibilities to staff and sought the counsel of staff. In contrast to ETs who sometimes 'ruled with an iron fist' , facilitators were more willing to entertain alternative points of view and to broker comprise deals with staff that opposed or resisted proposed strategic changes such as opening a new campus, changing course profile or introducing tuition fees. A deputy vice-chancellor articulated the role of a facilitator: 'I see my role is to facilitate the work of all of our stars out there so that they can achieve without hindrance whatever they can achieve'. A vice-chancellor said 'I do the job because I enjoy drawing out the capacity of others, rather than running my own race. That is what sucks anybody into a management role and that is a very rewarding thing, trying to produce effective outcomes and get people to reach their full potential'. The following response from a deputy vice-chancellor illustrates how a facilitator deals with resistance to the university's proposed strategic directions:

> We all resist change except when it is initiated by ourselves but if it is initiated by somebody else then you will find resistance. So resistance to change is just human nature. Dealing with resistance comes down to leadership and team work, the management of change. You need a leader who is knowledgeable, who is empathetic and who is to an extent charismatic, they can communicate the need for change well and build a team behind themselves who will sing the same song (deputy vice-chancellor).

When another deputy vice-chancellor was asked how he coped with resistance to change from staff he said 'jaw, jaw not war, war' I mean endless talking, endless persuasion, endless meetings. Just demonstrating that at all times that you know what they want and that you are there to support them and to remove all of the impediments towards them achieving what they want to achieve'.

Three leaders in this study displayed many of the characteristics of Weber's ideal type of bureaucrat. These leaders viewed their prime responsibility as fulfilling the tasks specified in their position description within the established boundaries of codified policies, procedures and established precedents. Hence bureaucrats focused on maintaining established order and modes of operating, they did not see it as their role or responsibility to transform the university or even to 'manage change'. This group of leaders did not strive to be charismatic figures instead they derived their authority and staff complied with their decisions because staff accepted that their appointments had been made in accordance with due process. As long as these leaders did not seek to expand their power and authority beyond the boundaries of their designated role their authority was deemed to be legitimate, exemplifying Weber's rational-legal mode of authority. The remarks made by a registrar (director) when asked how he managed change illustrate the bureaucratic leadership style: 'I have put in place a very comprehensive continuous improvement project now. The coordinator works with major divisions and departments and examines whether they have particular problems and how we could improve them. So she has looked at sixty or seventy processes now and written new policies and procedures to manage change'.

For a considerable period of time collegial leadership was the dominant mode of leadership for Australian universities (Marginson and Considine, 2000 p.62). Vice Chancellors, deputy vice- chancellors, deans and heads of department were viewed as 'the first amongst equals' and most of the significant decisions that were made within the university were debated at length in university councils and academic boards. Yet since the Dawkins reforms of 1987-90 there has been a shift to a more corporate managerialist style of executive leadership (Harman, 2005; Marginson and Considine, 2000; Meek, 2003). Hence it is not surprising that only one of the seventeen leaders in this study used a collegial style of leadership. This leader (a deputy vice-chancellor) did not see himself as the sole agent of power and authority. He sought to share decision-making authority for resource allocation, strategic goals and the priorities for goals amongst a group of senior colleagues and academics. When asked to describe how he viewed his role as a leader and manager and what his priorities were, this deputy vice chancellor responded:

> I think that it is important to show the staff that we care about them, that we value them and their contribution to the university. We must interact with staff in a meaningful way, we have to try and engage them. We are extremely fortunate we have an extremely loyal staff that are committed to the university; they see it as their university.

When this collegial leader was asked how he managed change he said that 'the most important thing is to have a lot of consultation, to involve as many people as possible in making decisions, and to deal with resistance by explaining to academics about the changes in the environment and why the changes are necessary, otherwise people will just go off completely disillusioned'. To conclude this discussion about the leadership style of the university executives in this study I will add the observation that there was no definitive association between a leader's seniority and leadership style, that is senior leaders (vice chancellors) were not necessarily ETs and lower ranked executives (directors and general managers) were not necessarily collegial leaders. The following conclusion explores the issue of whether it is possible to identify any links or connections between how the university executives conceived their university and their leadership style and offers some reflections on the study.

Conclusions

This work identifies several links between the theoretical conceptions of the university and university executives' leadership style. The strongest link between theory and empiricism demonstrated in this study is that most of the university executives described their leadership style as an entrepreneurial transformer (ET) and this leadership style illustrates many key aspects of Clark's conception of the entrepreneurial university. These aspects included accepting and striving for change in organizational structure, modes of operating, types of research undertaken, research partners, types of courses taught, modes of delivery, risk taking – entering new markets, changing hiring and pricing strategies, having a greater focus on competition, diversifying revenue streams, and making decisions quickly so as to respond to changes in markets rather than relying on more traditional committee and consultative decision-making patterns. This link is significant because it stands as evidence that several Australian universities are currently aspiring to become entrepreneurial universities. Of course Clark's observation stands, not every university has the capacity to be entrepreneurial and indeed not every university wants to be entrepreneurial.

A second link between theory and empiricism suggested by this study's findings is that because only one of the seventeen university executives in this study described himself as a bureaucratic leader, this implies that Australian universities may no longer be bureaucratic organizations. Yet we must be cautious, the sample size is small so it is not legitimate to offer definitive statements. It would be premature to declare the death of bureaucracy in the Australian university. Indeed a case can be made that the rise of managerialist initiatives such as quality assurance and key performance indicators for strategic planning have spurred growth in the number of bureaucrats working in Australian universities, and that there has been a shift of power from academics to bureaucrats, see (Meek, 2003). Indeed this points to an interesting paradox noted by Clark – whilst the emergence of the entrepreneurial university seems to have modified the traditional Weberian bureaucracy, a new form of bureaucracy has emerged, a bureaucracy that is more closely integrated with entrepreneurial initiatives in universities rather than one that operates in opposition to entrepreneurial goals (Clark, 2003 pp.108-109).

An absence in the data provides the third finding for this study. The fact that only three of the seventeen university leaders in this study acknowledged the existence of Ritzer's McDonaldization thesis and none of these leaders admitted to being agents for McDonaldization suggests that the McDonaldization thesis requires a codicil when applied to universities. Those who consume the products of the university (students) and those who deliver those products and services (employees) may support the McDonaldization thesis, yet it seems that university leaders who manage and control universities and their means of production are unlikely to acknowledge that their universities are being 'McDonaldized'.

Even though this research project was small scale and exploratory its findings demonstrate the complexity of the university. None of the leaders interviewed for this study viewed their university as completely aligned with any of the three theoretical conceptions of the university investigated in this work. Each of the universities displayed aspects of all three conceptions of the university. In addition this study focused on reporting executives' perceptions of their leadership style, identifying four styles of leadership: entrepreneurial transformers, facilitators, bureaucrats and collegial leaders. The study also pointed out that there can be a mixture of leadership styles within a university's executive groups and noted that even though leaders may believe they are using a particular leadership style their followers (employees) may view their leadership in a totally different way.

In disciplines such as Sociology and its specializations such as Higher Education Studies there is a distinct chasm between those who work with empirical realities and those who explore theoretical conceptions. All too often there is a lack of understanding and value of each type of work. Theoreticians often harshly critique empiricists' work asserting that it is merely descriptive and not explanatory. And in turn empiricists often view theoreticians' work as impenetrable, and devoid of all connections with reality. Some scholars hold an entrenched view that by definition theory is separate from empiricism. Yet this work illustrates that there are connections between theory and empiricism. Although it is important to note that these connections were complex and reflexive rather than unidirectional causes and effects. I contend that the boundaries between theoretical conceptions and empirical realities have a transilient fluidity, that they are indeed permeable. It is my view that integrating theory and empiricism is a useful endeavor because it enriches both domains. This project enables practitioners to operate with enhanced knowledge of theoretical conceptions that seek to explain situations and issues. While theoreticians who test their theories in empirical contexts can evaluate the analytical and explanatory power of their theories and modify, enhance or reject their theoretical conceptions in the light of knowledge gained from empirical contexts.

REFERENCES

Alfino, M., Caputo, J. S., and Wynward, R. (eds.). (1998). *McDonaldization Revisited:Critical Essays on Consumer Culture*. Westport: Praeger.

Avery, G. C. (2004). *Understanding Leadership: Paradigms and Cases*. London: Sage Publications.

Barker, R. A. (1997). How Can We Train Leaders if We Do Not Know What Leadership Is? *Human Relations, Vol.50* (No.4), pp. 343- 362.

Bryman, A. (1996). Leadership in Organizations. in S. Clegg, C. Hardy and W. Nord (eds.), *Handbook of Organization Studies* (pp. pp.276-292). London: Sage Publications.

Clark, B. (1998a). *Creating Entrepreneurial Universities: Organizational Pathways of Transformation*. Oxford: Pergamon.

Clark, B. (1998b). The Entrepreneurial University: Demand and Response. *Tertiary Education and Management, Vol.4* (No.1), pp.5-16.

Clark, B. R. (2003). Sustaining Change in Universities: Constituencies in Case Studies and Concepts. *Tertiary Education and Management, Vol.9* (No.2), pp.99-116.

Clark, B. R. (2004). *Sustaining Change in Universities: Continuities in Case Studies and Concepts*. Maidenhead: Society for Research into Higher Education and Open University Press.

Considine, M., and Painter, M. (1997). *Managerialism: The Great Debate*. Melbourne: Melbourne University Press.

Currie, J. (2004). The Neo-Liberal paradigm and Higher Education: A critique. In J. Odin and P. Manicus (eds.), *Globalization and Higher Education*. Honolulu: University of Hawaii Press.

de Zilwa, D. K. (2006). *Academic Units in the era of the Entrepreneurial University*. Melbourne: University of Melbourne.

DEST. (2005). *Selected Higher Education Statistics, Students*, from http://www.dest/ highereducation/publications/selected statistics.

Drucker, P. (2001). Leadership as Work. In P. Drucker (Ed.), *The Essential Drucker* (pp. pp.268-271). Oxford: Butterworth Heinemann.

Edles, L. D., and Applerouth, S. (2005). *Sociological Theory in the Classical Era: Texts and Readings*. Thousand Oaks: Pine Forge Press (Sage Publications).

Harman, G. (2005). Introducing Comprehensive National Higher Education Reforms:The Australian Reforms of Education Minister John Dawkins, 1987-90. In A. Gornitzka, M.

Kogan and A. Amaral (eds.), *Reform and Change in Higher Education: Analyzing Policy Implementation* (Vol.8, pp. pp.169-185). Dordrecht: Springer.

Hartley, D. (1995). The 'McDonaldization' of Higher Education: Food for Thought. *Oxford Review of Education, Vol. 21*(No.4), pp.409-423.

Hayes, D., and Wynward, R. (eds.). (2002). *The McDonalization of Higher Education*. Westport: Bergin and Garvey.

Henderson, A. R., and Parsons, T. (1947). *The Theory of Social and Economic Organization: By Max Weber*. London: William Hodge and Company Limited.

Hooijberg, R. (1996). A multidimensional approach toward leadership: an extension of the concept of behavioral complexity. *Human Relations, Vol.49* (No. 7), pp.917-946.

Kotter, J. P. (1999). *John.P Kotter on What Leaders Really Do*. Boston: Harvard Business Review.

Lakomski, G. (2005). *Managing without Leadership: Towards a Theory of Organizational Functioning*. Oxford: Elsevier.

Marginson, S. (2006). Dynamics of National and Global Competition in Higher Education. *Higher Education, Vol. 52*(No. 4), pp.1-39.

Marginson, S., and Considine, M. (2000). *The Enterprise University: Power, Governance and Reinvention in Australia*. Cambridge: Cambridge University Press.

Meek, V. L. (2002). On the Road to Mediocrity? Governance and Management of Australian Higher Education in the Marketplace. In A. Amaral, G. A. Jones and B. Karseth (Eds.), *Governing Higher Education:National Perspectives on Institutional Governance* (pp. pp.235-260). Dordrecht: Kluwer.

Meek, V. L. (2003). Governance and Management of Australian Higher Education: Enemies Within and Without. In A. Amaral, V. L. Meek and I. M. Larsen (eds.), *The Higher Education Managerial Revolution?* (Vol. Vol.3, pp. pp.179-201). Dordrecht: Kluwer Academic Publishers.

Monash University. (2000). *Global Development Framework*. Melbourne: Monash University.

Morgan, G. (2006). *Images of Organization*. Thousand Oaks: Sage.

Parker, M., and Jary, D. (1995). The McUniversity:Organization, Management and Academic Subjectivity. *Organization, Vol.2* (No.2), pp.319-338.

Ritzer, G. (1993). *The Mc Donaldization of Society*. Thousand Oaks: Pine Forge Press.

Ritzer, G. (1998). *The McDonaldization Thesis: Explorations and Extensions*. London: Sage.

Ritzer, G. (2000). *The McDonaldization of Society*. Thousand Oaks, California: Pine Forge Press.

Ritzer, G. (2002). Enchanting McUniversity: Toward a Spectacularly Irrational University Quotidian. In D. Hayes and R. Wynward (Eds.), *The McDonaldization of Higher Education*. Westport: Bergin and Garvey.

Ritzer, G. (2004). *The McDonaldization of Society*. Thousand Oaks: Pine Forge Press.

Ritzer, G. (2006). *McDonaldization: The Reader*. Thousand Oaks: Pine Forge Press.

Roth, G., and Wittich, C. (eds.). (1978). *Max Weber Economy and Society: An Outline of Interpretative Sociology* (Vol. Vol.2). Berkeley: University of California Press.

Shils, E. (ed.). (1973). *Max Weber: On Universities: The Power of the State and the Dignity of the Academic Calling in Imperial Germany*. Chicago: The University of Chicago Press.

Weber, M. (1930). *The Protestant Ethic and the Spirit of Capitalism*. London: Allen and Unwin.

In: Australia: Economic, Political and Social Issues
Editors: Lachlan J. Williams and Ethan N. Lee
ISBN: 978-1-60456-856-1

Chapter 2

THE IMPACT OF UNIVERSITY RESEARCH AND DEVELOPMENT ON AUSTRALIAN REGIONAL DEVELOPMENT

Claudia Burgio-Ficca and Hristos Doucouliagos[1]
School of Accounting, Economics and Finance
Faculty of Business and Law
Deakin University

ABSTRACT

Recent years have seen growing interest in research and development (R&D) in Australia. Unfortunately, little is know about the contributions of R&D to Australian economic performance. Even less is known about the contributions of university R&D. This paper examines the impact of both university and non-university R&D on output levels in Australia, using data for Australian states, for the period 1979 to 2003. Both Cobb-Douglas and Translog versions of the production function are estimated. The results indicate that while both types of R&D make important contributions to the generation of output, not all university R&D has a positive effect. Pure basic and applied university R&D both have had a positive effect on regional output. However, this is in sharp contrast to the impact of strategic basic and experimental R&D, which are shown to have a negative effect on output.

I. INTRODUCTION

The idea that research and development (hereafter referred to as R&D) is an important and vital input into the production process has been emphasized by economists for at least the last 40 years. Internationally, the topic of R&D and its impact on productivity and growth has been extensively explored and documented. Studies by Mansfield (1972), Nadiri (1980),

[1] Corresponding author. Email: douc@deakin.edu.au. Mailing address: School of Accounting, Economics and Finance, Faculty of Business and Law, Deakin University, 221 Burwood Highway, 3125, Victoria, Australia.

Griliches (1992) and Coe and Helpman (1995), to name but a few, have all concluded that R&D expenditure contributes substantially to the growth of output. However, reviews by Dowrick (1994) and the Industry Commission (1995) indicate that Australian studies in this area are limited and have largely been confined to the agricultural and manufacturing industries. Moreover, most of the extant Australian research has been in the form of case studies, as opposed to econometric studies.

In recent years, the Commonwealth Government has commissioned a number of reports into the current and future status of R&D in Australia. These reports have included *The Virtuous Cycle: Working together for health and medical research* (Health and Medical Research Strategic Review, 1999), *Knowledge and Innovation: A policy statement on research and research training* (Kemp, 1999), *The Chance to Change* (Batterham, 2000) and *Backing Australia's Ability* (Commonwealth of Australia, 2001). While these reports provide a review of current funding levels for various fields of research, and have proposed a number of new initiatives for the future of R&D, they have done little to analyze the current impact R&D has on Australian output. Such an assessment is long overdue and we hope to add to this, even in a small way, in this paper.

In Australia, the greatest proportion of R&D comes from the private sector, with the university sector being the second greatest contributor, followed by the government sector in third place. Even so, in 2002-03, most (about 86%) of university R&D was funded by the Commonwealth Government, with about 5% of the funding coming from the private sector (Year Book Australia 2005).

This paper's main aim is to examine the impact of university R&D on Australia's development, as proxied by output. This is achieved by estimating production functions using a panel data set of six Australian states for the period 1979 to 2003. The paper is set out as follows. Section II provides a brief review of previous research in this area. Section III outlines the estimation procedure undertaken, while Section IV discusses the data. Section V presents the results. Concluding comments are made in Section VI.

II. Previous Research

Early econometric analyses linking R&D to productivity were conducted by Terleckyj (1958), Minasian (1962), Griliches (1964) and Mansfield (1965). Terleckyj (1958) used the total factor productivity (TFP) approach, relating R&D intensity to the rate of growth in the residual output (controlling for the contributions of labor and physical capital). Terleckyj concluded that the intensity of R&D may contribute to productivity. Minasian (1962) also used the TFP approach and found that R&D expenditure was a highly significant independent variable in determining the rate of growth in productivity in a cross-section of firms in the chemical and allied products industries and in the drug and pharmaceutical industries. Griliches (1964) used an unrestricted Cobb-Douglas production function and concluded that public expenditure on agricultural research had a positive and significant affect on agricultural output.

Since these early works, there has been an abundance of studies exploring the impact of R&D on productivity. Noteworthy contributions were made by Griliches (1979) and Jaffe (1986). Applications of the TFP method include Goto and Suzuki (1989), Griliches (1994) and Sterlacchini (1989). Some of the more important reviews of this literature are provided by Mairesse and Sassenou (1991), Nadiri (1993), the Industry Commission (1995), Mairesse and Mohnen (1994) and Mohnen (1996).

Unfortunately, the impact of university research on productivity has received only scant attention, in comparison to the wider attention of R&D in general. The existing research focuses mainly on the existence of spillovers from university R&D and the impact of university R&D on innovation. These are important *indirect* channels through which university R&D can affect output. However, very little is known about the *direct* effect of total university R&D on output. Even less is known about the direct impact of different types of university R&D.

An early study on university R&D was conducted by Jaffe (1989). Jaffe's analysis aimed to examine the production of corporate patents and how this was influenced by industry and university R&D. The model included 29 U.S. states over the period 1972-1981 and incorporated a breakdown of university research by academic departments. Jaffe used a Cobb-Douglas specification estimated by both OLS and Generalized Least Squares (GLS). GLS produced better results for both the industry R&D and university R&D variables. Overall, Jaffe found that university expenditure on drugs and medical technology produced the statistically strongest effect, while chemical technology ranked second, followed by electronic, optical and nuclear technology. Importantly, Jaffe's study found that there was only a weak relationship between the location of the R&D spillovers and the location of the university and research laboratories, and that spillovers of R&D were limited to specific research areas. Anselin, Varga and Acs (1997, 2000) later disputed the findings on the location of R&D spillovers and the location of university and research laboratories.

Commenting on Jaffe (1989), Acs, Audretsch and Feldam (1992) argue that: "the knowledge created at university laboratories spills over to contribute to the generation of commercial innovations by private enterprises". Acs, Audretsch and Feldam (1994a) examined the degree to which university and corporate R&D spills over to innovative activity at the state level. Their analysis was based on the same data set as Jaffe (1989), however instead of investigating the contribution of university R&D to corporate patents, innovations were introduced as the dependent variable. They found that substituting patent data with a measure of innovative activity generally strengthened Jaffe's (1989) arguments and findings. In fact, unlike Jaffe (1989), Acs, Audretsch and Feldam (1992) conclude that spillovers were affected by the geographic location of universities and research laboratories.

Acs, Audretsch and Feldam (1994b) examined the degree to which university and corporate R&D spills over into firms. They concluded that R&D undertaken by university laboratories spilled over and impacted upon the innovative activity of small firms, whilst corporate R&D affected larger firms. Anselin, Varga & Acs (2000) extended their 1997 paper in which spillovers generated by universities was disaggregated at the sectoral level. Their findings indicate that local university spillovers were constrained to specific industries.

The link between research and innovation was examined also by Nelson (1986). Using a survey of research managers, Nelson concluded that university research was an important source of innovation in some industries. Link & Rees (1990) compared the university based research relationship between small and large firms in an attempt to explain why small firms are more innovative. Their analysis of 209 innovating firms concluded that larger firms were in fact more active in university based research, but were unable to exploit this association to the degree achievable by smaller firms. Anselin, Varga and Acs (1997) used the number of high technology innovations as their dependent variable, and found a positive and statistically significant relationship between university research and innovative activity.

In recent years various authors from the Melbourne Institute of Applied and Social Research have contributed papers to a collaborative research program. For example, Fenney and Rogers (2001) compared the performance of firms relative to their innovative activity. Their results show that innovation leads to increased firm performance. Using a cross-country regression approach, Rogers (2001) examined the economic growth of 61 countries between 1965 and 1985. With the trend growth in GDP per worker as the dependent variable, Rogers added each of the absorptive capacity proxies (20 in total) individually to the baseline regression. The absorptive capacity proxies were grouped under 5 main categories which comprised students studying abroad, telecommunications (i.e. main telephone lines per population), publications (i.e. periodicals published), patents (per thousand worker) and trade data (i.e. imports/export variables). The overall results suggest that absorptive capabilities (i.e. patents etc) affected the determination of economic growth.

Rogers (2002) analysed how innovative activity affected firm profitability in a sample of Australian firms. The study examined innovative activity from 1994 to 1998. The results revealed that patenting activity was never significantly associated with market value, implying that either patent applications were a poor proxy for innovative activity or more important that the stock market failed to recognise such value.

Unfortunately, none of these industry studies explores the impact of R&D on aggregate sectoral output. It is this lacuna that we wish to address.

III. Estimation Procedure

Our analytical approach is to estimate a set of production functions. The production function relates the quantity of output to the inputs used in the production process. In this framework, labor and capital are mandatory. In following with previous studies, research capital is introduced as a third input (see, for example, Coe and Helpman 1995, Griliches and Mairesse 1984 and Nadiri 1980). The Cobb-Douglas version of the basic production function is given by:

$$\ln(Y_{it}) = \alpha_0 + \alpha_1\ln(L_{it}) + \alpha_2\ln(K_{it}) + \alpha_3\ln(TRD_{it}) + \alpha_z\mathbf{Z}_{it} + u_i \qquad (1)$$

where Y is output (in our case Gross State Product), L is labor, K is the stock of physical capital, TRD is the stock of total R&D capital, **Z** is a vector of other variables, u are the residuals and the subscript i is an index for each state, at time period t.

Separating higher education R&D from non-university R&D results in equation 2:

$$\ln(Y_{it}) = \gamma_0 + \gamma_1\ln(L_{it}) + \gamma_2\ln(K_{it}) + \gamma_3\ln(NURD_{it}) + \gamma_4\ln(URD_{it}) + \gamma_z\mathbf{Z}_{it} + v_i \qquad (2)$$

where NURD is R&D capital from the non-university sector (mainly the private sector), and URD is university R&D capital. Equation 2 can be extended by separating out the different types of university R&D:

$$\ln(Y_{it}) = \delta_0 + \delta_1\ln(L_{it}) + \delta_2\ln(K_{it}) + \delta_3\ln(NURD_{it}) + \delta_4\ln(P_{it}) + \delta_5\ln(S_{it}) + \delta_6\ln(A_{it}) + \delta_7\ln(E_{it}) + \delta_z\mathbf{Z}_{it} + \varepsilon_i \quad (3)$$

where the stock of higher education R&D is disaggregated into four major categories: pure basic (P), strategic basic (S), applied (A) and experimental (E)[2]. It is reasonable to assume that given a very high degree of factor mobility and competition, that the production process is the same across each Australian state. Hence, it is assumed that all the variables have the same coefficient in each state, as well as over time[3]. The Translog versions of equations 1 to 3 include interactive terms.

Equations 1, 2 and 3 assume errors that are free of technical inefficiency – the production process is assumed to be fully efficient. In preliminary analysis, we estimated various Stochastic Production Frontiers. In no case was technical efficiency identified.[4] Equations 1 to 3 do not include a time trend, which is usually incorporated to represent disembodied technical change. In this paper, R&D is used instead of a time trend, as R&D is a broader measure that captures also technical change, and this is preferable to a simple time counter[5].

It is important to note that our focus in this paper is on only one aspect of the university research process - R&D. The impact of scholarship, communication of research findings and research training in general, especially higher degrees by research degrees, may all make important contributions to output, that are not included in the above specifications and are, hence, not considered in this paper. Moreover, knowledge created by universities can affect a society's welfare through its wider impact on education and culture. There are clearly many possible extensions to this paper.

Numerous factors affect the performance of the Australian economic landscape such as business cycles, government policies, regulatory reform, general world economic conditions, and technological change. Ideally one would like to account for all of these factors, so that the regression results provide the truest reflection of the impact on various variables on the Australian output. However, data and measurement issues prevent the vast majority of such factors being accounted for directly. We do however include two important control variables as part of the **Z** vector: the effect of industrial relations and deregulation on Australia's production process.

Unions and industrial relations issues in general have been a key feature of the industrial landscape in Australia. For example, the Australian Council of Trade Unions (ACTU) has had a significant impact on economic and social policy in Australia, both through its own actions and through its links with the Australian Labour Party (Brambles, 2001 and Briggs, 2001). There exists a voluminous theoretical and empirical literature on the economic effects of unions (see, for example, Turnbull 2003, Addison and Belfield 2004 and Hirsch 2004). In general, unions may be viewed as a having 'two-faces' (Freeman & Medoff, 1984). Unions are able to increase wage levels and impose employment restrictions. However unions are also able to increase productivity levels through strengthening communication between

[2] A definition of each category is provided below in Section IV.

[3] Similar assumptions were made by Acs, Audretsch & Feldman (1994a, 1994b), Anselin, Varga and Acs (1997), Griliches (1964) and Jaffe (1989).

[4] This does not, however, mean that Australian states are not inefficient relative to other countries or regions in other countries.

[5] Preliminary results revealed that the inclusion of a time trend caused both the time trend and the R&D variable to become statistically insignificant. As a result the time trend was omitted from the analysis. Similar problems were encountered by Nadiri (1980).

management and employees. The literature has failed to draw firm conclusions regarding the impact of unions. A recent meta-analysis of the literature concluded that for the U.S. there was a small positive effect on output levels, while for the U.K. the effect of unions was negative (Doucouliagos and Laroche 2003). A small group of studies has explored the impact of Australian unions (e.g. Alexander & Green: 1992, Drago & Wooden: 1992, Drago, Wooden & Sloan: 1992 and Phipps and Sheen: 1994). The verdict appears to be that Australian unions have had an adverse effect on production.

Another area of interest in the Australian context is the impact of deregulation of the financial system on the production process. This has been an extensive process, involving the floating of the Australian dollar in 1983, followed by the removal of a number of regulatory measures (e.g. exchange rate controls and deregulation of the banking sector), together with the privatisation of numerous government corporations. These events have significantly impacted upon the structure of the economy and as such their inclusion in the production function is warranted. Most of the extant research in this area has focussed on the impact of deregulation on specific industries (e.g. Doucouliagos & Hone 2000 and Lie, Brooks & Faff 2000), although there have also been some studies exploring the broader impact on the economy (Groenewold 2003). We expect to find that deregulation has had a positive effect on production.

IV. Data

The data used in this analysis was primarily sourced from the Australian Bureau of Statistics (ABS) for the six Australian states of New South Wales (NSW), Victorian (VIC), Queensland (QLD), Western Australia (WA), South Australia (SA) and Tasmania (TAS) between 1979[6] and 2003. Due to a lack of data, the regions of Northern Territory and ACT were eliminated from the analysis. Hence, this paper constructs a panel data analysis of six states and a twenty-five year span, resulting in 150 observations.[7]

The definitions of the variables used are as follows:

Output: While output levels are only one aspect of development, it is certainly an important one. We use the level of output at the state level as our broad measure of regional development. We used two measures of output. First, we used Gross State Product (GSP) deflated into constant 2002-03 dollars using the associated Gross State Product deflator. Second, we also used the Gross State Product Chain Volume Index series. The results are similar and we focus here on the results using the Chain Volume Index series.

[6] 1978-89 is the initial year the Australian Bureau of Statistics commenced collecting R&D expenditure data.

[7] It is important to note that the Australian Bureau of Statistics provides data on R&D expenditure in Australia only biannually. In the absence of complete data, an average of the two years was taken for missing years data. A similar methodology was utilised by Olley and Pakes (1996).

Labor: measured as the total number of workers employed in each state.

Union Density: measured as the proportion of the workforce who are trade union members.

Deregulation: In the last two decades the Australian economy has experienced a process of deregulation in various industries through tariff reductions and industry protection. As there is no index available on deregulation in Australia, the focus of this paper is on the post-1983 period during which the majority of the deregulations were implemented. Hence, events such as the floating of the Australian dollar and financial deregulations are accounted for through a dummy variable equivalent to zero for the years between 1979 and 1983 and one for the years 1984 to 2003. An alternative measure is to use the Fraser Institute measure of economic freedom (Gwartney and Lawson 2003). The results regarding R&D are not altered when this measure is used.

R&D Stock: In Australia, R&D is conducted by a number of institutions and governing bodies, including business enterprises, general government, higher education institutions and private non-profit organisations. The focus of this paper is on R&D conducted by higher education organizations (URD), compared to that arising from the other sectors (NURD). R&D has been defined as: 'creative work undertake on a systematic basis in order to increase the stock of knowledge – including knowledge of man, culture and society – and the use of this knowledge to devise new applications'[8]. However, what is of more importance for our purpose is the *stock* of knowledge generated by the R&D. In the absence of a stock series from the ABS, stock data[9] was constructed for the required variables: physical capital, total R&D, higher education R&D and the four various types of higher education R&D (pure, strategic, applied and experimental).

The stock of R&D for each of these variables was calculated using the perpetual inventory method (PIM) (see Coe and Helpman 1995). Under the PIM, R&D capital stock in any period is a function of the value of the R&D capital stock in the previous period, less any depreciation that has occurred plus the level of R&D expenditure in the previous period[10]. The PIM also requires the calculation of an initial stock of capital which is based on the growth of R&D and the assumed rate of depreciation[11]. Like all capital, the stock of accumulated knowledge from R&D expenditure depreciates (Mohnen, 1990). In this paper, it is assumed that R&D expenditure depreciates at the rate of 10 percent per annum. According

---

[8] OECD (1980).

[9] Stock data is a more accurate measure as it takes into consideration the depreciable/obsolete nature of R&D and provides a more accurate representation of the R&D available as an input into the production process.

[10] $S_t = (1-\delta)\, S_{t-1} + R_{t-1}$

where: S_t = the stock of R&D capital at the beginning of the period

S_{t-1} = the stock of R&D capital at the beginning of period t-1

R_{t-1} = the expenditure on R&D during period t-1

δ = the depreciation or obsolescence in the rate of knowledge.

[11] $S_o = R_o/(g + \delta)$

where: S_o = the stock of R&D capital at the beginning of the first year for which R&D expenditure data is available.

R_o = the expenditure on R&D during the first year for which it is available.

g = the average annual logarithmic growth of R&D expenditures over the period for which published R&D data were available, in this case 1978-79 to 2002-03.

δ = the depreciation or obsolescence rate of knowledge, in this case 10 percent.

to Griliches (1979), a rate of 10 percent is appropriate given that most private knowledge becomes obsolete after ten years. This rate was also adopted by Mohnen, Nadiri and Prucha (1986) in their analysis of manufacturing sectors in the US, Japan and Germany, and by Bernstein (1989) in his analysis of inter-industry spill-overs in Canada. Moreover, in preliminary analysis of the Australian panel data, we found that using depreciation rates of 8 and 15 percent did not alter the results significantly. Expenditure figures for total R&D were extracted from ABS, Cat. No. 8111.0 whilst figures relating to university R&D were sourced from ABS, Cat No. 8112.0.

According to the ABS (Cat No. 8112), the following definitions apply to the different components of R&D. *Pure basic research* is defined as: "Experimental and theoretical work undertaken primarily to acquire new knowledge without a specific application in view." *Strategic basic research* is defined as research that is: "directed into specified broad areas in the expectation of useful discoveries. It provides the broad base of knowledge for the solution of recognised practical problems." *Applied research* is: "Original work undertaken in order to acquire new knowledge with a specific application in view. It is undertaken either to determine possible uses for the findings of basic research or to determine new methods or ways of achieving some specific and predetermined objectives." Finally, *Experimental research* is: "Systematic work, using existing knowledge gained from research or practical experience, for the purpose of creating new or improved products/processes."

Capital: PIM was also used to calculate the stock of physical capital for each Australian state. It was assumed that the asset life of plant and equipment was 12 years, while buildings would last 40 year[12]. The stock for these two variables was calculated separately and combined to represent the stock of total physical capital (expenditure figures extracted from ABS, Cat. No. 5242.0)

Descriptive statistics for the data used in this analysis are presented in Table 1. In 2002-03, experimental R&D was the largest R&D activity (39% of total R&D), with applied research being 36% of total, and only 10% coming from pure basic research. Almost 80% of the pure basic research originates from the university sector. This contrasts with the bulk (about 86%) of experimental R&D being conducted by the business sector, and roughly one third of applied research coming from the business sector (see ABS Cat. No. 8112).

Table 1: Descriptive Statistics, 1978-79 to 2002-2003

	NSW	VIC	QLD	WA	SA	TAS
Gross State Product						
Mean	201296	143810	86726	55507	41113	11507
Std.Dev	48407	29469	24803	16875	7875	1747
Employed						
Mean	2594	1978	1327	628	745	189
Std.Dev	306	205	279	46	137	12

[12] Bureau of Industry Economics (1995).

	NSW	VIC	QLD	WA	SA	TAS
Capital Stock						
Mean	152848	106608	63555	54888	27098	7090
Std.Dev	24235	17797	14468	18435	8761	1156
Total R&D Stock						
Mean	14096	13507	4991	3351	3946	1982
Std.Dev	5858	5345	2315	1932	1396	1373
University R&D Stock						
Mean	3913	2793	1613	1030	1110	294
Std.Dev	1356	1045	834	491	340	118
Non-University R&D Stock						
Mean	10182	10714	3379	2321	2836	1688
Std.Dev	4507	4302	1484	1441	1063	1285
Pure R&D Stock						
Mean	1552	949	462	305	396	102
Std.Dev	547	336	212	129	96	32
Strategic R&D Stock						
Mean	839	711	399	276	299	78
Std.Dev	284	247	205	152	95	38
Applied R&D Stock						
Mean	1210	962	650	383	351	102
Std.Dev	416	405	371	186	131	47
Experimental						
Mean	311	171	102	66	64	11
Std.Dev	112	62	51	27	24	4
Union Density						
Mean	38	38	37	32	40	46
Std.Dev	9	10	9	9	8	10

Std.Dev = standard deviation

V. RESULTS

The Cobb-Douglas and Translog versions of the Australian states production function were estimated using both pooled Least Squares and Estimated Generalised Least Squares (EGLS), but we present and discuss only the latter set of results. The EGLS estimated here corrects for both cross-section heteroscedasticity, as well as contemporaneous correlation between the cross-sections.[13] According to Beck & Katz (1995), this approach is valid when contemporaneous correlation is present and when the time span is at least three times greater than the number of cross-sections. Both of these conditions are met for out dataset.

[13] All of the regression analysis was performed using Eviews 5.0.

The results from estimating the Cobb-Douglas version of the Australian states production function are presented in Table 2. Column 1 presents the basic production function without R&D. The total stock of R&D is added in column 2. As expected, the coefficients on capital stock, labor and total R&D stock were all found to be positive and statistically significant. R&D in Australia is an important input into the production process. Note, however, that the contribution of total R&D is lower than either labor or physical capital. Similar results are reported in column 3, where the total R&D stock variable is replaced by separate variables for the stock of university and non-university R&D. In column 4, university R&D is disaggregated into the four major categories, with the aim of highlighting which types of R&D are the most productive. Unionization and deregulation are introduced in the results reported in column 5.

Unfortunately, our preferred specification reported in column 5 has several coefficients with rather surprising results. If these results are to be believed, non-university R&D has a negative effect on output levels, union density has a positive effect and deregulation had no effect at all. All these are opposite of what we expected and are in sharp contrast to the findings of other researchers.

Table 2: Cobb-Douglas Production Function, Australian States, 1978-79 to 2002-2003, Pooled Estimated Generalized Least Squares, (Dependent variable = lnGross State Product)

Variable	(1)	(2)	(3)	(4)	(5)
Constant	2.151 (81.35)***	2.130 (33.62)***	2.380 (46.65)***	1.845 (41.16)***	1.792 (39.93)***
ln(Capital)	0.520 (76.56)***	0.467 (34.03)***	0.433 (47.08)***	0.483 (63.45)***	0.490 (73.56)***
ln(Labor)	0.484 (64.92)***	0.434 (44.46)***	0.367 (34.11)***	0.348 (23.09)***	0.313 (17.00) ***
ln(Total R&D)	-	0.111 (16.98)***	-	-	-
ln(Non-University R&D)	-	-	0.022 (4.43)***	-0.019 (-2.23)**	-0.020 (-2.49)**
ln(University R&D)	-	-	0.186 (19.00)***	-	-
ln(Pure R&D)	-	-	-	0.244 (13.73)***	0.228 (10.81)***
ln(Applied R&D)	-	-	-	0.308 (10.67)***	0.331 (10.47)***
ln(Experimental R&D)	-	-	-	-0.203 (-9.86)***	-0.188 (-9.28)***
ln(Strategic R&D)	-	-	-	-0.118 (-3.47)***	-0.109 (-3.14)***
Union Density	-	-	-	-	0.002 (3.42)***
Deregulation	-	-	-	-	0.009 (1.03)

*, **, *** statistically significant at the 10%, 5% and 1% levels, respectively. t-statistics using robust standard errors reported in brackets.

Given the restrictive nature of the Cobb-Douglas, we prefer the results from the Translog. Table 3 reports the results from estimating the Translog version of the production function, allowing for important interactions among the variables. Column 1 presents the basic regression results, using Total R&D. Interestingly, none of the Total R&D variables are individually statistically significant[14]. Total R&D is separated into university and non-university R&D in column 2. Column 3 reports the results from disaggregating university R&D into the four types, but without allowing for interaction effects between these types. The results from the full Translog model are presented in column 4. These are our preferred results.

Table 3: Translog Production Function, Australian States, 1978-79 to 2002-2003, Pooled Estimated Generalized Least Squares, (Dependent variable = lnGross State Product)

Variable	(1)	(2)	(3)	(4)
Constant	9.07 (17.61)***	10.696 (6.54)***	24.631 (7.71)***	38.642 (7.08)***
ln(Capital)	-1.820 (-8.29)***	-3.289 (-5.44)***	-6.300 (-7.06)***	-6.283 (-6.48)***
ln(Labor)	2.348 (9.72)***	2.794 (10.78)***	3.462 (5.63)***	1.024 (1.11)
ln(Total R&D)	-0.156 (-1.25)	-	-	-
ln(Total R&D) Squared	0.004 (0.52)	-	-	-
ln(Capital)*ln(Total R&D)	0.031 (0.72)	-	-	-
ln(Labor)* ln(Total R&D)	-0.027 (-0.60)	-	-	-
ln(Capital) squared	0.227 (5.69)***	0.659 (9.36)***	0.576 (6.30)***	0.469 (5.36)***
ln(Labor) squared	0.219 (5.68)***	0.363 (5.32)***	0.666 (5.21)***	0.816 (6.30)***
ln(Capital)*ln(Labor)	-0.424 (-6.55)***	-0.897 (-11.24)***	-0.806 (-5.55)***	-0.799 (-5.40)***
ln(Non-University R&D)	-	-2.311 (-6.58)***	-1.913 (-4.11)***	-1.112 (-2.07)**
ln(University R&D)	-	3.701 (7.38)***	-	-
ln(Capital)*ln(University R&D)	-	-1.700 (-8.45)***	-	
ln(Labor)*ln(University R&D)	-	1.403 (6.98)***	-	
ln(University R&D)*ln(Non-University R&D)	-	-0.085 (-2.05)**	-	
ln(Capital)*ln(Non-University R&D)	-	0.968 (6.77)***	1.120 (10.13)***	0.804 (6.28)***
ln(Labor)*ln(Non-University R&D)	-	-0.932 (-5.99)***	-1.483 (-9.62)***	-1.362 (-8.47)***
ln(Non-University R&D) squared	-	-0.060 (-3.85)***	-0.075 (-2.06)**	-0.134 (-4.05)***
ln(University R&D) squared	-	0.385 (6.26)***	-	
ln(Pure R&D)	-	-	1.644 (1.65)	-2.747 (-1.23)
ln(Applied R&D)	-	-	-0.345 (-0.58)	-6.881 (-4.22)***
ln(Experimental R&D)	-	-	2.814 (2.82)***	10.988 (4.03)***
ln(Strategic R&D)	-	-	0.441 (0.52)	2.670 (1.69)*
ln(Pure R&D)* ln(Capital)	-	-	-0.573 (-3.33)***	0.048 (0.20)
ln(Applied R&D)* ln(Capital)	-	-	0.181 (1.35)	0.833 (4.52)***
ln(Strategic R&D)* ln(Capital)	-	-	-0.888 (-5.75)***	-0.947 (-5.36)***
ln(Experimental R&D)* ln(Capital)	-	-	-0.370 (-3.12)***	-0.966 (-5.67)***
ln(Pure R&D)* ln(Labor)	-	-	0.223 (1.18)	0.201 (0.86)
ln(Applied R&D)* ln(Labor)	-	-	-0.671 (-4.18)***	-0.394 (-1.97)*

[14] However, a Wald test rejects the Null hypothesis that the four Total R&D variables are jointly statistically non-significant (Chi-square = 86.64, prob value = 0.00).

Table 3. (Continued)

Variable	(1)	(2)	(3)	(4)
ln(Strategic R&D)* ln(Labor)	-	-	2.059 (10.86)***	2.006 (9.24)***
ln(Experimental R&D)* ln(Labor)	-	-	-0.128 (-1.04)	-0.560 (-2.66)***
ln(Pure R&D)*ln(Non-University R&D)	-	-	0.143 (0.62)	0.392 (1.71)*
ln(Applied R&D)*ln(Non-University R&D)	-	-	-0.256 (-1.78)*	0.188 (1.27)
ln(Strategic R&D)*ln(Non-University R&D)	-	-	0.200 (2.73)***	0.115 (1.01)
ln(Experimental R&D)*ln(Non-University R&D)	-	-	0.201 (2.05)**	-0.032 (-0.27)
ln(Pure R&D) squared	-	-	0.157 (1.06)	0.338 (1.33)
ln(Applied R&D) squared	-	-	0.426 (5.25)***	1.061 (2.26)**
ln(Experimental R&D) squared	-	-	0.045 (0.54)	0.721 (2.19)**
ln(Strategic R&D) squared	-	-	-0.594 (-6.14)***	-0.096 (-0.21)
ln(Pure R&D)*ln(Applied R&D)	-	-	-	-0.665 (-1.67)*
ln(Pure R&D)*ln(Strategic R&D)	-	-	-	-0.221 (-0.59)
ln(Pure R&D)*ln(Experiment R&D)	-	-	-	-0.243 (-0.57)
ln(Applied R&D)*ln(Strategic R&D)	-	-	-	-1.159 (-1.28)
ln(Applied R&D)*ln(Experiment R&D)	-	-	-	-0.705 (-2.14)**
ln(Strategic R&D)*ln(Experiment R&D)	-	-	-	0.510 (1.23)
Union Density	-0.003 (-8.79)***	-0.002 (-1.73)*	-0.001 (-1.45)	-0.002 (-2.50)**
Deregulation	0.019 (2.56)**	0.041 (5.97)***	0.042 (6.44)***	0.048 (6.03)***

*, **, *** statistically significant at the 10%, 5% and 1% levels, respectively. t-statistics using robust standard errors reported in brackets.

While some of the results are similar, there are also important differences between the results from the Cobb-Douglas and the Translog specifications. The key elasticities are compared in Table 4 (the elasticities for the Translog are calculated at the sample means). In both cases, the elasticity of capital is greater than it is for labor. In both cases, pure basic and applied R&D have a positive impact on output, while strategic basic and experimental R&D have an adverse effect on output. The Translog indicates a lower elasticity associated with Pure and Applied R&D. The key differences are the elasticity of non-university R&D and university R&D. The Cobb-Douglas specification suggests a small negative non-university R&D elasticity, while the Translog suggests a more plausible positive elasticity. Importantly, the Cobb-Douglas specification suggests a positive university R&D elasticity, while the Translog suggests a small negative elasticity.[15]

While it is of small magnitude, the negative elasticity of output with respect to university R&D is of some concern, especially from a policy perspective. It is clear, however, that this is driven by the negative elasticities associated with strategic and experimental R&D. The results on both applied and experimental are not surprising. We expect that R&D effort devoted towards applications of basic research should have positive payoffs. Experimental may be expected to go either way, although those who initiate it would expect to get returns from it. However, pure basic R&D is not directed towards long term benefits and is undertaken for the sake of advancing knowledge. Hence, it is heartening to find that the advancement of knowledge *per se* has a positive effect on the economy. It was surprising to

[15] That is, if pure, applied, strategic and experimental R&D all rise by 1 percent, Australian state output will, on average, decline by 0.03 percent.

us that strategic basic R&D had a robust negative effect (regardless of the specification used). The reasons for this are beyond the scope of this paper, but do warrant a full examination.

Table 4: Australian Gross State Product (GSP) Elasticities, Various Specifications

Elasticity	Cobb-Douglas (Table 2, column 5)	Translog (Table 3, column 4)
Elasticity of GSP w.r.t Capital	0.49 [5411.29]***	0.62 [2157.89]***
Elasticity of GSP w.r.t Labor	0.31 [288.91]***	0.37 [287.97]***
Elasticity of GSP w.r.t Non-University R&D	-0.02 [6.18]**	0.11 [197.82]***
Elasticity of GSP w.r.t University R&D	0.26 [324.85]***	-0.03 [307.90]***
Elasticity of GSP w.r.t University Pure R&D	0.23 [116.85]***	0.15 [44.48]***
Elasticity of GSP w.r.t University Applied R&D	0.33 [109.57]***	0.10 [196.91]***
Elasticity of GSP w.r.t University Strategic R&D	-0.11 [9.86]***	-0.17 [203.22]***
Elasticity of GSP w.r.t University Experimental R&D	-0.19 [-86.16]***	-0.10 [75.61]***

Figures in squared brackets are Wald tests, testing whether the associated elasticity is equal to zero. **, *** statistically significant at the 5% and 1% levels, respectively.

The reasons for this are beyond the scope of this paper, but do warrant a full examination.

Over the period studied, unionization had a consistently negative impact on state output, but the effect was small.[16] The results presented here also indicate that deregulation of the financial sector had a favorable impact on state output. State output is about 5 percent higher in the post deregulation period.

Additional insights into the responsiveness of output with respect to university R&D can be gleamed from the interaction effects. These are summarized in Table 5.

Table 5: Substitution and Complementarity in Australian State Output, 1979-2003

	Capital (1)	Labor (2)	Non-University R&D (3)	Pure (4)	Applied (5)	Strategic (6)	Experimental (7)
Capital	Comp	Sub	Comp	Neutral	Comp	Sub	Sub
Labor	Sub	Comp	Sub	Neutral	Sub	Comp	Sub
Non-University R&D	Comp	Sub	Sub	Comp	Neutral	Neutral	Neutral
Pure	Neutral	Neutral	Comp	Neutral	Sub	Neutral	Neutral
Applied	Comp	Sub	Neutral	Sub	Comp	Neutral	Sub
Strategic	Sub	Comp	Neutral	Neutral	Sub	Neutral	Neutral
Experimental	Sub	Sub	Neutral	Neutral	Sub	Neutral	Comp

Sub = substitute. Comp = complement. All Sub and Comp associations are statistically significant.

16 We do not address, however, other effects of unions, such as provision of benefits to employees, safety in workplaces etc. These issues need to be addressed in future research. Rogers (2000) also briefly address the issue of unions. Using probit regressions, union presence was represented by a dummy variable. The results indicated that firms with unions had a higher probability of reporting to be innovative.

There are three sets of important university R&D interactions: with factor inputs; with non-university R&D; and among the different types of R&D.

Impact on Marginal Productivity of Labor and Capital

As expected, capital and labor are substitutes. Non-university R&D is a complement with capital and a substitute with labor. Pure R&D has no effect at all on the marginal productivity of either capital or labor. Applied R&D is complementary with capital but is a substitute with labor. Hence, its effect is the same as non-university R&D. Strategic R&D has the opposite effect. Experimental R&D is a substitute with both factors.

Impact on Marginal Productivity of Non-University R&D

Pure is the only type of university R&D that has an impact on non-university R&D. Pure R&D is complementary with non-university R&D. Increasing pure university R&D has a positive effect on the contribution of non-university R&D to output. Since the other types of university R&D are neutral, we conclude that university R&D has a positive spillover effect on non-university R&D.

Non-Linearities

The squared input terms capture the existence of non-linear effects. The contributions of capital and labor are greater at higher levels of input usage. However, non-university R&D's contribution declines at higher levels of non-university R&D. Both strategic and pure research are neutral, while applied and experimental are both complementary. That is, the contributions of applied R&D to production are higher at higher levels of applied R&D.

Interactions between University R&D

The only effect pure research has is on applied R&D, where it is, surprisingly, a substitute in the production process. Applied R&D is a substitute also with experimental R&D. Experimental and strategic are neutral with respect to each other's impact on production.

Given these results, it is beneficial to briefly examine the relative share of each of the four types of university R&D. Data for selected years is presented in Table 6. Over the 1979-2003 time period, the relative share of pure R&D undertaken by the university section has decreased. This decrease will have had a negative effect on output levels. This has been offset by the corresponding increase in the share of applied R&D. The increase in applied R&D will have had a positive effect on output levels. In light of the results presented here, it is tempting to conclude that the university sector should shift the focus away from experimental and particularly strategic research and towards pure and applied research areas, which have a positive impact on Australia's overall productivity. However, it is possible that strategic and experimental R&D may have other long-run benefits to production. These need to be considered before firmer inferences can be drawn to guide policy.[17]

---

[17] For example, it is possible that strategic R&D contributes to applied R&D and, hence, has a positive indirect effect on output.

Table 6: Relative Share of University R&D Stocks, by type, selected years

Types of Research	1978-79 %	1988-89 %	2002-03
Pure	35	35	30
Strategic	25	25	26
Applied	34	34	38
Experimental	6	6	6

Table 7 uses the parameter estimates from Table 3 and the growth accounting framework to identify the sources of regional growth. The first row reports the average annual rate of output growth, and the other rows report the contributions of the various inputs and sources of R&D. For example, NSW GSP grew at an average annual rate of 3.32%. Of this, 1.34% (or 40 percent of NSW's growth) can be attributed to growth in physical capital, 0.60% to growth in labor, 0.72% to growth in non-university R&D and 1.20% to growth in pure and applied university R&D. In most cases, the contributions of non-university R&D were larger than those of labor. In the case of Tasmania, non-university R&D was more important than even physical capital formation. Interestingly, with the exception of Tasmania, the contributions of university pure and applied R&D were higher than those from the non-university sector.

Table 7: Contributions of Factor Inputs and R&D to Australian State Output Growth, 1979-2003 (all figures are percentages)

	NSW	VIC	QLD	WA	SA	TAS
Output	3.32	2.83	3.96	4.40	2.70	2.10
Capital	1.34	1.42	1.91	2.95	2.74	1.42
Labor	0.60	0.52	1.11	0.39	0.95	0.30
Non-University R&D	0.72	0.64	0.68	1.00	0.60	1.48
Total University R&D	-0.12	-0.10	-0.20	-0.27	-0.16	-0.32
- Applied and Pure R&D	1.20	1.33	1.73	1.63	0.98	1.33
- Strategic and Experimental R&D	-1.32	-1.43	-1.93	-1.90	-1.14	-1.65

VI. Concluding Comments

The importance of R&D to the production process has long been a source of considerable discussion and evaluation. Numerous international studies have highlighted its contribution to productivity and have concluded that it is an important source of economic growth. A review of Australian literature in this field reveals that relatively little has been written on the topic outside of agriculture and manufacturing industries. Furthermore, to date, the impact of higher education R&D on Australian productivity has been an area which has been largely ignored.

This paper has examined the impact of R&D on Australian state production, and in particular that conducted by the higher education sector, through Cobb-Douglas and Translog production functions. The results confirm that, in addition to capital and labor, R&D is an important and vital input in the production process.

Analysis of the four types of R&D carried out by higher education organizations revealed that both pure and applied R&D have a statistically significant positive impact on Australian regional economic performance. However, strategic and experimental R&D have had an adverse effect, although that they may have other payoffs that remain unexplored. Nevertheless, over the last two decades the majority of research undertaken by the higher education sector in Australia has been in the form of pure and applied research, and these have contributed to regional development.

The results are robust and show that, on average, experimental and strategic basic R&D have negative returns, while pure basic and applied research have positive returns. This is, of course, an average effect, and there could be many projects that fall in the first two categories that have positive payoffs. However, it is clear from the results that Australian regional production benefits more from universities' pure basic research than from strategic basic research. This is an interesting finding that warrants further investigation. An interesting extension would be to compare strategic basic research conducted in the non-university sector to that conducted in the university sector, with the view of exploring the productivity differences between the two.

It is important to note that the production function framework we have used informs on the marginal productivity of factors and how university R&D affects this. This is the direct effect. Additionally, there may be important indirect effects. For example, university R&D may stimulate non-university R&D and may also have important factor accumulation effects. These need to be modeled and explored before firm conclusions can be reached regarding the total effect of university R&D on output.

The focus in this paper has been on total R&D. It would be very interesting to extend the analysis to compare the productivity effects of R&D expenditure across different fields, such as engineering, sciences, information systems and medicine. Furthermore, it would be interesting to compare the impact of different objectives. For example, most of the R&D is directed towards economic development, while other R&D is directed towards defense, environment, health and general societal objectives. Comparing the economic impact of these types of R&D would provide a more complete analysis of the effects of university R&D.

References

Acs, Z., Audretsch, D. and Feldman, P. (1992) 'Real Effects of Academic Research', *American Economic Review* vol. 82, no. 1, pp. 363-67.

- (1994a) 'R&D Spillovers and Innovative Activity', *Managerial and Decision Economics*, vol. 15, no. 2, pp.131-138.

- (1994b) 'R&D Spillovers and Receipt Firm Size', *The Review of Economics and Statistics*, vol. 76, no.2, pp. 336-40.

Addison, J. and C. Belfield. (2004). 'Union Voice', *Journal of Labor Research*, vol. 25, no. 4, pp. 563-96.

Alexander, M. and Green, R. (1992) 'Workplace Productivity and Joint Consultation', *Australian Bulletin of Labour,* vol. 18, no.2, pp.95-118.

Anselin, L., Varga, A. and Acs, Z. (1997) 'Local Geographic Spillovers Between University Research and High Technology Innovations', *Journal of Urban Economics*, vol. 42, no. 3, pp. 422-448.

- (2000) 'Geographic Spillovers and University Research: A spatial econometric perspective', *Growth and Change*, vol. 31, no. 4, pp.501-15.

Australian Bureau of Statistics (various dates) *Research and Experimental Development, Higher Education Organisations, Australia*, Cat. No, 8110.0, AGPS, Canberra.

Australian Bureau of Statistics, *All Sector Summary, Australia, 2002-03*, Cat. No. 8112.0.

Batterham, R. (2000) *The Chance to Change: Final report by the Chief Scientist*, Department of Industry, Science and Resources, Canberra.

Beck, N and Katz, J. (1995) 'What to do (and Not to Do) with Time-Series Cross-Section Data', *American Political Science Review*, vol. 89, no. 3, pp. 634-647.

Bernstein, J. (1988) 'Costs of Production, Intra- and Interindustry R&D Spillover: Canadian evidence' *The Canadian Journal of Economics,* vol. 21, no.2, pp.324-47.

- (1989) 'The Structure of Canadian Inter-industry R&D Spillovers, and the Rates of Return to R&D' *The Journal of Industrial Economics,* vol. 37, no. 3, pp.315-328.

Bernstein, J. and Nadiri, M. (1988) 'Interindustry R&D Spillovers, Rates of Return and Production in High-Tech Industries' *American Economic Review,* vol. 78, no. 2, pp. 429-434.

Brambles, T. (2001) 'Australian Union Strategies Since 1945', *Labour and Industry,* vol.11, no. 3, pp. 1-26.

Briggs, C. (2001) 'Australian Exceptionalism: The role of trade unions in the emergence of Enterprise Bargaining', *Journal of Industrial Relations,* vol. 43, no. 1, pp. 27-43.

Cabalu, H., Kenyon, P. and Koshy, P. (2000) *Of Dollars and Cents: Valuing the Economic Contribution of Universities to the Australian Economy*, Commissioned Report (Business/Higher Education Round Table): no.5.

Coe, D. and Helpman, E. (1995) 'International R&D Spillovers', *European Economic Review,* vol. 39, no. 5, pp. 859-887.

Coe, D. and Moghadam, R. (1993) 'Capital and trade as engines of growth in France: An application of Johansen's cointegration methodology', *IMF Staff Papers,* vol. 40, no. 3, pp. 542-66.

Cuneo, P. and Mairesse, J. (1984) 'Productivity and R&D at the Firm Level in French Manufacturing', in Z. Griliches (ed) *R&D Patents and Productivity,* University of Chicago Press, Chicago.

Commonwealth of Australia (2001) *Backing Australia's Ability: An Innovation Action Plan for the Future*, Commonwealth of Australia, Canberra.

Doucouliagos, C. and Hone, P. (2000) 'Deregulation and Subequilibrium in the Australian Dairy Processing Industry', *The Economic Record*, vol. 76, no. 233, pp. 152-62.

Doucouliagos C. & Laroche P. (2003), 'What do unions do to productivity? A meta-analysis', *Industrial Relations*, vol. 42, no. 4, pp. 650-691.

Dowrick, S. (1994) '*The Role of R&D in Growth: A Survey of the New Growth Theory and Evidence'*, Industry Commission.

Drago, R. and Wooden, M. (1992) 'The Australian Workplace Industrial Relations Survey and Workplace Performance', *The Australian Bulletin of Labour*, vol. 18, no. 2, pp. 142-167.

Drago, R., Wooden, M. and Sloan, J. (1992) *Productive relations? Australian Industrial Relations and Workplace performance,* Allen & Unwin, Sydney.

Fenney, S. and Rogers, M. (2001) 'Innovation and Performance: Benchmarking Australian firms', *Melbourne Institute of Applied Economics and Social Research,* Working Paper No. 7/01.

Freeman, R. and Medoff, J. (1984) *What do unions do?*, Basic Books, New York.

Goto, A. and Suzuki, K. (1989) 'R&D Capital, Rate of Return on R&D Investment and Spillover of R&D in Japanese Manufacturing Industries' *The Review of Economics and Statistics,* vol. 71, no. 4, pp. 555-564.

Griliches, Z. (1964) 'Research Expenditure, Education and the Aggregate Agricultural Production Function', *American Economic Review,* vol. 54, no. 6, pp.961-974.

- (1973) 'Research Expenditure and Growth Accounting', in B.R. Williams (ed) *Science and Technology in Economic Growth,* John Wiley & Sons, Halsted Press, New York.

- (1979) 'Issues in Assessing the Contribution of Research and Development to Productivity Growth', *Bell Journal of Economics,* vol. 10, no. 1, no. 92-116.

- (1990) 'Patent Statistics as Economic Indicators: A Survey', *Journal of Economic Literature,* vol. 28, no. 4, pp.1661-1707.

- (1992) 'The Search for R&D Spillovers', *The Scandinavian Journal of Economics,* (Supplement), vol. 94, no. 0, pp. S29-47.

- (1994) 'Productivity, R&D and Data Constraints', *American Economic Review,* vol.84, no. 1, 1-23.

Griliches, Z. and Mairesse, J. (1984) 'Productivity and R&D at the Firm Level', chapter 17 in Z. Griliches (Ed) *R&D, Patents and Productivity,* University of Chicago Press, Chicago.

Groenewold, N. (2003), 'Financial Deregulation and the Relationship between the Economy and the Share Market in Australia' *Australian Economic Papers,* vol. 42, no. 4, pp. 454-77.

Gwartney, J. and R. Lawson. (2003) *Economic Freedom of the World Annual Report.* The Fraser Institute, Vancouver, BC.

Health and Medical Research Strategic Review (1999) *The Virtuous Cycle: Working together for health and medical research,* Department of Health & Aged Care, Canberra.

Hirsch, B. 2004. 'What Do Unions Do for Economic Performance?' *Journal of Labor Research,* vol. 25, no. 3, pp. 415-55.

Industry Commission (1995) *Research and Development,* Report No 44, May 15, vol. 3, Government Publishing Services, Canberra.

Jaffe, A. (1986) 'Technological Opportunity and Spillovers of R&D: Evidence from firms' patents, profits and market value', *American Economic Review,* vol. 76, no. 5, pp. 984-1001.

- (1989) 'Real Effects of Academic Research' *American Economic Review,* vol.79, no. 5, pp.957-970.

Kemp, D. (1999) *Knowledge and Innovation: A policy statement on research and research training,* Department of Education, Training and Youth Affairs, Canberra.

Lie, F., Brooks, R. and Faff, R. (2000) 'Modelling the Equity Beta Risk of Australian Financial Sector Companies', *Australian Economic Papers,* vol. 39, no.3. pp.301-311.

Link, A. & Rees, J. (1990) 'Firm Size, University-Based Research and the Returns to R&D' *Small Business Economics,* vol. 2, no. 1, pp.25-32.

Mairesse, J. and Mohnen, P. (1994) 'R&D and Productivity Growth: What have we learned from econometric studies?' In *Proceedings of the EUNETIC (European Network on the Economics of Technological and Institutional Change) Conference on Evolutionary Economics of Technological Change: Assessment of Results for the New Frontiers* Strasbourg: BETA Strasbourg Communaute Urbaine.

Mairesse, J. and Sassenou, M. (1991) 'R&D and Productivity: A survey of econometric studies at the firm level', *Science-Technology Industry Review*, vol. 8, pp. 9-43.

Mansfield, E. (1965) 'Rates of Return from Industrial R&D', *American Economic Review,* vol. 70, pp. 863-873.

- (1972) *Contribution of Research and Development to Economic Growth in the United States,* Papers and Proceedings of a Colloquium on Research and Development and Economic Growth Productivity, National Science Foundation, Washington D.C.

- (1984) 'Comments on Using Linked Patent and R&D Data to Measure Interindustry Technology Flows', in Griliches, Z (ed) *R&D Patents and Productivity*, University of Chicago Press, Chicago.

Minasian, J.R. (1962) 'The Economics of Research and Development', in R.R. Nelson (ed) *The Rate of and Direction of Inventive Activity: Economics and Social Factors*, NBER Special Conference vol. 13, Princeton University Press, Princeton.

Mohnen, P. (1990) *R&D and Productivity Growth: A survey of the literature,* CERPE – Cahier de Recherche no 57, Centre de Recherche sur les Politiques Economiques, Universite du Quebec a Montreal.

- (1996) 'R&D Externalities and Productivity Growth', *Science-Technology Industry Review,* vol. 18, pp. 39-66.

Mohnen, P and Lepine, N. (1988) *Payments for Technology as a Factor of Production,* Cahier n. 8810, Departement des Sciences Economiques, Universite du Quebec a Montreal.

- (1991) 'R&D, R&D Spillovers and Payments for Technology: Canadian Evidence', *Structural Change and Economic Dynamics,* vol. 2, no. 1, pp. 213-28.

Mohnen, P., Nadiri, M. and Prucha, I. (1986) 'R&D, Production Structure and Rates of Return in US, Japanese and German Manufacturing Sectors: A non-separable dynamic factor demand model', *European Economic Review*, vol. 30, no. 4, pp. 749-772

Nadiri, M.I. (1980) 'Sectoral Productivity Slowdown', *American Economic Review*, vol. 70, no. 2, pp. 349-52.

- (1993) 'Innovations and Technological Spillovers', *NBER Working Paper no. 4423*, National Bureau of Economic Research, Cambridge.

Nelson, R. (1986) 'R&D, Innovation and Public Policy', *American Economic Review,* vol. 76, pp.186-89.

OECD (1980) *The Measurement of Scientific Technical Activities: Proposed Standard Practice for Surveys of Research and Experimental Development - Frascati Manual*

Olley, S. and Pakes, A. (1996) 'The Dynamic of Productivity in the Telecommunications Equipment Industry', *Econometrica*, vol. 64, no. 6, pp. 1263-1297.

Phipps, A. and Sheen, J. (1992) 'Unionisation, Industrial Relations and Labour Productivity Growth in Australia: A pooled time-series/cross section analysis of TFP growth', *Labour of Economics and Productivity*, vol. 6, pp.54-77.

Rogers (2000) 'Understanding Innovative Firms: An Empirical Analysis of the GAPS' *Melbourne Institute of Applied and Social Research,* Working Paper No. 8/00.

Rogers, M. (2001) 'The International Diffusion of Technology: Technological catch-up and economic growth', in Bloch, H. and Kenyon, P. (eds), *Creating an Internationally Competitive Economy,* Palgrave, New York.

- (2002) 'Firm Performance and Investment in R&D and Intellectual Property', *Melbourne Institute of Applied and Social Research,* Working Paper No. 15/02.

Sarafoglou, N. and Hayes, K. (1996) 'University Productivity in Sweden: A demonstration and explanatory analysis for economics and business programs', *The Annals of Regional Science*, vol. 30, pp. 285-304.

Scherer, F. (1983) 'The Propensity to Patent', *International Journal of Industrial Organization*, vol. 1, no. 1, pp. 107-128.

Sterlacchini, A. (1989) 'R&D, Innovations, and Total Factor Productivity Growth in British Manufacturing', *Applied Economics*, vol. 21, no. 1, pp. 1549-62.

Terleckyj, N. (1958) 'Factors Underlying Productivity: Some empirical observations', *Journal of the American Statistics Association*, vol. 53, pp. 593.

- (1974) *Effects of R&D on the Productivity of Growth of Industries: An exploratory study*, National Planning Association, Washington.

Turnbull, P. (2003). 'What Do Unions Do Now?', *Journal of Labor Research*, vol. 24, no. 3, pp.491-527.

In: Australia: Economic, Political and Social Issues
Editors: Lachlan J. Williams and Ethan N. Lee
ISBN: 978-1-60456-856-1

Chapter 3

HIGH PRISON POPULATION IN QUEENSLAND, AUSTRALIA: ITS IMPLICATIONS AND PUBLIC POLICY CHOICES

*Wing Hong Chui**
School of Law, The Chinese University of Hong Kong, School of Social Science, The University of Queensland, Australia

INTRODUCTION

The size and growth of Australia's prison population is a concern to political leaders and the public (Brown, 1998; Carcach and Grant, 2000; Heggie, 2005; Indyk and Donnelly, 2007). The latest figure released by the Australian Bureau of Statistics (ABS) (2006) reported that there were 25,790 sentenced and unsentenced prisoners in Australian prisons as of 30th June 2006, which translates to an imprisonment rate of 163 prisoners per 100,000 adult population.[1] A rise in the number of people in prison has also been documented in many other countries such as the United States (Merlo, 1997; Tonry, 1999, 2004a; Mauer, 2001; Smith, 2004; Welch, 2005; Doob and Webster, 2006; Stucky, Heimer and Lang, 2007), England and Wales (Matthews, 1999; Cavadino and Dignan, 2002; Liebling, 2006; Morgan and Liebling, 2007), and New Zealand (Pratt, 2006). For example, Hooks, Mosher, Rotolo and Labo (2004) report that the national incarceration rates grew by almost 400 per cent between 1980 (N=329,821) and 1998 (N=1,302,019) in the United States. The 1998 figure translates 'to an incarceration rate of 668 prisoners per 100,000 citizens' (Hooks et al., 2004: 40). Similarly a recent survey conducted by Aebi and Stadnic (2007) indicates that there was an increase in

* E-mail: w.chui@uq.edu.au

[1] The imprisonment rate of prisoners per 100,000 head of population has been used as one measurement of the use of imprisonment in common law jurisdictions (Indyk and Donnelly, 2007: 7). However, it is important to emphasize that the exact counting rule and procedure varies across Australian jurisdictions and countries (Chappell, 1992). For instance, the imprisonment rate per 100,000 usually refers to the average daily populations which include both sentence prisoners and those on remand in the Australian adult correctional facilities. Countries such as England and the United States include juvenile and young offenders in detention when calculating the rates (Indyk and Donnelly, 2007: 8). Therefore, caution should be taken when comparing imprisonment rates both nationally and internationally.

prison population rates amongst a number of European countries such as Albania, Croatia, Luxembourg and England and Wales between 2000 and 2005 (see Table 1). The adult prisoner numbers had grown 42 per cent in the last ten years.

Table 1. Prison Populations in 2000 and 2005 in Selected European States

	2000		2005		% change***
	(a)*	(b)**	(a)	(b)	
Albania	1467	43.5	3425	109.3	151.2
Austria	6896	83.1	8767	106.8	28.6
Belgium	8671	84.7	9371	89.7	5.9
Bulgaria	9424	115	12240	157.7	37.1
Croatia	2027	44.4	3485	78.5	76.8
Czech Republic	22489	219	19052	186.4	-14.9
Denmark	3279	61.5	4132	76.4	24.2
Estonia	4720	328	4410	327.4	-0.2
Finland	2703	52.3	3823	73.0	39.6
France	48835	80.1	57582	91.8	14.6
Greece	8038	76.2	9589	86.6	13.6
Hungary	15821	158	16394	162.4	2.8
Iceland	82	29	119	40.5	39.8
Italy	53481	92.7	59649	102.0	10.1
Latvia	8555	353	7228	313.4	-11.2
Lithuania	8867	240	7993	233.4	-2.8
Luxemburg	394	90.4	693	152.3	68.5
Netherlands	13847	90.1	21826	133.9	48.6
Norway	2643	59	3097	67.2	14.0
Poland	65336	169	82656	216.5	28.1
Romania	49682	221	37929	175.1	-20.8
Slovak Republic	7128	297	9289	172.5	-41.9
Slovenia	1136	57.3	1132	56.7	-1.1
Spain	45044	114	61269	142.4	24.9
Sweden	5678	64.1	7054	78.3	22.1
Switzerland	6390	89.2	6111	82.4	-7.6
(The Former Yugoslav Republic of) Macedonia	1394	69	2132	104.8	51.8
Turkey	71860	110	54296	75.8	-31.1
UK: England and Wales	65666	124	76190	142.7	15.1

* (a) Total number of prisoners (including pre-trial detainees) on 1st September of each year (For some countries, the reference date may vary across years. See the full report of SPACE 1)

** (b) Prison population rate per 100,000 inhabitants on 1st September of each year (For some countries, the reference date may vary across years. See the full report of SPACE 1)

*** % Change 2000-2005 = Evolution (in percentage) of prison population rates between 2000 and 2005

Source: Adapted and modified from Aebi and Stadnic (2007: Table 1.3).

In recent years, some researchers such as Neapolitan (2001) and Listokin (2003) have attempted to examine the link between imprisonment rates and crime rates. The mechanical theory of crime and incarceration believes that the rising prison population reflects in an increase in total crime rates, especially those violent and serious crimes. On the contrary other commentators believe that the growth in prison populations is a function of policy such as changes in sentencing and parole practice (Young, 1986; Brown, 1998; Caplow and Simon, 1999; Tonry and Petersilia, 1999; Mauer, 2001). Those who do not support the mechanical theory of crime and incarceration hold the view that growth in prison populations has little or nothing to do with changes in crime rates. Rather it is primarily influenced by the political responses to crime and social control (Garland, 2001). At a public policy level, decisions made by political leaders, judicial officers and criminal justice personnel will determine the likelihood of prosecution, sentencing practice, rates of incarceration, and types and length of various community and custodial sentences. For instance, the New Labour's crime control policy has become punitive and mean-spirited. Part of the reason to adopt such a tough measure on crime is to respond to the increasing media and public support for severe punishment on criminals. The shift a rational penal policy to 'populist punitiveness' or 'new punitiveness' has been driven by the attempt to win electoral favour (Bottoms, 1995; Ryan, 1999; Johnstone, 2000). Tonry (2004b: 5) comments:

> The Labour government has apparently decided that an end it values – its own perpetuation in power – justifies undesirable means ... Tony Blair has himself quoted in the press as acknowledging that his government's proposal for locking up 12- to 15-year-olds in secure facilities are 'horrible', but necessary because the politics of law and order require it (Paveley, 2002).

So what are the major reasons for the increasing incarceration rates? An examination of this increase is vital. The knowledge gained from the present research can be used to inform the decisions of criminal justice personnel and policy makers, by offering a better explanation of how and why more people are held in prisons and questioning whether incarceration is the right way to achieve crime prevention and public safety. More specifically, this paper investigates the reasons for the increasing prison population in Queensland, Australia. While the discussion is primarily focused on the Queensland prison system, examples from other industrialized countries such as England and Wales and the United States and references to the National prison population in Australia are incorporated. For the purpose of this paper, the term 'prison' refers to all Queensland Corrective Services custodial establishments. It does not include juvenile offenders who are administered by a separate Government Department, nor does it include offenders who receive non-custodial or community sentences.

The paper is divided into four sections. The first section introduces the Queensland prison system that may provide a useful context for non-Australian readers. Recent trends in the Queensland prison population are examined in the second section. General trends are also examined in gender and race contexts, examining the composition of prison population. An extended examination of possible reasons for those trends comprises the third section of the paper before the final section, which argues for increased support in prison research. At the outset it must be emphasized that this paper is largely based on data from secondary sources such as the Queensland Corrective Services and the ABS. Relying extensively on secondary data is usually problematic, and, for example, different data sources may vary in their ways of operationalizing concepts and operational definitions may not be sufficiently specified (see Jupp, 1989; Riedel, 2000; May, 2001). Therefore, any conclusions drawn in this paper are tentative and require further investigation.

OVERVIEW OF THE QUEENSLAND CORRECTIVE SERVICES

In Australia, although offenders may be charged under Federal law, there are no Federal prisons. A sentenced offender will therefore serve his or her sentence in the State or Territory where the crime was committed. In Queensland, the State prison system is administered by the Minister for Police and Corrective Services. The then Department of Corrective Services was first established in May 1999 to replace the former Queensland Corrective Services Commission, and the Government owned corporation, Queensland Corrections (O'Toole, 2006). This structural change followed the acceptance of recommendations from a legally required five-yearly review of corrective services under the *Corrective Services (Administration) Act 1988* (see the Department of Corrective Services, 2001). The report from the Commission of Inquiry, *Corrections in the Balance – A Review of Corrective Services in Queensland*, identified a number of target areas for change (Corrective Services Review, 1999). Much of the development of this Department in the early 2000s was a consequence of this report. Notably, the enactment of the new *Corrective Services Act 2000* and the associated policy and procedures documents clarified the functions of the Department of Corrective Services. Developments include ongoing commitment to a partially privatized prison system; the expansion of one correctional centre, and the completion of an additional correctional centre; increased emphasis on addressing the specific needs of female offenders; an enhanced sentence management policy; a new Aboriginal and Torres Strait Islander recruitment strategy; and involvement in a number of projects regarding offenders on community supervision orders (see Department of Corrective Services, 2001).

Since August 2006, the Department of Corrective Services has been renamed as the Queensland Corrective Services. The *Corrective Services Act 2006* was passed by the parliament on 25 May 2006 and commenced on 28 August 2006. The new Act is based on the principles of providing for a safe and humane containment, supervision and rehabilitation of prisoners and ensuring the safety of the community and the staff who work in the correctional system (quoted in Queensland Corrective Services, 2006a). Under the *Corrective Services Act 2006*, all prisoners, including remand prisoners, are classified into three categories, namely maximum, high and low security upon admission to a correctional facility. The assessment criteria are: the nature of the offence for which the prisoner has been charged or convicted; the risk of the prisoner escaping, or attempting to escape, from custody; the risk of reoffending and potential impact on the community; and the risk the prisoner poses to themselves and the correctional staff (Queensland Corrective Services, 2006b). With reference to sections, 17, 66, 68 and 71 of the *Corrective Services Act 2006*, decisions about a prisoner's security classification, transfer or placement will not be reviewable under the *Judicial Review Act 1992.* According to Chapter 5 of the *Corrective Services Act 2006*, supervised parole is the only form of early release available to prisoners, replacing remission, conditional release, release to work and home detention. Three Parole Boards have been established to consider all these parole applications (Queensland Corrective Services, 2006a,

2006b). While this legislative change to empower the Parole Boards to make decisions on prisoners' release to parole, it is still early days to assess its impact on correctional outcomes and practice in Queensland.

Whilst acknowledging the recent legislative change, one of the major responsibilities of the Queensland Corrective Services has remained to supervise offenders through four main areas of operations, which can be seen as a continuum ranging from the most reliant on physical containment to the least. Prisoner movement through the continuum is dependent on satisfactory behaviour. The first is Secure Custody Correctional Centres (Queensland Corrective Services, 2006c). Approximately 70% of the State's incarcerated prisoners are held in ten correctional centres (of which two are privately operated, the remainder being government facilities). These centres ensure containment by means of a secure perimeter, within which prisoners are managed according to their assessed security classification and their particular needs (Department of Corrective Services, 2006c). Participation in education, work, vocational training and programmes that address offending behaviour provides opportunities for rehabilitation. The second type is the Open Custody Correctional Services which place less emphasis on physical containment than secure ones. Prisoners must be assessed as suitable and hold low/open security classification. These low or open security correctional centres are regarded as a step towards rehabilitation and graduated release. There is an encouragement to raise levels of self-responsibility and to participate in programmes similar to those available in the higher security centres. Approximately 13% of Queensland prisoners are held in six low security facilities, of which four are annexes to secure custody centres (Queensland Corrective Services, 2006c). The remaining 17% of prisoners in Queensland are held in various Community Custody Centres around Queensland participating in various prisoner rehabilitation programmes, for instance Work Camps. Prisoners in community custody centres can access leaves of absence to attend work, perform community services or visit families, and those who satisfactorily complete a period of community custody will progress to community supervision. In addition to three types of custodial corrections, the Queensland Corrective Services monitors offenders on community-based orders such as probation and parole, home detention with electronic monitoring, intensive drug rehabilitation orders, community service and fine option orders. Between 2005 and 2006, the Department supervised an average of 15,354 offenders on either community-based orders or post-prison community-based releases (Department of Corrective Services, 2006: 78). These offenders are case managed and supervised by correctional staff to whom they must report regularly.

It is apparent that the vast majority of Queensland prisoners are held in secure custody as opposed to open custody. The continuing reliance on imprisonment is evidenced by the recent increases in the capacity of the Queensland prison system. For instance, the Woodford Correctional Centre is a high security facility whose recent expansion increased its capacity and currently holds 988 prisoners. Although Rockhampton Correctional Centre, which held 336 prisoners in the secure compound and 14 in the low security farm, recently closed, it was replaced by Capricornia Correctional Centre, with a capacity for 300 secure prisoners, 100 prisoners in residential accommodation and 96 in farm/open security. This new centre also incorporates a maximum security unit. The most recent addition to the Queensland prison system however is the Maryborough multi-purpose high security facility that commenced operations in 2003. This prison houses 320 male prisoners in secure accommodation and 180 in residential, with state of the art technology such as drug and contraband scanners and equipment capable of detecting movement and sound around the perimeter (Queensland Corrective Services, 2006c). While a lot of money and resources have been consumed in increasing Queensland's capacity to contain offenders in prisons, the Queensland Corrective Services has also been involved in developing alternative means of offender supervision in the community. For example, the Drug Courts subject drug offenders to Intensive Drug Rehabilitation Orders under supervision in the community; the use of electronic monitoring allows some prisoners who may serve the post-prison portion of the custodial sentence in the community; and the State Penalties Enforcement Registry (SPER) offers a range of payment options to fine defaulters (Department of Corrective Services, 2001). Since the commencement of the Drug Courts in June 2000, 774 intensive drug rehabilitation orders have been supervised by the corrective services department in Queensland (Department of Corrective Services, 2006). The last two alternatives are intended to reduce the number of offenders in prison, and especially in the case of SPER, the Department (2001) saw this initiative effective and attributes to its implementation 'the significant decline in total number of offenders subject to fine option order' (p. 32).

Recent Trends in the Queensland Prison Population

The increase in prison population at a rate higher than that in the general population is a trend that has been evident over the last few decades (Criminal Justice Commission (CJC), 2000). During the period between the 1950s and early 1990s, the Queensland annual average imprisonment rate varied between 85 and 120 per 100,000 adults, by 1997–98, this rate had grown to almost 165 per 100,000 adults in prison custody and in 2006 this figure had continued to rise to 181 per 100,000 (Australian Bureau of Statistics, 2006). The CJC (2000) went on to note 1993 as something of a benchmark year, and was unable to ascribe the growth in prison numbers since that time to any single factor. In fact, the average annual increase in the prison population (from 1992–3 to 1997–98) was almost 17%. During the same period, there was a 2% increase in the general adult population, a 4% increase in recorded crime, a 7% increase in convictions involving a sentence of imprisonment and a 14% increase in the number of admissions to prison. Based on these findings, the CJC speculated that the increase in convictions leading to imprisonment implies that the police were more successful in solving crime and the courts were tougher by imposing more prison sentences, and increasing their length. At the same time the disproportionate increase in admissions means that fewer were getting off an appeal, after being sentenced. These speculations are all the more noteworthy when it is considered that Queensland's high rate of imprisonment has occurred concurrently with its average levels of crime being below the national average (CJC, 2000).

Table 2 shows the number of prisoners and imprisonment rates per 100,000 population aged 18 years and over in Queensland and Australia from 1982 to 2006. These data were derived from two major sources, namely *Australian Prisoners* (Australian Institute of Criminology, 1982–1993) and *Prisoners in Australia* (Australian Bureau of Statistics, 1994–2006). The statistics show a phenomenal increase of prisoners in Queensland from 1,628 in 1982 to 5,392 in 2006. There was also an increase in the national prison population from 9,826 in 1982 to 25,800 in 2006.

Table 2. Numbers of Prisoners and Imprisonment Rates per 100,000 Population Aged 18 Years and Over in Queensland and Australia

Year	Queensland	Australia	Queensland	Australia
	Number of Prisoners		Rate per 100,000 Population of Imprisonable Age	
1982	1,638	9,826	95.4	89.8
1983	1,709	10,196	96.9	91.6
1984	1,881	9,694	104.4	85.6
1985	1,999	10,844	108.4	94.1
1986	2,185	11,497	115.0	97.6
1987	2,343	12,113	120.3	100.8
1988	2,374	12,321	118.4	100.4
1989	2,390	12,965	115.0	103.5
1990	2,296	14,305	107.4	112.2
1991	2,094	15,021	95.6	116.0
1992	2,017	15,559	89.5	118.3
1993	2,068	15,866	89.0	119.2
1994	2,491	16,944	104.0	125.5
1995	2,870	17,428	116.6	127.3
1996	3,528	18,193	139.6	130.9
1997	3,839	19,082	149.2	134.9
1998	4,466	19,906	171.3	139.2
1999	4,729	21538	177	145
2000	4,482	21,714	165.5	148
2001	4,517	22,458	163	151
2002	4721	22,492	167.3	148
2003	5,243	23,555	180.7	153
2004	5,240	24,171	177	157
2005	5,354	25,400	176.7	163
2006	5,392*	25,800	181*	163

Source: Statistics for years 1982-1998 modified from Carcach and Grant (1999: 3); those for years 1999-2006 taken from the Australian Bureau of Statistics (various issues).

* Numbers are taken from the latest release from ABS (2007).

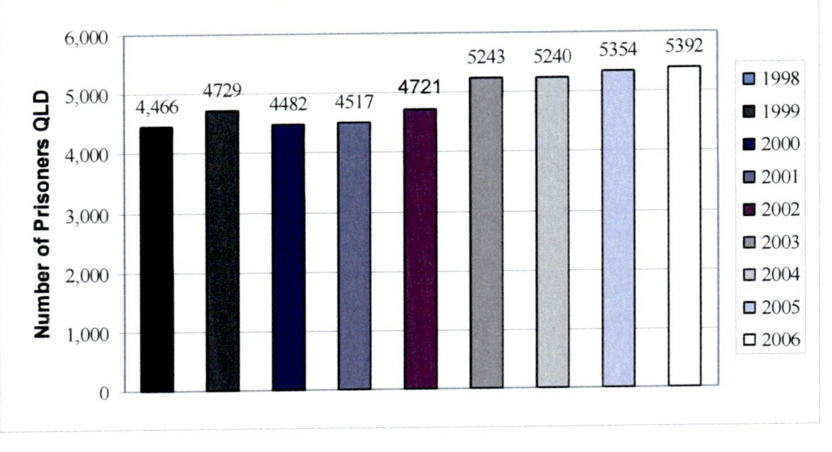

Source: ABS (1998–2006).

Figure 1. Annual Number of Prisoners for the Period 1998–2006 in Queensland.

Figure 1 shows the annual number of prisoners in Queensland from 1998 to 2006 based on the official figures published by the ABS (1998–2006). It shows a steady increase in the prison population over an eight year period. On the contrary, community-based supervision orders significantly decreased in 2006 as shown in Figure 2.

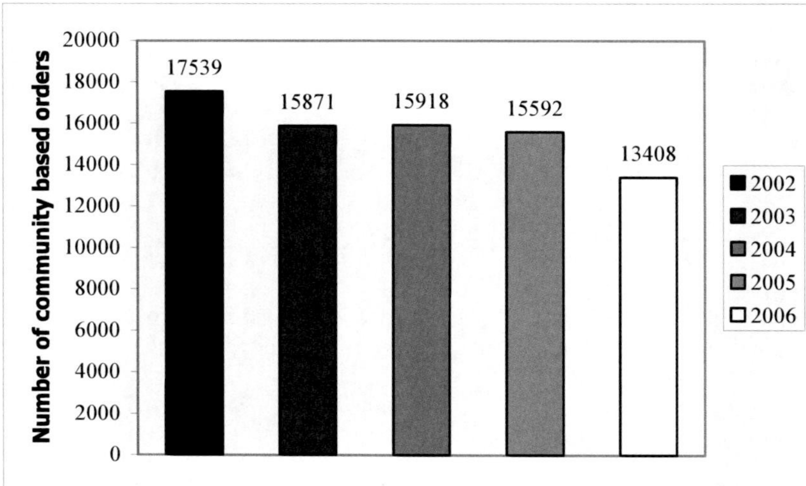

Source: Derived data from the Department of Corrective Services (2002–2006).
Figure 2. Annual Number of Community-based Orders for the Period 2002–2006 in Queensland.

In order to provide a more detailed picture of the trends exhibited by the Queensland prison population, it is helpful to break it down by gender and indigenous status. The minority status of women in the prison system has led to their virtual invisibility (Faith, 1993; Devlin, 1998; Carlen, 2002). It is only recently that the needs of incarcerated women have begun to be recognized and addressed as distinct from those of their male counterparts, and initiatives have been set up to developing the gender-specific rehabilitative programmes for women offenders. Unless otherwise stated, all the data used were derived from the report entitled *Profile of Female Offenders* (Women's Policy Unit, 2000). The following lists the most notable female trends in Queensland prison populations. Firstly, in the period 1994–1999, the growth of the female prison population was 173%, that is an annual growth of 22%, far in excess of the male rate (15%). Women in secure and open custodial centres comprised 5.8% of the entire prison population, a total of 273 women. Secondly, there were more women (N=4,331) on community supervision orders than on custodial orders (N=273). This is a proportion of 21.63% of all offenders serving community supervision orders. Thirdly, the Queensland rate of imprisonment of women was 16.7 per 100,000 female adults, well in excess of the national rate of 12.5 per 100,000 for female offenders. Fourthly, Indigenous women comprised 22.3% of all women prisoners, a significant over-representation. Indigenous women did not have access to community custody options to the same extent as non-Indigenous prisoners. Fifthly, the pattern of female offending was distinct from the male. Compared to male prisoners, drug offences comprised a greater proportion of all offences committed by women prisoners. Proportionally fewer females than males were convicted of violent offences, and homicide offences had decreased between 1994 and 1999, although robbery and break and enter offences had increased. These figures have continued to increase with females accounting for 6.7% of the population of prisoners in Queensland in 2005, a total of 358 women (Office of Economic and Statistical Research, 2005). Indigenous women increased to 26.5% of female prisoners in Queensland in 2005 also (Department of Corrective Services, 2005).

Indigenous prisoners represent 27% of all prisoners (Department of Corrective Services, 2006), showing an increase of 2% from the previous year (Department of Corrective Services, 2005). As shown in Figure 3, the actual numbers of Indigenous offenders in prison has displayed a steady growth since 1991, peaked in 1999 and shown a small decrease in 1999/2000 (Office of the Government Statistician, 2001). Between 1992 and 1999, the Indigenous rate of imprisonment increased by 13% per year, a higher rate than that of overall imprisonment which increased by 10% annually during the same period. From 1999 to 2000, the rate of imprisonment decreased both overall, and for Indigenous offenders, by 7% and 8% respectively (Office of the Government Statistician, 2001). For the March quarter of 2001, Indigenous prisoners represented 21.2% or 974 persons. For that same quarter, the rate of imprisonment of Indigenous persons was 1,465.6 per 100,000 Indigenous population, 10.7 times the rate for non-Indigenous Australians. It should be noted however, that despite the obvious over-representation of Indigenous people, Queensland's rate was lower than the national Indigenous imprisonment rate of 1,689.8 per 100,000 population (Office of Economic and Statistical Research, 2001).

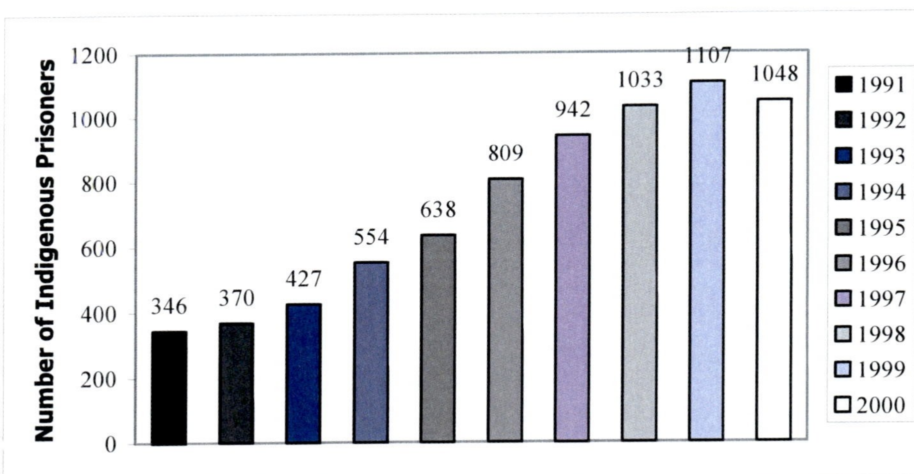

Source: Derived data from the Office of the Government Statistician (2001: Table 3.3).
Figure 3. Indigenous Prisoner Population at 30 June 1991–2000 in Queensland.

By analyzing the 1997 Census data, the Office of Statistical and Economic Research (2001) found that the median age of Indigenous prisoners was 25 years, three years younger than that of the overall Queensland prison population; Indigenous prisoners were more likely to have been incarcerated previously (only 56% of non-Indigenous prisoners had served a prior custodial sentence, compared to 73% of Indigenous prisoners); Indigenous prisoners were generally serving shorter sentences than the whole prison population – the median time an Indigenous prisoner expected to serve was 13 months, compared to 3.3 years for the general prison population – and only 29% of Indigenous prisoners were serving sentences of five years or more, compared to 48% of non-Indigenous prisoners. Significant differences in the proportion of Indigenous and non-Indigenous prisoners serving sentences for non-violent offences were also apparent. For example, there were more than twice as many non-Indigenous prisoners (3.9%) serving a sentence for fraud and misappropriation, as there were Indigenous (1.2%). The proportion of Indigenous prisoners convicted of drug offences was 2%, compared to the non-Indigenous prisoners, proportion of 9.2% (see Office of Economic and Statistical Research, 1999).

Possible Explanations for the Trend

The reasons for this increasing prison population are complex, and indeed, it is not easy to give an unequivocal explanation. According to Young (1986), prison populations may be determined by factors extrinsic to the system and by policy choices. To explain the prison population explosion in Queensland, the deterministic approach can be interpreted as the factors extrinsic to the criminal justice system such as crime rates. Put simply, 'crime rates increased and carried punishments with them' (Tonry, 2004a: 23). On the contrary, the policy choice model alludes to the law and order ideology which emphasizes the increasing use of punitive crime control and punishment policies in the contemporary society. The tougher penalties may be driven by the public's fear of crime and feeling of insecurity in a so-called 'risk society' (Tonry, 2004a: 23). In order to increase the public confidence in the Government, civil servants and politicians intentionally demonstrated their abilities to achieve outcomes in dealing with emotional issues such as crime, welfare, illegal immigration and terrorism. Their actions in turn will win the voters' support by being 'tough on criminals and the causes of crime' (Tonry, 2004a). Likewise, Greenwood (1998) comments: 'In recent years, it has become fashionable for just about every candidate for public office to have a position on crime, and the only position worth having is appearing to be tougher than your opponent' (p. 138).

At the outset, it is important to acknowledge that several criminologists such as Christie (2000), Garland (2001) and Tonry (2004a) have attempted to analyze how and why penal policies and practices in western countries developed as they did. They agreed that any attempt to single out one explanation is wrong and it is very difficult to disentangle all factors and processes affecting the size of the prison population in many western countries. In this respect, this chapter by no means offers a straightforward answer to explain the growing prison population in the Queensland correctional system in the past decade. Rather it is seen as a starting point to generate more academic interest and research to examine this complex and essential subject area in the Australian context. The focus of this chapter is an exploration of the sense in which rising prison population in Queensland is becoming a policy issue and the policy options being canvassed.

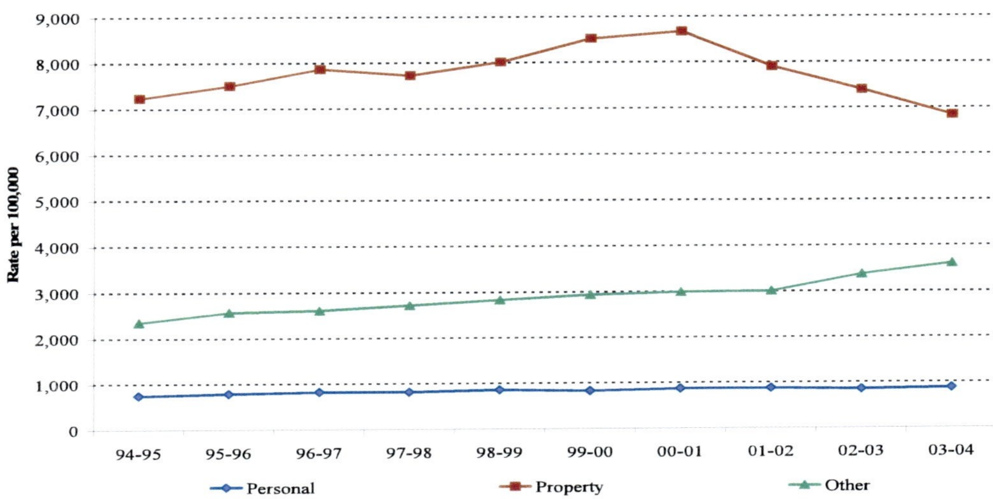

Source: ABS Statistical Reviews (cited in Department of Premier and Cabinet, 2005: 5).

Figure 4. Rate per 100,000 Population: Recorded Crime by Offence Category, Queensland, 1994-95 to 2003-04.

With reference to the deterministic approach, a greater level of recorded crime and the increasing number of serious offences result in a higher use of incarceration. It is generally believed that 'more crime leads to more incarceration' (Listokin, 2003: 182). As shown in Figure 4, the Queensland police statistics show that property crimes accounted for the majority of offences in Queensland, and they decreased significantly between 2000/01 and 2003/4. Offences against the person had increased since 1994/95 but remained fairly stable in recent years. However, there was a remarkable increase in recorded crime involving offences classified 'other', and the majority of these offences were drug offences, traffic and related offences, good order offences, breaches of domestic violence protection orders, prostitution, trespassing, weapons and liquor offences, and gaming, racing and betting offences (Department of Premier and Cabinet, 2005).

Based upon the official data, it appears that the number of recorded crimes have been fairly stable between 2000/01 and 2003/04. The latest police statistics also shows an insignificant increase in the total number of reported offences between 2004/05 and 2005/06. The percentage of the number reported per 100,000 population for the offences against the person is a reduction of 4%; for the offences against the person is a 3% increase; and for other offences is a 6% increase (Queensland Police Service, 2006: 2–7). In contrast, as shown in Table 2 and Figure 2, the number of prisoners aged 18 years and over in Queensland has increased in a more substantial way than the overall recorded crime rate. Indeed several commentators confirm that there is a lack of empirical evidence which proves the direct link between crime and imprisonment (Bowker, 1981; Blumstein, 1998; Tonry, 1999). For instance, Bowker (1981) sees little or almost no relationship between crime and imprisonment, and convincing empirical examples such as West Germany and Scandinavia show that the recorded crime rate went up while the prison rate went down in the late twentieth century (see, for example, Graham, 1990; Mathiesen, 1990).

In Queensland, according to the Office of Economic and Statistical Research (1999), rises in the rates of serious crime might be linked to the rise in incarceration levels; the proportion of prisoners serving sentences for violent offences increased from 40% in 1982 to 55% in 1997 (see Figure 5). The report shows that the proportion of offenders for assault increased from 5% to 13%; for robbery and extortion increased from 9% to 15%; and for driving and related offences declined from 17% to 5% (Office of Economic and Statistical Research, 1999: 2). Nevertheless, caution should be exercised when interpreting these statistics. Firstly, legislative changes have affected the way offences have been defined, classified and recorded. Secondly, the relationship between the rates of serious crime and imprisonment is often mediated by other factors such as the efficiency of law enforcement agencies, and changing patterns of prosecution and sentencing activity. For example, longer sentences and the possibility of early release programmes for specific groups of offenders affect the size of the prison.

The rise in prison population could however have been interpreted as a consequence of policy choice rather than a reflection of an increase in recorded crime rate or serious crime in particular. Christie (2000) contends that the size of prison population is man-made and is a result of political decisions. In fact, the CJC (2000) report titled *Prisoner Numbers in Queensland: An Examination of Population Trends in Queensland's Correctional Institutions* found little support to the mechanical theory of crime and imprisonment. Six possible factors were identified to explain the dramatic growth in the prison population between 1993 and 1998. The six factors identified were changes in police practice, changing legislations, declining use of community-based orders, increase in the number of fine deafulters being apprehended, increased recidivism, and increase in the number of short-term prisoners as well as longer sentences.

As argued by the CJC (2000: 16), police enforcement had focused substantially on apprehending a large volume of minor drug offences, good order offences, enforcement of order offences (such as breach of bail conditions and fine defaulters) and executing outstanding warrants since early 1990s. This changing police activity in some areas in Queensland contributed to the remarkable increase of short-term prisoners. Another two possible factors which affect the size of prison are the legislative change and changing sentencing practice. For example, it has been observed between 1989 and 1993 courts appeared more willing to sentence offenders to community-based orders in Queensland. Since the enactment of the *Penalties and Sentences Act 1992*, their willingness to do so has declined (CJC, 2000). Two significant changes from the existing law which incorporate in the *Penalties and Sentences Act 1992* were 'the creation of entirely new sentencing options, such as intensive corrective orders and indefinite sentences, and the reintroduction of sentencing options that had previously been diluted and/or fallen into disuse, such as 'suspended sentences' and 'a change to how default periods of imprisonment for non-payment of a fine were required to be served' (CJC, 2000: 18). The introduction of the *Penalties and Sentences Act 1992* in one way or another is in line with a 'law and order' ideology, which is the belief that society should be governed by law and crime effectively controlled. To sustain public confidence, the government has displayed an ongoing commitment to crack down on the increase in recorded crime. The changes resulting from the *Penalties and Sentences Act 1992* seemed likely to have contributed to the increased number of people sentenced to custody.

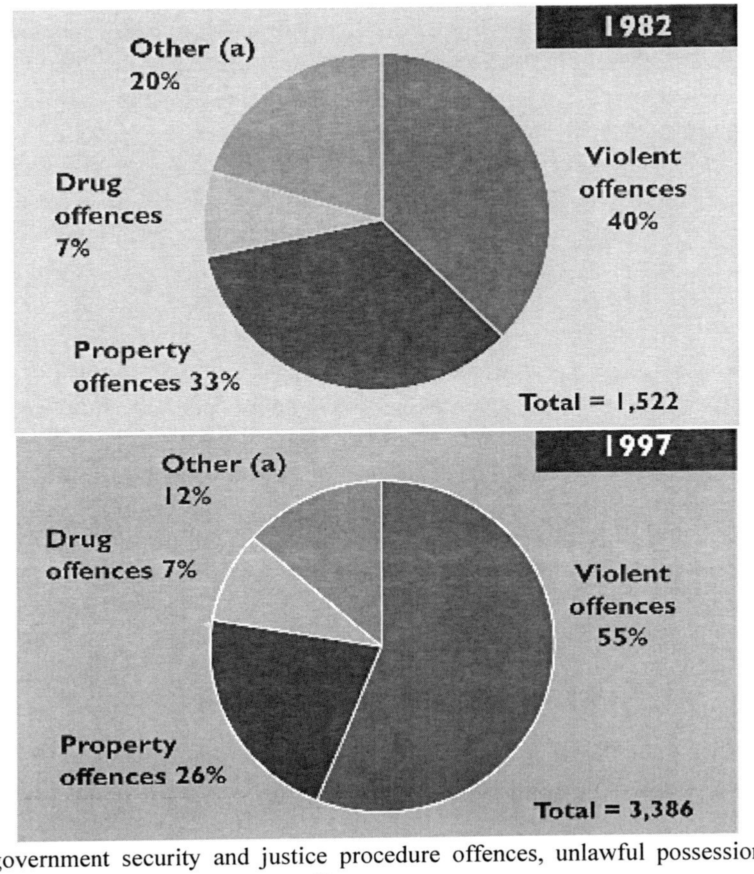

(a) Includes government security and justice procedure offences, unlawful possession of weapons, driving and related offences, and other offences.

Source: Office of Economic and Statistical Research (1999: Figure 2).

Figure 5. Sentenced prisoners by most serious offence at 30 June 1982 and 1997.

Two other factors affecting the prison population are the increase in the average length of time to which an offender is sentenced and the increased proportion of prison sentence that an offender is likely to serve (CJC, 2000). The CJC found that the policies and practices of the formerly Department of Corrective Services operated to increase the duration of a prisoner's stay through declining use of early release mechanisms, stricter criteria applied to parole applications, and decreasing the number of prisoners reaching the requisite low security classification necessary for early release (CJC, 2000). This last point regarding low security classification has been an issue of contention since the corporatization of corrective services. In 1996/1997, the Office of Sentence Management was created to oversee many aspects of sentence management within custodial settings. Many prisoners complained that they have been held at higher classifications on the basis of risk despite there being no supporting evidence of greater risk. In addition, risk assessment by the Office of Sentence Management was based on the completion of programmes despite the fact that some programmes were not readily available to inmates, while others had long waiting lists (cited in CJC, 2000). In this respect, it took some prisoners longer than the other to be eligible for an application for parole.

In recent years, two specific pieces of legislation have been enacted, namely the *Dangerous Prisoners (Sexual Offenders) Act 2003* and *Corrective Services Act 2006*. These laws delegated more power to the Queensland Government to make decisions regarding the length of the prison sentence and the outcome of the parole application. The *Dangerous Prisoners (Sexual Offenders) Act 2003* applies to offenders serving a period of imprisonment for a serious sexual offence involving violence or against children. Section 5 of the *Dangerous Prisoners (Sexual Offenders) Act 2003* states that the Attorney General may apply to the Supreme Court for the continuing detention of these offenders. Indeed similar laws in other states in Australia have been used to allow the authorities to decide whether or not to apply for the continued detention orders for high risk offenders (McSherry, 2006). Under the *Dangerous Prisoners (Sexual Offenders) Act 2003*, electronic monitoring is now a condition of release for all offenders under supervision. With the inception of the *Corrective Services Act 2006*, 'the ability for prisoners to request a review under the *Judicial Review Act 1991* of a decision made about security classification, transfer or placement has been removed (Queensland Corrective Services, 2006d: 7). All these legislative changes are examples to illustrate the Government's attempt to intensify the controlling and punitive elements in corrections.

Implications of the Increasing Prison Population

In order to accommodate the rapidly increasing prisoner numbers, the current Queensland Premier The Honourable Peter Beattie has announced in the Parliament that the Gatton shire had been chosen a preferred location for the new $500 million Queensland correctional precinct on 29 November 2006. In the press release, Beattie said, "This Government makes no apology for being tough on crime and incarcerating those who commit serious crimes" (see Queensland Corrective Services, 2006e). The proposed establishment is planned to accommodate 3,000 people. One may question whether building more prisons is the most effective way to reduce crime and protect community safely. Or is it the most visible option to indicate to the voters the Government has taken this action in the best interest of the public? Increasing prison capacity will mean that there are more people to be locked up.

The average cost of keeping a prisoner in high security is $116 per day and in open custody $64 per day, whereas the average daily cost of community supervision orders is $4 (Steering Committee for the Review of Commonwealth/State Service Provision, 1999). The excessive use of imprisonment is thus diverting resources from more effective methods of reducing crime such as local crime prevention initiatives. However the former Director-General, Frank Peach, chose to continue to expand prison capacity throughout the State and clearly said in the foreword of an annual report of Department of Corrective Services (2000: 2) that '[t]he expansion of correctional facilities is designed to reduce overcrowding and provide for future growth in prisoner numbers'. This policy choice has remained unchanged in Queensland as there are numerous proposals to modernize the 'older' prisons and build more larger prisons. One vexed question is, besides building more jails, what else we can and should do to establish a safer community? Drawing from their success in other countries, the following are some recommendations to address the possible ever-increasing prison population in Queensland.

Continued preference for imprisonment overlooks the potential of community-based treatment as an effective alternative. In order to halt this development, three basic approaches, namely a front-door approach, back-door approach and capacity expansion, will be suggested (Blumstein, 1988; Skovron, 1988; Tonry, 2003). The front-door approach involves reducing prison admissions or diverting people to sentences other than imprisonment. Prison is not only expensive but also unsuitable for the great majority of such offenders as the mentally disordered, the young and petty, and pregnant women, who should all be directed into more worthwhile, constructive and cheaper punishments, such as community service or probation which are not intended for the most serious offenders. Evaluation research in the United Kingdom has proved that community penalties such as probation and community service are as effective as or at least not worse than prison in reducing reoffending behaviour (see Bottoms, 1987; Raynor, 1988; Mair, 1997; Bottoms, Gelsthorpe and Rex, 2001). Likewise, Underdown (1995) is aware of the rich potential of employing community supervision as an alternative to custody, though an unintended consequence of the development of alternatives has been a widening 'net' of penal control (McMahon, 1990). Furthermore, bail should be granted more frequently to reduce the remands in custody. The ABS reported in 2006 that unsentenced prisoners accounted for 22% of the total prison population in Australia, a figure that had risen 9% from the previous year (ABS, 2006). Admittedly assessment of the effectiveness of the various penal measures in Queensland is non-existent and very few programmes for offenders are properly evaluated. This may partly explain why decisions made by the politicians and policymakers are based on intuition and morals rather than evidence.

The back-door approach involves reducing sentence lengths to relieve the high prison population. There is evidence that longer sentences do not produce greater benefits in reducing further offences than shorter ones (Gottfredson, Gottfredson and Garofalo, 1977 cited in Song and Lieb, 1993). In addition to reducing prison crowding, the shock incarceration programme that found in Louisiana serves as a good example of the development of a short, intensive therapeutic programme to treat prisoners (MacKenzie and Parent, 1991). Low security classifications and thus, the possibility of early release, is extended to those inmates who successfully participate in institutional programmes and industries, and for their good conduct. The provision of such programmes must be sufficient that prisoners who are willing and able to participate are not prevented from doing so by unavailability or inordinately long waiting lists. There is evidence that early release had no impact on overall recidivism rates (Berecochea and Jaman, 1981; Austin, 1986 cited in Song and Lieb, 1993).

Additional prison capacity would permit keeping prisoners under more acceptable conditions. Community prisons, that are close to the prisoners' homes and are small in size, are regarded as the ideal prison type for reducing the recidivism rate (Farrington and Nuttall, 1980; Cooke, 1991). There is however the danger that prison building programmes send a wrong signal to the police, prosecutors and sentencers, in which there are cells waiting to be filled. The danger becomes especially evident when expansion of the prison service is combined with heightened anxieties about crime and public order (Rutherford, 1986; Mauer, 2001). Prison construction is not a panacea for the crowding problem, and it is a costly short term solution. Instead, more specialized facilities are urged to cater to the needs of treatment and psychiatric help for mentally disordered prisoners; and more gender and culture specific programmes should be delivered to address the needs and problems of female offenders and

Indigenous persons. Provision of additional prison capacity should be concurrent with the promotion of alternative means of protecting society and reforming offending behaviour.

These three approaches are not mutually exclusive in reducing the size of the prison population and improving prison conditions. Nor are they as radical as Mathiesen's (1986, 1990, 1991) proposals for the abolition of prison. Incarceration is sometimes a necessary means for society to express its sincere disapproval of a criminal act, particularly true in a country that does not use capital punishment (Zirming and Hawkins, 1995; Matthews, 1999). Instead of abolishing incarceration, it should be used more carefully and for shorter periods (Brydensholt, 1992). Other initiatives or insights in relation to reducing the prison population can be generated by learning from past mistakes and from other countries' experience.

More active co-operation between the courts, the prosecution service, the probation service and the prison service is needed in order to reduce the number of people remanded in custody and to limit the periods of time on remand. A substitute for remand would be the requirement to report to the local police. The recent Italian legislation can serve as a good model: if the prosecution, the trial or the appeal proceedings are not completed within certain time limits, the suspect has to be released from remand in prison (Feest, 1991).

All these ideas are admirable and worth implementing, but a major reduction in the use of prison will require more than this. It will require a change of heart and a move away from traditional views on what imprisonment is for, what it contributes to protecting the public and reducing crime, and how much of it should be used at any one time for any particular offender. It will take considerable time to bring about this change of heart which will require action on many fronts at once (Stern, 1993: 196; CJC, 2000). From the former West Germany's experience, changing the attitudes, beliefs and practices of lawyers, the judiciary and the prosecution is crucial in reducing the prison population (Feest, 1988, 1991). There must be a shared vision between politicians and the public to question the role and value of imprisonment in a modern society.

References

Aebi, M. F. and Stadnic, N. (2007) *Council of Europe Annual Penal Statistics SPACE I: 2005 Survey on Prison Populations*, Strasbourg: Council of Europe.

Austin, J. (1986) 'Using early release to relieve prison crowding: A dilemma for public policy', *Crime and Delinquency*, 32(4), 404-502.

Australian Bureau of Statistics (ABS) (1994–2006) *Prisoners in Australia*, Canberra, ACT: ABS.

ABS (2007) *Corrective Services, Australia, Dec 2006* (Cat. No. 4512.0), Canberra, ACT: ABS. Available at: http://www.abs.gov.au/AUSSTATS/abs@.nsf/ViewContent?readform&view=ProductsbyReleaseDate&Action=Expand&Num=1.2

Australian Institute of Criminology (1982–1993) *National Prison Census*, Canberra: Australian Institute of Criminology.

Berecochea, J. and Jaman, D. (1981) *Time Served in Prison and Parole Outcome: An Experimental Study* (Report No. 2), Sacramento, CA: California Department of Corrections.

Blumstein, A. (1988) 'Prison populations: A system out of control', in M. Tonry and N. Morris (Eds.) *Crime and Justice: A Review of Research, Volume 10* (pp. 231-266), Chicago: The University of Chicago Press.

Blumstein, A. (1998) 'U.S. criminal justice conundrum: Rising prison populations and stable crime rates', *Crime and Delinquency*, 44(1), 127-135.

Bottoms, A. E. (1987) 'Limiting prison use: Experience in England and Wales', *Howard Journal of Criminal Justice*, 26 (3), 177-202.

Bottoms, A. E. (1995) 'The philosophy and politics of punishment and sentencing', in C. Clarkson and R. Morgan (Eds.) *The Politics of Sentencing Reform* (pp. 17-49), Oxford: Clarendon Press.

Bottoms, A. E., Gelsthorpe, L. and Rex, S. (Eds.) (2001) *Community Penalties: Policy, Practice and Future Directions*, Cullompton, Devon: Willan.

Bowker, L. H. (1981) 'Crime and the use of prisons in the United States: A time series analysis', *Crime and Delinquency*, 27 (2), 206-212.

Brown, D. (1998) 'Penality and imprisonment in Australia', in R. P. Weiss and N. South (Eds.) *Comparing Prison Systems: Towards a Comparative and International Penology* (pp. 367-400), Amsterdam: Gordon and Breach Publishers.

Brydensholt, H. H. (1992) 'Crime policy in Denmark: How we managed to reduce the prison population', in M. K. Carlie and K. I. Minor (Eds.) *Prisons Around the World* (pp. 185-191), Dubuque: Wm. C. Brown.

Caplow, T. and Simon, J. (1999) 'Understanding prison policy and population trends', in M. Tonry and J. Petersilia (Eds.) *Prisons* (pp. 63-120), Chicago: The University of Chicago Press.

Carcach, C. and Grant, A. (1999) 'Imprisonment in Australia: Trends in prison populations and imprisonment rates 1982–1998', *Trends and Issues in Crime and Criminal Justice, No. 130*, Canberra: Australian Institute of Criminology.

Carcach, C. and Grant, A. (2000) 'Australian corrections: Main demographic characteristics of prison population', *Trends and Issues in Crime and Criminal Justice, No. 150*, Canberra: Australian Institute of Criminology.

Carlen, P. (Ed.) (2002) *Women and Punishment: The Struggle of Justice*, Cullompton, Devon: Willan.

Cavadino, M. and Dignan, J. (2002) *The Penal System: An Introduction* (3rd ed.), London: Sage.

Chappell, D. (1992) 'Sentencing of offenders: A consideration of the issues of severity, consistency and cost', *Australian Law Journal*, 66(7), 423-439.

Christie, N. (2000) *Crime Control as Industry* (3rd ed.), London: Routledge.

Cooke, D. J. (1991) 'Violence in prisons: The influence of regimes factors', *Howard Journal of Criminal Justice*, 30 (2), 95-109.

Corrective Services Review (1999) *Corrections in the Balance: A Review of Corrective Services in Queensland (A Commission of Inquiry)*, Brisbane, QLD: Department of Corrective Services.

Criminal Justice Commission (CJC) (2000) *Prisoner Numbers in Queensland: An Examination of Population Trends in Queensland's Correctional Institutions*, Brisbane, QLD: CJC.

Department of Corrective Services (various issues, 2000–2006) *Annual Report*, Brisbane, QLD: Department of Corrective Services. Available at: http://www.dcs.qld.gov.au/

docs/index.shtml Department of Premier and Cabinet (2005) *Queensland's Criminal Justice System Bulletin 2003-04*, Brisbane, QLD: Department of Premier and Cabinet, Available at: http://www.premiers.qld.gov.au/policy/research/cjresearch/#publications

Devlin, A. (1998) *Invisible Women: What's Wrong With Women's Prisons?*, Winchester: Waterside.

Doob, A. N. and Webster, C. M. (2006) 'Countering punitiveness: Understanding stability in Canada's imprisonment rate', *Law and Society Review*, 40(2), 325-367.

Faith, K. (1993) *Unruly Women: The Politics of Confinement and Resistance*, Vancouver: Press Gang.

Farrington, D. P. and Nuttall, C. P. (1980) 'Prison size, overcrowding, prison violence, and recidivism', *Journal of Criminal Justice*, 8, 221-231.

Feest, J. (1988) *Reducing the Prison Population: Lessons from the West German Experience?*, London: National Association for the Care and Resettlement of Offenders.

Feest, J. (1991) 'Reducing the prison population: Lessons from the West German experience?', in J. Muncie and R. Sparks (Eds.) *Imprisonment: European Perspectives* (pp. 131-145), Hemel Hempstead, Hertfordshire: Harvester Wheatsheaf.

Garland, D. (2001) *The Culture of Control: Crime and Social Order in Contemporary Society*, Oxford: Oxford University Press.

Graham, J. (1990) 'Decarceration in the Federal Republic of Germany', *British Journal of Criminology*, 30 (2), 150-170.

Gottfredson, D. M., Gottfredson, M. R. and Garofalo, J. (1997) 'Time served in prison and parole outcomes among parolee risk categories', *Journal of Criminal Justice*, 5(1), 1-12.

Greenwood, P. W. (1998) 'Investing in prisons or prevention: The state policy makers' dilemma', *Crime and Delinquency*, 44(1), 136-142.

Heggie, K. (2005) 'Prison populations in Australia', in S. O'Toole and S. Eyland (Eds.) *Corrections Criminology* (pp. 17-21), Annandale, NSW: Hawkins Press.

Hooks, G., Mosher, C., Rotolo, T. and Lobao, L. (2004) 'The prison industry: Carceral expansion and employment in US counties, 1969-1994', *Social Science Quarterly*, 85(1), 37-57.

Indyk, S. and Donnelly, H. (2007) *Full-time Imprisonment in New South Wales and Other Jurisdictions: A National and International Comparison*, Sydney, NSW: Judicial Commission of New South Wales.

Johnstone, G. (2000) 'Penal policy making', *Punishment and Society*, 2(2), 161-180.

Jupp, V. (1989) *Methods of Criminological Research*, London: Unwin Hyman.

Liebling, A. (2006) 'Prisons in transition', *International Journal of Law and Psychiatry*, 29 (5), 422-430.

Listokin, Y. (2003) 'Does more crime mean more prisoners? An instrumental variables approach', *Journal of Law and Economics*, 46(1), 181-206.

MacKenzie, D. L. and Parent, D. G. (1991) 'Shock incarceration and prison crowding in Louisiana', *Journal of Criminal Justice*, 19 (3), 225-237.

Mair, G. (Ed.) (1997) *Evaluating the Effectiveness of Community Penalties*, Aldershot: Avebury.

Mathiesen, T. (1986) 'The politics of abolition', *Contemporary Crises*, 10(1), 81-94.

Mathiesen, T. (1990) *Prison on Trial*, London: Sage.

Mathiesen, T. (1991) 'The argument against building more prisons', in J. Muncie and R. Sparks (Eds.) *Imprisonment: European Perspectives* (pp. 177-184), Hemel Hempstead, Hertfordshire: Harvester Wheatsheaf.

Matthews, R. (1999) *Doing Time: An Introduction to the Sociology of Imprisonment*, London: Macmillan.

Mauer, M. (2001) 'The causes and consequences of prison growth in the United States', in D. Garland (Ed.) *Mass Imprisonment: Social Causes and Consequences* (pp. 4-14), London: Sage.

May, T. (2001) *Social Research: Issues, Methods and Process* (3rd ed.), Buckingham: Open University Press.

McMahon, M. (1990) 'Net-widening: Vagaries in the use of a concept', *British Journal of Criminology*, 30 (2), 121-149.

McSherry, B. (2006) *High-risk Offenders: Continued Detention and Supervision Options Community Issues Paper*, Victoria, Melbourne: Sentencing Advisory Council.

Merlo, A. V. (1997) 'The crisis and consequences of prison overcrowding', in J. M. Pollock (Ed.) *Prisons: Today and Tomorrow* (pp. 52-83), Gaithersburg, Maryland: Aspen.

Morgan, R. and Liebling, A. (2007) 'Imprisonment: An expanding scene', in M. Maguire, R. Morgan and R. Reiner (Eds.) *The Oxford Handbook of Criminology* (4th ed.) (pp. 1100-1138), Oxford: Oxford University Press.

Neapolitan, J.L. (2001) 'An examination of cross-national variation in punitiveness', *International Journal of Offender Therapy and Comparative Criminology*, 45(6), 691-710.

Office of Economic and Statistical Research (1999) Crime Statistics Bulletin No. 5: Prisoners in Queensland, Brisbane, QLD: Office of Economic and Statistical Research.

Office of Economic and Statistical Research (2001) Information Brief Queensland Corrective Services: March Quarter 2001, Brisbane, QLD: Office of Economic and Statistical Research.

Office of Economic and Statistical Research (2005) Information Brief Prisoners in Australia: 2005, Brisbane, QLD: Office of Economic and Statistical Research.

Office of the Government Statistician (2001) *Crime and Justice Statistics, Queensland, 1999-2000,* Brisbane, QLD: Go-Print.

O'Toole, S. (2006) *The History of Australian Corrections*, Sydney, NSW: University of New South Wales Press.

Paveley, R. (2002) 'Child muggers behind rise in crime to be locked up', *Daily Mail*, 26 February.

Pratt, J. (2006) 'The dark side of imprisonment – Explaining New Zealand's history of high imprisonment', *British Journal of Criminology*, 46(4), 541-560.

Queensland Corrective Services (2006a) *Legislation Update*, Brisbane, QLD: Queensland Corrective Services.

Queensland Corrective Services (2006b) *Queensland Corrective Services: A Guide to the Correctional Services Act 2006*, Brisbane, QLD: Queensland Corrective Services.

Queensland Corrective Services (2006c) *Custodial Corrections*, Brisbane, QLD: Queensland Corrective Services.

Queensland Corrective Services (2006d) *A Guide to the Queensland Corrective Services Act 2006*, Brisbane, QLD: Queensland Corrective Services.

Queensland Corrective Services (2006e) *Media Statements – Gatton Shire Named as a preferred Location for New SEQ Jail*, Brisbane, QLD: Queensland Corrective Services. Available at: http://www.dcs.qld.gov.au/Publications/Media_Statements/Ministerial_Media_Releases/gatton.shtml

Queensland Police Service (2006) *Queensland Police Service Annual Statistical Review 2005-06*, Brisbane, QLD: Queensland Police Service. Available at: http://www.police.qld.gov.au/services/reportsPublications/statisticalReview/0506/

Raynor, P. (1988) *Probation as an Alternative to Custody: A Case Study*, Aldershot, Hants: Avebury.

Riedel, M. (2000) *Research Strategies for Secondary Data: A Perspective for Criminology and Criminal Justice*, Thousand Oaks, CA: Sage.

Rutherford, A. (1986) *Growing Out of Crime*, Harmondsworth: Penguin.

Ryan, M. (1999) 'Penal policy making towards the Millennium: Elites and populists; New Labour and the new criminology', *International Journal of the Sociology of Law*, 27(1), 1-22.

Skovron, S. E. (1988) 'Prison crowding: The dimension of the problem and strategies of population control', in J. E. Scott and T. Hirschi (Eds.) *Controversial Issues in Crime and Justice* (pp. 183-198), Newbury Park, CA: Sage.

Smith, K. B. (2004) 'The politics of punishment: Evaluating political explanations of incarceration rates', *Journal of Politics*, 66(3), 925-938.

Song, L. and Lieb, R. (1993) *Recidivism: The Effect of Incarceration and Length of Time Served* (Document No.: 93-09-1201), Olympia, WA: Washington State Institute for Public Policy.

Steering Committee for the Review of Commonwealth/State Service Provision (1999) *Report on Government Services*, Melbourne, VIC: Steering Committee for the Review of Commonwealth/State Service Provision.

Stern, V. (1993) *Bricks of Shame: Britain's Prisons*, London: Penguin.

Stucky, T.D., Heimer, K. and Lang, J.B. (2007) 'A bigger piece of the pie?: State corrections spending and the politics of social order', *Journal of Research in Crime and Delinquency*, 44 (1), 91-123.

Tonry, M. (1999) 'Why are U.S. incarceration rates so high?', *Crime and Delinquency*, 45 (4), 419-437.

Tonry, M. (2003) 'Reducing the prison population', in M. Tonry (Ed.) *Confronting Crime: Crime Control Policy Under New Labour* (pp. 211-223), Cullompton, Devon: Willan.

Tonry, M. (2004a) *Thinking About Crime: Sense and Sensibility in American Penal Culture*, New York: Oxford University Press.

Tonry, M. (2004b) *Punishment and Politics: Evidence and Emulation in the Making of English Crime Control Policy*, Cullompton, Devon: Willan.

Tonry, M. and Petersilia, J. (1999) 'American prisons at the beginning of the twenty-first century', in M. Tonry and J. Petersilia (Eds.) *Prisons* (pp. 1-16), Chicago: The University of Chicago Press.

Underdown, A. (1995) *Effectiveness for Community Supervision: Performance and Potential*, Manchester: Greater Manchester Probation Service.

Welch, M. (2005) *Ironies of Imprisonment*, Thousand Oaks, CA: Sage.

Women's Policy Unit (2000) *Profile of Female Offenders under Community and Custodial Supervision in Queensland*, Brisbane, QLD: Department of Corrective Services.

Young, W. (1986) 'Influences upon the use of imprisonment: A review of literature', *Howard Journal of Criminal Justice*, 25 (2), 125-136.

Zirming, F. E. and Hawkins, G. (1995) *Incapacitation: Penal Confinement and the Restraint of Crime*, New York: Oxford University Press.

Legislation Cited

Corrective Services Act 2000 (Qld)
Corrective Services Act 2006 (Qld)
Corrective Services (Administration) Act 1988 (Qld)
Dangerous Prisoners (Sexual Offenders) Act 2003 (Qld)
Judicial Review Act 1992 (Qld)
Penalties and Sentences Act 1992 (Qld)

In: Australia: Economic, Political and Social Issues
Editors: Lachlan J. Williams and Ethan N. Lee
ISBN: 978-1-60456-856-1

Chapter 4

Working from Within: A Comparison of Feminist Intervention in the Bureaucracy in Australia, Canada and the United Kingdom

Louise Chappell
Gender Studies
University of Hull, UK

Abstract

Why do political activists operating in similar polities experience different degrees of success in pursuit of the same strategy? What role do institutions play in shaping the success of activists strategies? This chapter considers these questions through a study of feminist activists engagement with the bureaucracy in three parliamentary democracies – Australia, Canada and the United Kingdom. It analyses why certain Australian feminists have had a relatively high degree of success with a 'femocrat' strategy, compared to counterparts in Canada and the UK. The chapter argues that internal institutional factors as well as the interaction between institutions and political parties best explain this outcome. The argument advanced in the chapter illustrates not only the importance of taking institutions seriously in explaining political activists' strategies, but also the need to pay careful attention to the differences between similar institutions across polities and variations in the political contexts in which they operate.

Introduction

Attempts to explain the strategic choices made by political actors have long been a focus of political science research. This chapter contributes to this work by considering the extent to which political strategies are shaped by the opportunities and barriers present within political institutions in a given polity. It examines attempts by certain feminist activists to engage with the bureaucracy in three Westminster parliamentary democracies: Australia, Canada and the United Kingdom. Specifically, it seeks to explain why these activists who are operating in similar institutional environments experience different degrees of success in pursuit of the same strategy – bureaucratic 'entrism' or what will be referred to as the 'femocrat' strategy. It considers why feminist activists in Australia have found it easier to engage with this arm of the state and have had a greater degree of success in exploiting bureaucratic institutions to develop feminist-inspired policies compared to their counterparts in the other two countries. The chapter suggests that despite obvious similarities in bureaucratic structures across these polities, important differences also exist and these factors, along with the intervention of political parties, have shaped the political opportunities open to feminist activists in each country.

The discussion begins by defining the nature of the activists involved in this strategy and by providing a brief outline of the features and location of feminist bureaucrats and women's policy machinery in the three countries. It compares the outcomes of the 'femocrat' strategy in terms of the degree of *institutionalisation* and the relative influence of these state actors. The second section of the chapter considers explanations for the variations in the degree of success of this strategy between each country. It contends that it has been a combination of institutional norms, structures and political parties, rather than anything intrinsic to each of the feminist movements, which have influenced the success of this strategy. Here it is suggested that the political opportunity structure open to feminist activists in the bureaucratic realm is dependent upon three factors: the influence of federal versus unitary structures, the nature of the political parties in office and differences in the operation of bureaucratic norms.

In analysing feminist intervention in the state, this work engages with two approaches within political science. The first is feminist political science where there has been a growing interest in feminist engagement with the state[1]. An important focus of this work is on the way feminists have intervened in political institutions, especially the bureaucracy. There is now a growing literature on feminists' engagement with the bureaucracy in various *domestic* settings including Australia[2] and Canada[3]. More recently, work is being undertaken which considers the *international* dimension of gender policy making, and which takes an over-arching view of these developments[4]. There is also a great deal of work on unravelling the gender dimensions of public policy within and between across states [5] and now comparative work is beginning to emerge on women as policy-makers. Stetson and Mazur's edited volume entitled *Comparative State Feminisms* is an important contribution that looks at the role of feminists in policy-making positions in western and developing countries. The argument presented in this chapter follows this comparative approach. It adopts a most 'similar'

---

1 See Suzanne Franzway et al., *Staking a Claim: Feminist Interventions in the State* (Sydney: Allen and Unwin, 1989) and Joy Misra and Frances Akins, 'The Welfare State, Structure, Agency, and Diversity' *Social Politics* Fall (1998): 259-85.

2 See Marian Sawer, *Sisters in Suits: Women and Public Policy in Australia* (Sydney: Allen and Unwin, 1990) and Hester Eisenstein *Inside Agitators: Australian Femocrats and the Australian State* (Sydney: Allen and Unwin, 1996).

3 See Maureen O'Neil and Sharon Sutherland, 'The Machinery of Women's Policy: Implementing the RCSW' in Caroline Andrew and Sanda Rogers eds., *Women and the Canadian State/ Les femmes et l'Etat canadien* Kingston: McGill University Press, 1997).

4 See Jacqui True and Michael Mintrom. 'Transnational Networks and Policy Diffusion: The Case of Gender Mainstreaming' *International Studies Quarterly* 45 (1:2001): 27-57.

5 Examples include Janine Brodie ed., Women and Canadian Public Policy (Canada: Harcourt Brace and Company, 1996), Moria Gatens and Alison MacKinnon eds., *Gender and Institutions* (Cambridge: Cambridge University Press, 1998), Julia O'Connor, Ann Shola Orloff and Sheila Shaver. *States, Markets, Families: Gender, Liberalism and Social Policy in Australia, Canada, Great Britain and the United States.* (Cambridge: Cambridge University Press, 1999).

comparative methodology, looking at the engagement of feminist activists within three western, liberal, Westminster parliamentary systems. In using this method, the chapter seeks to examine how and why feminists operating in similar systems have such different experiences of engaging with the bureaucratic arm of the state. While the study makes it possible to develop a specific argument about the nature of feminist activists and the bureaucracy in these three countries, it also seeks to make some broader conclusions and raise questions that might be useful to consider in future research in the field.

The second set of literature that this chapter draws upon relates to what is broadly known as 'neo-institutionalism'. The approach can be seen to have stemmed from efforts to 'bring the state back in' to political science. In its broadest sense, neo-institutionalism is interested in examining the way state institutional arrangements shape political behaviour. In using this term, it is important to be aware that there are many new institutionalisms - in economics, organisation theory, political science and public choice, history and sociology[6]. Each of these vary in the extent to which they emphasise the formal and informal aspects of institutions and the degree to which they see institutions as presenting constraints or opportunities for social actors[7]. The variant used in this chapter fits most closely with the historical-institutional approach which suggests that role of actors within a political system can only be understood by investigating the nature of the institutions within that system over time[8].

A number of features of historical neo-institutionalism can be seen to have direct bearing on the arguments presented in this chapter. First, it takes up the call of neo-institutionalists to *disaggregate* the state by emphasising both the importance of differences between institutions within a particular polity, and also, variations between similar institutions in different polities[9]. The chapter is specifically interested in how a single institution – the bureaucracy – operates differently across time and place and the effect that this has on feminist political actors. Second, it stresses the importance of the interaction *between* institutions within a given polity in influencing the relationship between the state and social actors. Specifically, the chapter is interested in examining how the bureaucracy and federalism interact in each polity and what effect these varying configurations have on the opportunities open to feminists. Thirdly, it is interested in the political context in which institutions operate and the interaction between institutions and political parties on the prevailing political opportunity structure. Finally, it draws on the new institutionalist view of state institutions being both *embedded* in society and *dynamic*: it postulates that state institutions are only partially autonomous and are shaped through their interaction with social actors[10]. The chapter suggests that social actors, such as feminist activists, can influence changes in the very institutions that help shape their behaviour.

---

6 For a full discussion see B Guy Peters, *Institutional Theory in Political Science: the new institutionalism* (London: Pinter, 1999).

7 Hans Keman, 'Approaches to the Analysis of Institutions' in Bernard Steunenberg and Frans van Vught eds. *Political Institutions and public policy: perspectives on European decision making* (Boston: Kluwer Academic Publishers, 1997), 1-2.

8 Ibid, 12.

9 Kathleen Thelen and Sven Steinmo, 'Historical institutionalism in comparative politics' in Sven Steinmo, Kathleen Thelen and Frank Longstreth eds., *Structuring Politics: Historical Institutionalism in Comparative Analysis.* (Cambridge: Cambridge University Press, 1992).

10 Alan Cairns 'The Embedded State: State-Society Relations in Canada' in Douglas E. Williams ed. *Reconfigurations: Canadian Citizenship and Constitutional Change* (Toronto: McLelland and Stewart, 1995).

PART I: FEMINIST ACTIVISTS, ISSUES AND STRATEGIES

Defining Feminist Activists

This chapter is interested in exploring the way *feminist activists* have engaged with the bureaucracy in each of the three countries under review. But, who exactly are we referring to by this term? The notion of an all-encompassing feminist 'sisterhood' has long been rejected by feminists as a highly problematic concept which glosses over important differences not only in ideology, but especially in relation to identity including race, class and sexuality[11]. In each country under review the term feminist encompasses women from a variety of different ideological positions including those from socialist, marxist, liberal and post-modernist perspectives. Moreover, within each community, feminists have followed various strategic paths ranging from those who have eschewed involvement with the state to those who have been willing to directly enter state institutions as politicians or bureaucrats in an attempt to achieve their aims.

In each place we can also discern majoritarian and minority strands of the feminist movement - strands which are differentiated along identity lines. In Canada, two majoritarian strands are evident - Anglo-feminists who operate outside Quebec and Francophone feminists who operate inside Quebec. These two strands have adopted quite different positions on key questions such as constitutional reform, the power of the Federal government vis-a-vis the provinces and approaches to the state. Aside from these two majoritarian strands, 'minority' feminist groups also exist within Canada such as those within the Native community, and those from other 'visible minority groups'. These groups have worked with, but also sometimes in opposition to, the majoritarian strands depending upon the issue. For instance, Native groups have taken quite a distinct position on the constitution, arguing for an acknowledgment of collective over individual rights. Similarly, in Australia and in the UK, it is impossible to talk of a single feminist movement. In these countries a majoritarian strand which reflects the views of predominantly Anglo, middle-class feminists, operates alongside other groups who come from lesbian and non-English speaking backgrounds. In Australia, indigenous women have often shunned the feminist label but have created their own organisations to address specific 'women's issues' such as child-care and violence against women. In the UK, women from black and Asian communities have created organisations to represent 'women's issues' as they are defined within their particular racial and ethnic identities.

It is not the intention of this chapter to analyse the various identities, ideas and strategies used by those who adopt the feminist appellation in each country. Rather, it focuses the efforts of particular feminists, drawn primarily from the Anglo-majoritarian strands of each feminist community, in pursuing a particular strategy - 'bureaucratic entrism'. This is not to say that other segments of the feminist community or different strategies do not exist or are unimportant, only that they are different stories which need to be told elsewhere.

What is examined here is entry into the bureaucracy of *feminist* activists. To be precise, the focus is on those who have become known as 'femocrats' and their strategy of state

[11] For a good discussion see Valerie Bryson *Feminist Debates: Issues of Theory and Political Practice* (London: Macmillan 1999).

feminism[12] or 'bureaucratic entrism'. The term 'femocrat' is an Australian neologism. The term refers specifically to *feminist* bureaucrats, not women in the bureaucracy *per se*. The term has been applied in a number of senses. It has been used pejoratively by conservatives who see these women as representing a select band of 'special interests' in the bureaucracy. Other feminists have also used it as a term of derision and abuse, seeing those within the bureaucracy as selling out the women's movement and profiting from women's disadvantage [13]. However, some femocrats have appropriated the phrase to define themselves, and have imbued the term with a more positive meaning. According to Eisenstein, the sense in which the term is used by femocrats reflects their praxis. In its 'original' usage, it referred to: 'a feminist woman who had entered the public service bureaucracy to advance the cause of women and whose responsibilities were defined in this manner by male bureaucrats or politicians who appointed her' [14]. Due to the movement of femocrats out of designated 'women's policy' positions into the mainstream of the bureaucracy, the term has undergone a redefinition. It has come to be understood by the practitioners themselves as 'a powerful woman within government administration, with an ideological and political commitment to feminism' [15]. The sense in which the terms femocrat and the 'femocrat strategy' will be used in the following discussion draws on this definition, referring to the entry of feminists into all areas of the bureaucracy in an effort to influence public policy making through an explicitly feminist perspective.

Defining 'Women's Issues'

Just as it is important to be precise about the activists who are the subject of this chapter, so too is it necessary to be clear what is meant by the term 'women's issues' which these activists seek to promote. The feminist literature is alive with debates surrounding whether there are indeed particular women's needs, interests and issues[16]. Given the challenge presented by women from various identity groups about what constitutes a 'woman', feminists scholars and practitioners are increasingly reluctant to hold on to universalist concepts and suggest that there is one identifiable set of women's issues. Women, like men, have widely diverse interests and cannot be treated as a monolithic block. Women's diversity presents a dilemma for those arguing for increasing women's representation, whether in a corporeal sense or in terms of 'interests' in political institutions such as the parliament or the bureaucracy. As Phillips point out, 'the representation of women *as women* potentially founders on both the difficulties of defining shared values of women and difficulties of establishing mechanisms through which these interests are voiced'[17].

---

[12] See Dorothy McBride Stetson, and Amy G.Mazur eds. *Comparative State Feminism* (Thousand Oaks, California: Sage Publications, 1995).

[13] Anne Summers, 'Mandarins or Missionaries?: Women in the Federal Bureaucracy' in Norma Grieve and Alisa Burns eds. *Australian Women: New Feminist Perspectives (*Melbourne: Oxford University Press, 1986) 60.

[14] Eisenstein, 68.

[15] Ibid.

[16] See for example Elizabeth van Acker, *Different Voices: Gender and Politics in Australia* (Melbourne: Macmillan, 1999) 32-6; Jill Vickers 'Toward a Feminist Understanding of Representation' in Jane Arscott and Linda Trimble eds. *In the Presence of Women: Representation in Canadian Governments* (Toronto: Harcourt Brace & Company Canada: 1997).

[17] Anne Phillips *Engendering Democracy* (Cambridge: Polity Press, 1991)

The question of what constitutes women's interests is particularly pertinent to this study which judges the success or failure of the femocrat strategy, at least in part, on the basis of whether these policy-makers have been able to promote 'women's issues' through public policies once inside the bureaucracy. But how are these issues to be understood? One place to start, according to Vickers, is to differentiate between policies which are *women-friendly* and *women-focussed*. The former are policies which are not specifically designed for women but have positive effects for them, such as general increases in the minimum wage or welfare benefits. The latter are specifically designed by women with the aim of promoting 'women's interests'[18].

Femocrats have been directly engaged in pursuing *women-focussed* policies. Indeed, this is their *raison d'etre*. Through their practice, it is possible to identify two levels at which femocrats have understood and operationalised the concept of women's interests. The first relates to women's unique and common biological characteristics or what could be defined as sex-based commonalities. The fact that women share a similar reproductive system and potential has provided the basis for feminist bureaucrats to argue for specialist reproductive and health services including access to abortion, assisted reproductive technology, maternity leave provisions and services and the like. Aside from the vexed moral question of abortion, claims for specific policies based on biological arguments have been *relatively* uncontentious, no doubt in part because these differences are difficult to refute.

More controversial has been the second sense in which the term 'women's interests' has been understood and applied by feminist policy-makers. This relates to those specific interests arising from women's particular historical and social position[19]. In this view, women have a set of common interests because of the historical fact of women's relegation to the private world and men's predominance in the public sphere. This historical, patriarchal, division between the public and private spheres resulted in unequal power relations between the sexes with women being economically and emotionally dependent on men, as well as less educated. Moreover, it has meant that women have been under-represented in all area of the public realm including corporate and political life. These historical distinctions, and the ongoing attitudes and norms which stem from them, are not founded in any natural, biological difference between men and women but are *gender-based*. That is, they are socially constructed and are therefore presumably able to be changed. Femocrats have seen public-policy as a vehicle to alter these gender-based inequalities between men and women. The introduction of childcare facilities, girls and women's education programs, equal pay and affirmative action in employment, anti-violence against women measures are all examples these efforts.

Arguments about the existence of common women's interests, especially those related to gender-based distinctions between men and women, have been controversial. Challenges have come from a number of directions. Some feminists, particularly those outside the majoritarian strand of the movement, have argued that the analysis of women's specific needs has failed to incorporate the division between women based on race, class and sexuality[20]. Efforts to

---

[18] Jill Vickers, *Reinventing Political Science* (Halifax: Fernwood, 1997).

[19] For a good discussion see Vickers 'Reinventing' Chapter 6

[20] For examples of this in Australia see Eisenstein, 'Inside' Chapter 8, in Canada see Ruth Roach Pierson, 'The Mainstream Women's Movement and the Politics of Difference' in Ruth Roach Pierson, Majorie Griffin Cohen, Phillinda Masters, Philinda eds. *Canadian Women's Issues: Strong Voices Vol 1* (Toronto:James Lorimer and Co., 1993).

redress these historical, social imbalances have also presented a broader challenge the social *status quo*. Not surprisingly, many men and women wanting to uphold traditional roles have been highly critical of feminist activists assessment of 'women's issues' claiming that feminists do not speak on behalf of all women[21].

Despite the controversies around the notion of 'women's interests', the concept has been an important discursive tool for activists. The extent to which femocrats have used this concept, in both its sex and gender-based variants, is a focus of the following discussion. It is interested in evaluating the extent to which femocrats have been able to use the concept to create an *entrenched* position in the bureaucracy and then to *influence* policies to advance what they define as 'women's interests'. Drawing on Malloy's work on advocacy structures in the Ontario Civil Service, the term *influence* is understood to relate to 'the power to develop policy, compel co-ordination, and ensure implementation'[22].

The Femocrat Strategy: Institutional Position

If we judge the strategy by the extent to which feminist activists have been able to achieve a degree of entrenchment within the bureaucracy and influence public policy decisions, it becomes obvious that Australian feminists have achieved a much greater degree of success than their Canadian or UK counterparts. In terms of personnel, since the early 1970s until recently, the women's policy machinery that has been created has been staffed by women who have had an overt commitment to feminist principles and who have used their positions within these agencies to influence policies to reflect these principles [23]. Many of the first 'femocrats' were drawn directly from existing feminist organisations and although over time these direct links have been weakened, there has been an ongoing dialogue between these 'inside agitators' and feminists in community organisations[24].

In relation to their institutional position, since 1972 femocrats in Australia have been able to secure a strong institutional position at the heart of the bureaucracy. At the federal level, the Office of the Status of Women in the Department of Prime Minister and Cabinet has existed in some form since 1974, and similar women's agencies in Premier's departments in most states. But the growth of women's policy machinery did not end with these 'hubs'. Femocrats were very keen to ensure that there was no one agency which became the 'waste-paper basket' for all women's issues and efforts were made from the 1970s to create 'spokes' – women's policy agencies in key line departments[25]. The object of these agencies was to provide expertise in gender policy at the source of policy development.

The benefits of this 'wheel' structure for the Australian femocrat strategy have been numerous. It has enabled them to have access to, and potential input into, all issues dealt with by the Cabinet - the central co-ordination body in the Westminster system. Having a core co-ordinating body located in a central agency has meant that femocrats have also often been

---

21 For a discussion of anti-feminist women's groups in Australia see van Acker, 'Different Voices', 66.

22 Malloy, Jonathon 'What Makes a State Advocacy Structure Effective? Conflicts Between Bureaucratic and Social Movement Criteria' *Governance* 12, (3:1999): 268.

23 Eisenstein, 'Inside Agitators'.

24 Marian Sawer and Abigail Groves, 'The Women's Lobby: Networks, Coalition Building and the Women of middle Australia' *Australian Journal of Political Science* Vol 29 (1994): 435- 459.

25 See Sawer 'Sisters'.

able to enjoy the privilege (and exploit the political advantage) of having the imprimatur of the Prime Minister of the day.

Since the 1995 UN Beijing Women's Conference, there has been a greater emphasis in Australia and internationally on 'mainstreaming' gender policy issues throughout the bureaucracy. This refers to efforts to move away from specific 'women's issues' to bring a gender-based perspective to all policies. As True and Mintrom state, 'mainstreaming is the on-going process by which public policies that are know to have a large impact on society, from macro-economic to housing policy, are devised by taking into account the specific interests and values of both men and women'[26]. The existing wheel model has not conflicted with this effort. Indeed, it fits neatly with UN guidelines for women's policy machinery which recommends that a central co-ordinating agency oversees the work in other departments[27]. With the wheel model in place, existing gender policy experts in central agencies have been able to co-ordinate the efforts within line agencies whilst those femocrats within mainstream departments have lent support and expertise to those new to incorporating gender concerns into policy-development for the first time[28].

In neither Canada nor the UK have feminists been able to secure such a prominent institutional position. In Canada, feminists have had a much lower degree of success in terms of entering bureaucratic agencies and, for those who do make it inside, to create agencies and mechanisms to address women's issues as they defined them. Initially there was an attempt to draw feminists from the community sector into the bureaucracy. This was especially the case with the Women's Program[29]. Generally though, staff in these agencies tended to operate as career public servants, without any overt commitment to feminist principles[30]. According to two senior bureaucrats in the SWC, in recent years most appointees to positions in women's agencies in Ottawa have had an interest in, and knowledge of feminism, but it has not been usual for them to be outwardly feminist, or to use this term to define themselves[31]

By contrast, the women's policy machinery that has been developed in Canada has been relatively weak. When the first key women's policy agency was established in 1971 it was located in the central Privy Council Office. However, it was soon transferred to the periphery as a stand-alone-agency – Status of Women Canada (SWC). Women's agencies were established in other departments, the most important of which for the feminist community was the Women's Program in the Secretary of State Department which provided funding to women's organisations. Women's machinery has also been established in most provinces, but again tends to be located in peripheral rather than central agencies[32]. As a result of its location, women's machinery in Canada has been hampered by both a lack of political clout and co-ordination capacity. In the words of former feminist bureaucrat, Maureen O'Neil:

---

26 True and Mintrom, 'Transnational Networks'

27 Ibid

28 For these developments in New South Wales see Louise Chappell 'Women's Policy' in Martin Laffin and Martin Painter *Reform and Reversal: Lessons from the Coalition Government in New South Wales 1988-1995.* (Melbourne: Macmillan, 1995).

29 Sue Findlay, *Democracy and the Politics of Representation: Feminist Struggles and the Canadian State*, (University of Toronto, Unpublished PhD Thesis, 1995).

30 Linda Geller-Schwartz, 'An Array of Agencies: Feminism and the State in Canada' in Dorothy McBride Stetson and Amy G.Mazur eds., *Comparative State Feminism* (Thousand Oaks, California: Sage Publications, 1995), 57.

31 Interview Zeynap Karman, Status of Women Canada, Ottawa 4 October 1995; interview Jacquie Claxton, Status of Women Canada, Ottawa 27 November 1995.

32 See Katherine Teghtsoonian, 'Gendering Policy Analysis in the Government of British Columbia: Strategies, Possibilities and Constraints'. *Studies in Political Economy*, No. 61 (2000):105-127 and Malloy, 'What makes'.

> The simple fact is that Canadian governments have never created an in-house capacity to deliver policy on women. There is no organisation below the Minister Responsible - only a certain amount of goodwill. A proliferation of small and weak agencies at the margins of policy-making and of central administration will undo in confusion...what they can contribute in dedication[33].

The federal government in Canada has in recent years also picked up on the international trend toward gender-mainstreaming. However, operating on the periphery without access to Cabinet documents, the SWC has been unable to play the prominent co-ordination role which the UN considers is necessary to enhance this approach.

In the UK, feminists wanting to pursue policy reform from within the civil service have found it difficult to achieve a degree of institutionalisation. Throughout eighteen years of Conservative government from 1979, there was no women's policy agency to speak of, while appointments to the position of Women's Minister had no feminist credentials and tended to be male[34]. Initially Labour broke the mould by appointing Harriet Harman, a prominent feminist to the position of Minister for Women. However, after twelve months, Labour reverted back to the previous pattern in appointing the Baroness Jay to the portfolio. Although Jay was known to be a savvy political operator, she was not known for her feminist credentials. Indeed, she came to the post proclaiming to be 'not a feminist'[35]. According to one senior policy officer in the Women's Unit, Jay 'is implacably opposed to any initiatives which smack of feminism' [36]. Moreover, those women who staff the Women's Unit have no overt links with the feminist movement. Indeed, as one senior staff member commented 'women committed to feminist principles working the unit, tend to keep their views to themselves'[37].

The UK Women's policy machinery is also weak and marginal. Although the Thatcher Conservative Government appointed a minister for women and a cabinet committee on women, these measures were little more than 'window dressing' with the committee meeting only once per year [38]. It was not until 1997, with the election of the Blair Labour Government that the first women's unit was created. The unit was initially located on the periphery, in the Department of Social Security; it's location having more to do with the fact that the Minister responsible for women, Harriet Harman, had joint responsibility for social security, than any policy logic. According to one analyst, the Unit was 'set up without much forethought and provided weak and patchy service' [39]. When in 1998 Harman was replaced as women's minister by leader of the House of Lords, Baroness Jay, the unit was relocated to the Cabinet Office. The move to a central agency was seen as an attempt to enhance its co-ordination role, but there is little evidence that this has been achieved. A senior staff member of the unit who I interviewed in 1999, was of the view that it had few resources and was lacking in political

---

[33] O'Neil and Sutherland, 'The Machinery', 216.
[34] Coote, 'The longest'.
[35] Melissa Benn, 'Short March through the institutions: reflections on New Labour's gender machinery' in Anna Coote, ed. *New Gender Agenda* (London: Institute of Public Policy Research, 2000), 41.40.
[36] Interview with senior policy officer, UK Women's Unit June 1999.
[37] Ibid.
[38] Anna Coote, 'The longest revolution: Women and the New Labour Government in Britain', in Linda Hancock ed. *Women, Public Policy and the State*, (Melbourne: Macmillan 1999), 249.
[39] Ibid, 256-7.

clout. Another commentator has noted: 'there is a suspicion that No10 [the Prime Minister's residence] is simply waiting for the unit to wither away from neglect' [40].

The Femocrat Strategy: Policy Influence

There have also been significant differences between the three countries in terms of feminists being able to exercise influence within the bureaucracy to create policies to address women's interests whether they are defined in a sex or gender sense. Again, on this measure we find that Australian femocrats have made the most progress. In terms of policy outputs, Australian femocrats have been successful in extending the purview of government to address issues relating to both women's specific biological nature and their social position. One of the earliest successes of NSW femocrats was to argue for and secure federal government funding for the establishment of a specific women's health centre in Sydney. After its initial success, state and government support for these centres grew, and by 1989, sixty such centres existed[41]. In the early 1990s in South Australia, femocrats worked hard to convince the state government to provide the first free-standing abortion clinic. According to the director of the Office of the Status of Women in that state, Carmel O'Laughlin, this policy was pushed entirely from within the women's unit of the bureaucracy due to opposition within the community and the parliament.

For many femocrats, such as Sara Dowse, the first director of the Women's Unit at the Commonwealth level, the greatest achievement of Australian femocrats was the creation of a national childcare system[42]. Childcare was seen as a threshold women's issue linked both to their reproductive needs and economic and social position in society. The pioneering work of Meredith Edwards, which discredited assumptions about income sharing within families upon which social security policies were made, is an example of the femocracy's foray into mainstream economic policy making [43]. Through their work, femocrats also demonstrated the structured nature of discrimination against women and gave definition to issues such as domestic violence, sex discrimination and the gender gap in wages. Faced with the evidence presented by femocrats, governments were no longer able to dismiss these problems as 'private' concerns, but were forced to see them as systemic problems which required a policy response [44].

Femocrats have had a direct influence on the development of measures to addressing women's experiences of violence and sexual assault. Femocrats actively pressured the government at the Federal and state level to support the development of refuges whilst others have been an active within state bureaucracies. A case in point relates to the NSW femocrat, Carmel Niland, who encouraged the Wran Labor Government to fund a refuge program. Femocrats influence on developing domestic violence policy has been evident during the past two decades at the Federal and state level. Throughout this period documents, it was standard to read in government documents feminist inspired statements such as: 'violence against

---

[40] Perkins in Benn 'Short march'
[41] Eisenstien, 'Inside Agitators', 50.
[42] In Ibid
[43] Sawer, 'Sisters', 58.
[44] Anne Summers 'The Importance of Naming' *Canberra Journal of Public Administration* 76, (April) (1994): 48-52

women is a manifestation of the historically unequal power relations between men and women; it reflects the inferior status and the paucity of respect afforded women'[45].

In contrast to Australian femocrats, policy-makers in Canadian women's agencies have not been able to exercise the same degree of autonomy and have found it more difficult to bring a feminists perspective to bear on key policy areas. One outstanding example of this relates to femocrats' inability to convince government to develop a universal, national, state-funded childcare system. According to Burt, external feminist groups were correct in thinking that femocrats had been ineffectual in relation to childcare. In her 1990 study of this policy area, Burt found that the SWC had been unable to provide any leadership on the issue and had left the running on the issues to 'a plurality of women's groups and day care associations' [46]. Senior SWC officer, Zeynap Karman has also hinted at the difficulty femocrats have had in instigating gender sensitive policy in particular areas. In a 1996 speech to the UN, Karman noted in relation to three key areas - women's unpaid work, child support and pension reform - that it was members of the external women's movement, rather than internal femocrats, who first identified the issue and called for government action. In each case, the role of the SWC was limited to an educational one rather than taking the initiative on these issues. It saw its role as 'sensitizing other policy makers to the importance of considering unpaid work in their policy development'; suggesting 'directions for change' in relation to child support; and, 'disseminating the available information on gender and providing analyses for use of the various players' involved in pension reform[47].

There is some evidence to suggest that Canadian femocrats have been able to achieve positive policy outcomes in a limited range of specifically designated 'status of women' areas such as wife battering, child sexual abuse and other forms of family violence[48]. They have put the issues of economic equality and the integration of work and family on the agenda of First Ministers Conferences. Like their Australian counterparts, Canadian femocrats have also been influential in the international arena, taking a leading role in United Nations women's agencies. For instance, they were responsible for initiating the resolution leading to the UN declaration on the Elimination of Violence against Women[49]. Nevertheless, where women's agencies have shown initiative, their efforts have often been criticised by members of the external women's movement who have perceived them as diluting proposals to fit with the economic and social agenda of the government or for doing 'too little too late'[50].

It may be too early to judge the policy outputs of the Women's Unit in the United Kingdom. However, the initial signs are that, like its institutional position, its ability to influence the policy agenda is weak. Since the being created, the work of the unit has reflected the position of the Minister, focussing on educative, rather than interventionist

---

45 NCVAW, *National Strategy on Violence Against Women* (Canberra: Australian Government Printing Service 1992),15.

46 For a discussion on childcare see Sandra Burt 'The Changing Patterns of Public Policy' in Sandra Burt and Lorraine Code eds. *Changing Patterns: Women in Canada second ed.* (Toronto:McClelland and Stewart Inc. 1993).

47 Zeynap Erden Karman. 'Feminist Initiatives to Gender Macro-Economic Policies in Canada'. Paper presented to the United Nations Research Institute for Social Development and Centre for Policy Dialogue Workshop, Rajendrapur, Bangladesh 26-28 November 1996.

48 Alena Heitlinger, *Women's Equality, Demography and Public Policies*. New (York: St Martin's Press, 1993).

49 Status of Women Canada. Canada's National report to the United Nations For the Fourth World Conference on Women, (Ottawa: Status of Women Canada, 1995), 63.

50 See Malloy, 'What makes', 278.

strategies[51]. In 1998-9 the unit undertook a large consultation with women in the community, culminating in a report *Voices,* which considered a range of issues including women and health, transport safety and education. The report was greeted with cynicism in the media and the broader feminist community for promoting the 'third-way' policies of the Blair government rather than addressing the needs of women[52]. Despite also stating a commitment to gender mainstreaming, there appears to be little evidence of the development of a gender-sensitive approach policy making in line departments. This was evidenced most dramatically when, despite strong lobbying from women within and outside the civil service, the government introduced a cut in the lone parent benefit – the beneficiaries of which were overwhelmingly women [53].

The variations in the relative success of feminists in intervening in the bureaucracy in these three countries are intriguing. This is not least because they are all Westminster parliamentary systems, where we might expect similar there to be similar outcomes. How can the differences between these three countries be explained? Some initial work comparing feminists' engagement with the bureaucracy has suggested that there is something intrinsic to the women's movements – primarily the nature of feminist ideology - which has influenced these outcomes. In a comparison of Australian and Canadian feminists and the state, Marian Sawer suggests that Australian feminists have adopted a more 'pro-statist' position than their Canadian counterparts, thus encouraging them to engage with the public service[54]. A similar argument has been advanced by Sophie Watson to explain why Australian and British feminists have responded so differently to the state. In her view, Australian feminists' pragmatic approach to the state has encouraged bureaucratic intervention, while the predominant Marxist, anti-statist position of British feminists has produced the opposite result – they have assiduously avoided engaging with the bureaucracy [55].

In both instances, these arguments have some credence. Certainly, ideology has been one influence on feminists' choice of strategies – perceptions about the nature of the state and potential obstacles and opportunities have made a difference to where and when feminists exert their energies. However, it would be wrong to over-emphasise this factor. As I have suggested elsewhere, Sawer's argument in relation to Australian/Canadian case loses some of its appeal when we look across the institutional spectrum. Here we discover it is not the degree of pro-statism that is different, so much as the particular institutions feminists engage with[56]. While Australian feminists have chosen the bureaucracy, Canadian feminists have adopted alternative strategies including lobbying parliamentarians and litigating under the Charter of Rights and Freedoms. Similarly, in relation to Watson's argument, we can suggest an alternative hypothesis, *viz*: that while feminists have been unwilling to engage with the central government, they have been prepared to intervene at the local government level: a critical level of the state in any unitary system. The following section of the chapter presents an alternative explanation for variations in the success of the femocrat strategy, suggesting

---

51 Benn, 'Short March', 41.
52 Ibid,41-2.
53 For a discussion see Coote, 'The longest', 252-254; Benn, 'Short March', 42.
54 See Marian Sawer 'Feminism and the State: Theory and Practice in Australia and Canada' *Australian Canadian Studies,* 12 (1) (1994): 49-68.
55 Sophie Watson, 'Femocratic Feminisms' in Mike Savage and Anne Witz, eds. *Gender and Bureaucracy* (Oxford: Blackwell/The Sociological Review: 1992).
56 see XXXX 1998.

that *institutional* factors combined with the nature of the political party in office best explain differences across the three countries.

Part II. Explaining the Success of the Femocrat Strategy: The Influence of Institutional Structures, Norms and Parties

The following discussion argues that femocrat experiences have been shaped by variations in opportunities and constraints within the civil service in the three countries. Although the bureaucracy in each country has its foundation in a Westminster tradition, each operates quite differently due to variations in the interplay *between* the bureaucracy and other institutions in each polity as well as its unique cultural and normative foundations. The following discussion focuses on three specific factors that have had a significant influence on feminists' strategic choices. These include the existence of federal versus unitary structures, the influence of political parties and the operation of bureaucratic norms.

Institutional Structures: Federalism and Political Parties

Federalism can be identified as a key institution which has influenced the success of the femocrat strategy. Its influence is obvious at two levels. The first relates to the operation of federalism in Australia and Canada and the existence of a unitary system in the UK which influence the nature of the bureaucracy in the three countries. The second concerns the interaction between the federal and sub-national levels of government and the role played by political parties in shaping this interaction. As will be outlined below, political parties have acted as an intervening variable between the bureaucracy and federal/state relations to shape the political opportunity structure open to femocrats.

Australian Federalism and Political Parties

It is possible to identify some aspects of Australian federalism which have had an independent and direct influence on the femocrat strategy. Perhaps the most important aspect is that, because of the nature of federal constitutional and fiscal arrangements, femocrats have had the opportunity to enjoy a system of 'double democracy'. Whilst the states have the constitutional authority to become involved in a range of 'women's' policy areas such as child care, equal opportunity policy, women's health and housing, the commonwealth government shares some constitutional authority, and more importantly has the fiscal autonomy, to enter these areas. As a result, at times when femocrat efforts have been stymied at the federal level, they have been able to pursue their objectives at the state level and vice versa. For instance, in the 1980s when the federal government withdrew funding from women's refuges, the state governments in New South Wales and Victoria picked up the cost. Meanwhile, when the Queensland and Tasmanian state governments refused to provide dedicated women's policy machinery, the federal government funded its own women's information services in these states.

Feminists have articulated the importance of having multiple levels of government to a bureaucratic strategy, emphasising the fact that it enables them to play a two-level strategic game. Long term activist and former femocrat, Eva Cox is one who adopts a favourable stance in relation to federalism arguing that it enables 'Feminists and other lobbyists [to] play off the different levels of government to gain advantages for the less powerful'[57]. For Cox and others, the fact that federal-state relations are often 'confused and overlapping' only facilitates this process. According to Carmel Flask and Betty Hounslow, feminists active in the women's services sector:

> The Australian federal system, with its different tiers of governments, not only creates complexity, it also allows further opportunity for manoeuvring. Times can be instanced when some battles have been won (and lost) because of the complexity of state and federal funding systems and the negotiations which occur between bureaucrats across departments [58].

Femocrats in Australia have also benefited from another, more recent development within Australian federalism, the growth in co-operative relations between the Australian federal and state governments. They have been particularly influenced by the creation of co-operative intergovernmental machinery under the Council of Australian Governments. Femocrats have been involved in the establishment of women's advisers meetings and the Council of Women's Minsters and have used these bodies to develop national women's policy programs. Since the late 1980s, femocrats in state jurisdictions have co-operated with those at the national level to fashion national polices concerning childcare, domestic violence, women's health and other areas which require joint state/federal action. Most recently, the Howard Liberal Government has joined with the states to implement a co-ordinated, national domestic violence program, known as the Partnerships Program, which provides funding for research on domestic violence at the commonwealth level as well as in each state [59].

The co-operative nature of state/federal relations in Australia has been enhanced by the operation of political parties. In Australia, two major parties dominate the political scene – the Australian Labor Party (ALP) and the Liberal Party. Of the two parties, the ALP is more progressive supporting a social democratic agenda whilst the Liberal party, which usually governs in coalition with the rural-based National Party, is a conservative political force. The party system in which these two organisations operate can be broadly defined as *symmetrical.* Although party membership is organised at a state level and both the major parties have separate state and national bodies, there are strong links between the national and sub-national units. In both cases, the national body of the party plays an important role in co-ordinating, if not integrating, policy across states[60].

The presence of a progressive party and the symmetrical nature of the party system have strongly influenced the opportunities open to femocrats within the federal system. In the

---

[57] Eva Cox *A truly civil society* 1995 Boyer Lectures (Sydney: ABC Books, 1995), 48.

[58] Carmel Flask and Betty Hounslow 'Government Interventional and Right-Wing Attacks on Feminist Services' *Scarlet Woman,* No. 11: 20.

[59] Louise Chappell, 'Federalism and Social Policy: The case of Domestic Violence' in *Australian Journal of Public Administration* Vol 60, 1 (2001) 59-69.

[60]. Ibid.

main, Australian femocrats have found that when the ALP is in office at the national or state level they have been able to make inroads through the bureaucracy. By the same token, shifts within these institutions, and their relationship to each other, has at times resulted in constraints for femocrats. This has tended to be the case when the more conservative Liberal Party is in office at either the state or commonwealth level.

The Role of the ALP

The Whitlam Labor government was the first federal government to respond to the demands of the contemporary women's movement and supported the entry of women from feminist backgrounds into the bureaucracy. During its period in office between 1972 and 1975, the reformist government used its fiscal capacity to introduce a national child care policy, provide direct funding for refuges on a national basis, and to establish the first women's health centres [61]. It also established an extensive array of women's policy-making agencies within the federal bureaucracy - agencies that later became models for the states. These initiatives were very important to Australian women, most of who were living under conservative state governments that had demonstrated an unwillingness to address policy issues from a gender perspective. During this time, South Australia, under the ALP premier Don Dunstan, was the only Labor state and the only state to introduce dedicated women's policy agencies and policies specifically designed to address women's needs.

The return of Labor to federal office in 1983 again saw Canberra respond to femocrat pressure and assert its presence in policy fields related to women, but with a difference. Prime Minister Hawke was less willing than Whitlam to take unilateral action to introduce his policy agenda, preferring to enter into joint funding agreements with the states. Hawke's approach was no doubt facilitated by the fact that ALP governments were in office in many of the states during this period. In July 1983, the Hawke government announced the resumption of the commonwealth's involvement in a range of women's policy areas. Through the Office of the Status of Women, it developed the National Agenda for Women, a five year plan through which a range of national women's policies were established including: the National Women's Health Program; the National Domestic Violence Strategy; the Australian Women's Employment Strategy as well as a National Childcare Strategy. The Keating ALP government, which came to office in late 1991, continued joint funding of national programs and in 1993 released a new National Agenda for Women. It also undertook reforms to strengthen the Sex Discrimination Act and, in 1995, released the National Women's Justice Statement, which was a response to the Australian Law Reform Commission's report into the position of women and the law [62].

Femocrats have faced a much less favourable opportunity structure at the federal level under conservative governments. After the Fraser Liberal government came to office in 1975, many of the Whitlam government's initiatives in relation to women, including federal women's agencies, were pared back. During this period the commonwealth also retreated from national women's programs: it reduced its commitment to child-care, and granted the

---

[61] Deborah Brennan, *The Politics of Australian Childcare: From Philanthropy to Feminism,* (Melbourne: Cambridge University Press, 1994), 77-8.

[62] Sue Wills, 'Sexual Equality' in M. Hogan, K. Dempsey eds. *Equity and Citizenship Under Keating* (Sydney: Public Affairs Research Centre, University of Sydney, 1995), 117.

states much greater control over the community health and refuge programs [63]. Similarly, under the current Howard Liberal Coalition government femocrats have faced a range of constraints at the federal level. Since coming to office in 1996, the Howard government has cut the budget for women's policy machinery at the federal level and has withdrawn funding for the Women's Statistics Unit. Subsidies to community-based childcare centres - which were the foundation of the national childcare system in Australia - have been abolished and substantial cutbacks have been made to the child-care rebate[64]. The only women's policy area that has not been abandoned by the Howard government is domestic violence, and even then, the policy as it is conceived at the federal level, has come to reflect the government's conservative family discourse[65].

A similar pattern of advancement under ALP governments and retreat under conservative governments has also been apparent at the state level. For instance, during the Fraser Liberal period, when the commonwealth 'dilly-dallied' on sex discrimination legalisation, all the states with ALP governments - which excluded Queensland and Tasmania - took action to introduce anti-discrimination legislation[66]. State ALP governments have also been prepared to respond to femocrat pressure to take the initiative in providing support for some women's services when they have been stalled by conservative governments at the national level. During the 1980s, ALP governments in South Australia agreed to provide 100 per cent of the funding for women's health centres[67].

The alliance that developed between the ALP and the femocracy was not without its costs: in return for a position within the bureaucracy, femocrats were expected to help 'sell' the government's policies to women in the wider community. However, without the influence of the ALP on the public service, it is unlikely that feminist activists would have had the same opportunity to use bureaucratic structures to advance its objectives.

Canadian Federalism and Political Parties

Canadian federalism is markedly different to that in Australia primarily because of its decentralised nature. In Canada, the provincial governments have higher degrees of both constitutional and fiscal autonomy than that of the states in Australia. And, although Ottawa is able to use funding to influence policy at the sub-national level, its authority in this area is no where near as strong that of Canberra. It might be supposed that the decentralised nature of Canadian federalism would be a boon to Canadian femocrats in that they should have even greater opportunities than their Australian counterparts to be able to enjoy a system of 'double democracy', making advances at the provincial level when blocked at the centre and vice versa. However, few activists see the situation in these positive terms. Canadian feminists

---

[63] Ludo Mc Ferren, 'Interpretation of a Frontline State: Australian Women's Refuges and the State' in Sophie Watson ed. *Playing the State: Australian feminist interventions in the State.* (Sydney: Allen and Unwin, 1990).

[64] Marian Sawer, 'Shooting the Messenger: Australia and CEDAW' G. Crowder, H. Manning, D.S. Mathieson, A. Parkin, L. Seabrooke, eds. *Australian Political Studies 1997: Proceedings of the 1997 APSA Conference* (Department of Politics, Flinders University of South Australia, 1997).

[65] Lee Fitzroy, 'State Responses to Violence Against Women' in Linda Hancock ed. *Women, Public Policy and the State*, (Melbourne: Macmillan, 1999), 168-9.

[66] Marian Simms, and Diane Stone. 'Women's Policy' in Christine Jennett and Randall Stewart eds *Hawke and Australian Public Policy.* (Melbourne: Macmillan, 1990), 289.

[67] Sawer, 'Sisters', 13.

outside Quebec, have largely eschewed engagement with the provincial level, including the bureaucracy, aside from a few exceptions. In the main, feminist activists have seen federal arrangements as an impediment, arguing that decentralisation creates a 'patchwork' of policies on important women's issues such as divorce law, childcare, and violence against women will develop across the country.[68]

The decentralised nature of Canadian federalism has operated, in its own right, as an obstacle to a femocrat project, but when combined with the features of the Canadian party system, it can be seen to be even more of a barrier to their efforts. In keeping with its decentralised federal system, Canada has an *asymmetrical* party system. That is, political parties, even those of the same political hue such as the Liberal or Conservative Party, are only very loosely connected at the federal and state level. Membership and policy remains a matter for each level to decide with no strong co-ordination between the two. Further, although progressive parties exist in Canada, such as the left-leaning New Democratic Party, these parties have only had success at the provincial level. In the main, the party system has tended to operate along brokerage lines battling over the middle-ground. The effect of these arrangements on femocrats have been numerous and mostly negative.

At the federal level, Canadian feminists wanting to enter the bureaucracy to pursue their objectives have been less fortunate than their Australian counterparts in being able to exploit the benefits of supportive, reformist governments. In Ottawa, party politics has been dominated by two parties – the Progressive Conservatives (PC) and Liberals. Operating in a brokerage system, and pre-occupied with territorial and constitutional issues including the 'Quebec question', neither party has been overly concerned to be seen to be advancing women's issues to attract additional votes [69]. Although PC and Liberal governments have created women's policy machinery at the federal level, they have not encouraged the entry of feminists into the bureaucracy to staff these agencies. Nor have they supported the development of the breadth of gender-sensitive policies in the way that occurred under the ALP in Australia. According to Findlay, in the 1970s the Trudeau government was disinterested in fostering a feminist policy perspective at the federal level[70]. Meanwhile, under the Mulroney PC government there was outright hostility to any feminist-based approach[71].

Feminists operating at the provincial level have a more varied story. At those times when there has been a sympathetic government in office, feminist bureaucrats have made some progress. This has been especially apparent under the Rae New Democratic Party (NDP) government in Ontario and the Harcourt NDP government in British Columbia. In both cases, staff for women's agencies were recruited directly from the feminist movement and policies emerging from these agencies had an overt feminist perspective[72]. The fact that feminists in Quebec have made the most advances with a femocrat strategy both in terms of developing a

---

[68] Judy Rebick, 'The Charlottetown Accord: A Faulty Framework and a Wrong-Headed Compromise' in Kenneth McRoberts and Patrick Monahan, Patrick eds. *The Charlottetown Accord: The Referendum and the Future of Canada*, (Toronto: University of Toronto Press,1993).

[69] Janine Brodie and Jane Jenson 'The Party System' in Michael S. Whittington and Glen Williams eds. *Canadian Politics in the 1990s* third ed. (Scarborough, Ontario: Nelson, Canada, 1990).

[70] Findlay *Democracy.*

[71] Sylvia Bashevkin, *Women on the Defensive: Living Through Conservative Times.* (Chicago: University of Chicago Press, 1998).

[72] see Malloy 'What makes' on Ontario and Teghtsoonian on BC.

secure institutional position as well as achieving a degree of autonomy within the service[73] can also be explained by the coincidence of federal structures with sympathetic nationalist governments. However, these opportunities have appeared infrequently in a minority of provinces. Conservative provincial governments, especially in central and western provinces, have enjoyed enough fiscal autonomy and constitutional authority to simply be able to resist pressure from the feminist community to create women's policy agencies. Moreover, due to the division of power within the Canadian federation, and the lack of co-operation between political parties at the national and sub-national governments, Ottawa (unlike Canberra) has not been able or willing to intervene in the provinces where there are unsympathetic governments to bring about uniformity in relation to women's issues.

British Political Parties and the Unitary System

In the UK, efforts to develop a femocrat strategy have been constrained by a combination of the nature of the party in government and the unitary system. The fact that the British Conservative Party was in office for 17 years from the end of the 1970s is, on its own, an important factor in explaining the absence of a UK femocrat strategy. The ideology and policies of the conservative governments of Thatcher and Major may have had ambiguous outcomes for *women* – especially in terms of their neo-liberal agenda which provided a boon to some individual women[74]. However, as far as *feminists* were concerned, the outcomes were unquestionably negative. Thatcher's opposition to any form of collective action, including that of the women's movement was overt. In Bashevkin's view, under Thatcher:

> Women's groups were linked at the level of ideas to the same collectivist ideology that Thatcher detested at the level of practice to unions, local governments and other troublesome interests. These opponents were wrapped together in a single rhetorical package by the government and supporters in the tabloid press. Protest groups were castigated as 'looney left', fringe advocates of both high government spending and morally decadent 'alternative lifestyles' [75].

Under the Blair Labour Government, it is questionable whether feminist fortunes have improved. A number of recent critiques of the government suggest that it is also hostile to a feminist agenda. In its attempt to attract swinging voters with its consensual 'third way' message, it has sought to freeze out feminism which it sees as divisive and a feature of the 'old politics' [76]. The Blair government has been reluctant to embrace feminist arguments that that men and women have separate needs based on biological and/or social differences, which justifies a gender sensitive approach to policy making,. Instead, it is focussed on encouraging

---

[73] see Jane Arscott, et al. 'Canadian Experiments with State Feminism: Status of Women Machinery in a Federal State', (unpublished).

[74] see Lovenduski and Randall, *Politics: Women and Power in Britain.* (Oxford: Oxford University Press, 1993), 41.

[75] Bashevkin, 'Challenging Times', 171.

[76] Anna Coote, 'Introduction' in Anna Coote ed. *New Gender Agenda*, (London: IPPR, 2000), 4.

a partnership between men and women which obviates the need for such an approach[77]. In the view of one commentator:

> ...no-one should make the mistake of thinking that, because there is a minister for women and Women's Unit in the Cabinet office, that this government is interested in feminism. The f-word is still the biggest turn-off in the corridors of power...[78].

Whilst feminist activists have had little support from either of the major political parties, they have also been disadvantaged by the unitary system in which they operate. This was especially obvious under the conservatives, when feminists not only had to confront a government which was ideologically opposed to their goals, but also one that closed off avenues for advancement. Traditionally, the UK women's movement, who feared co-option by the central state, looked to the local government level to pursue their objectives. During the 1970s and early 1980s many feminists concentrated their efforts on creating women's committees within local government which were designed 'both to promote women's rights and to bring a women's perspective to the policies and practices of local government' [79]. Mostly, these committees operated along 'femocrat' lines, staffed by feminists and with direct links with women's activists in the community[80]. These women's committees were mostly created under Labour dominated councils while Conservative councils 'almost invariably opposed such initiatives' [81]. Where these committees existed, they were able to achieve some significant outcomes, such as the development of sophisticated anti-domestic violence policies [82].

To the extent that UK feminists were able to intervene in the state through local government, the strategy unravelled during the Thatcher years. In the United Kingdom, Westminster maintains ultimate authority over sub-national government. Should the central government have the predisposition to restrict the powers of local government, it has the capacity to do so. Thatcher, who saw local government as 'free-spending, inefficient and out of step' [83], had such a predisposition and was not afraid to employ the central government's fiscal and political power to limit its autonomy. During her period in office, Thatcher abolished the Greater London Council and stripped other local governments of their decision-making authority[84]. This was disastrous for feminist activists who had put so much emphasis on addressing women's issues through this area of the state. The problem of operating in a unitary state was not lost on them. As one feminist activist noted:

> The lack of a federal system has limited us. The Margaret Thatcher regime enormously limited the power of municipal government overall, not just in London. She imposed tax

---

77 Jane Franklin, 'After modernisation: gender, the third way and the new politics' in Anna Coote ed. *New Gender Agenda* (London: IPPR, 2000).

78 Anne Perkins, 'Campaigning in an era of consensus: must women wear the velvet glove?' in Anna Coote ed. *New Gender Agenda* (London: IPPR, 2000).

79 Lovenduski and Randall, 'Politics', 192.

80 Ibid.

81 Ibid, 204.

82 For a full discussion see Sefania Abrar et al., 'Feminist Ideas and Domestic Violence Policy Change' *Political Studies* Vol 48 (2000): 239-262

83 Bashevkin, 'Challenging Times', 23.

84 Ibid, 15.

rate caps all over that prohibited local councillors who defied her from running for office[85].

During the Thatcher years, feminists were also blocked from using other avenues for advancement. The conservative government used its extensive power to limited access to, and the impact of, regional and international political forums. Thatcher and Major were well known for their hostility to Europe on the grounds that it was 'interventionist, collectivists and ultimately threatening to British sovereignty'[86]. Consecutive conservative governments refused to sign the Maastricht treaty, which included a social charter with important ramifications for women in terms of work and family issues. They also ignored other international developments led by the UN, such as the development of gender sensitive policy machinery. This meant that while its European neighbours such as France, the Netherlands, Spain and Portugal and former colonies including Australia and Canada were busy developing women's policy agencies through which feminists could engage with the state, the UK lagged well behind[87]. As Bashevkin notes: 'Conservative actions on local government and the European Union served to weaken alternate sources of power in a highly centralized system'[88].

In its first term in office, the Blair Labour Government may have proven to be less supportive of feminists than some may have hoped. Nevertheless, it has created, albeit at times inadvertently, some opportunities for feminist activists at the central, local and regional/international level. It has reinstated authority in local councils and, after signing the Maastricht treaty, has begun to pay greater heed to European standards on issues related to women such as family friendly work hours and equal pay[89]. Moreover, the recent shift towards devolution in the United Kingdom is potentially a crucial development in relation to feminists' engagement with the state.

Greater devolution provides grounds for optimism for three reasons. First, devolution has given Scotland, Wales and Northern Ireland new legislatures and bureaucratic structures that have control over important policy areas including gender equity and education. As new institutions, these structures do not carry the embedded masculine institutional norms that have operated as such a barrier in Whitehall, and thus we might expect there would be less resistance to gender sensitive policy proposals. Second, women have done exceedingly well in terms of achieving representation in the new parliaments[90]. Moreover, many of the new female members are overtly feminist in outlook. Since taking office, many have actively pursued 'women friendly' policies in relation to anti-sex discrimination, education and domestic violence and worked to develop gender sensitive mechanisms including a gender budget audit instrument and, in the case of Scotland, a cross-party women's caucus.[91] Third, these new institutions go someway in breaking down one of the barriers to feminists advancement in the UK - the centralisation of power in Westminster. A greater diffusion of power means that when feminist efforts are blocked at the central level (or by the central

---

[85] Drew in Ibid, 139.
[86] Ibid, 23.
[87] see True and Mintrom, 'Transnational Networks'.
[88] Bashevkin, 'Challenging Times', 23.
[89] See Coote, 'The longest' 256.
[90] 37.2% of the Scottish parliament are women, while over 50% of the members of the Welsh parliament are women.
[91] For an outline of current activities in Scotland see http://www.engender.org.uk/.

government at the local level) they have another avenue through which they can pursue their aims. As we have seen in Australia, and to a lesser extent in Canada, the combination of a supportive political party and multi-tiered government can prove to be advantageous for feminists wanting to engage directly with the bureaucratic arm of the state.

Federalism and political parties have obviously had an important impact upon the experiences of femocrats in the three countries. Whilst it is obvious in each case that federal structures had some independent influence on shaping the opportunities between femocrats and the bureaucracy, a more important factor has been the interaction between national and sub-national jurisdictions and the political party system. The nature of political parties and the degree of co-ordination between them at the different levels of government have had a strong influence over whether femocrats have been able to take advantage of a system of 'double democracy'.

Bureaucratic Norms

However, these institutional and political relationships are not the sole explanation for the differences between femocrat experiences across the three polities. It is also possible to identify a factor within the bureaucratic arena which has profoundly shaped the political opportunities in each place – that is, the operation of bureaucratic norms.

Australian Bureaucratic Norms

On entering the Australian bureaucracy in the early 1970s, Australian feminists were confronted with a highly gendered institution. Underlying gender norms were evident at a number of levels. The long-term practice of positive discrimination for men through policies such as preference in employment for returned soldiers and a marriage bar for women was being dismantled. Nevertheless, its effect in terms of the profile of public service personnel was still being felt. The notion of a career service was firmly in place. This work pattern was premised not only on public servants having a full-time, unbroken work history, but also being able to rely on a dependent, full-time homemaker – both of which reinforced men's public and women's private roles[92]. Egalitarian ideals that came to be the 'backbone' of the Australian bureaucratic culture, served to protect the position of the 'common man' within the service and to exclude groups which fell outside this definition, including women [93].

One traditional normative aspect of the Westminster bureaucratic system that was not so strongly enforced in the Australian context was that of *neutrality*. As Kernaghan notes, the concept of bureaucratic neutrality as it is applied in Westminster systems has six aspects. Included within this definition is an understanding that public servants do not engage in partisan political activities; do not express their personal views on government policies or administration; and, execute policy decisions loyally and irrespective of the party in power and regardless of their personal opinions[94]. As with other bureaucratic norms, the concept of

---

[92] Clare Burton, *The Promise and the Price: The struggle for equal opportunity in women's employment*, (Sydney: Allen and Unwin, 1991).

[93] Gerald Caiden, 'Australia's Changing Administrative Ethos: An exploration' in Kouzmin, Alexander and Scott Nicholas eds. *Dynamics in Australian Public Management: Selected Essays.* (Melbourne: Macmillan, 1990), 3.

[94] Kenneth Kernaghan, in Peter Aucoin, ed. *Regional Responsiveness and the National Administrative State*, (Toronto: University of Toronto Press, 1985).

neutrality also has a gender dimension. Neutrality suggests that 'administrators can rise above their own beliefs and the political fray to fix their sights on the public interest, broadly conceived' [95]. In Stivers' view, this gives the term a masculine bias because it suggests that there is a set of universal norms that can be used to look at the world. However, when considered in detail, these norms reflect underlying gender assumptions. For instance, the importance of individuals being able to detach themselves from situations and act with 'dispassionate objectivity' reflects an emphasis on traditional masculine traits [96]. Meanwhile, values such as emotion, sensibility or passion, in other words those that have been identified as 'feminine' values, are regarded as excessive and laden with bias[97].

Traditionally in Australia, bureaucrats followed the Westminster model of non-partisanship and remaining above the political fray. But this was partially undercut by a competing tradition of tolerance of *advocates* within the bureaucracy. Traditionally, internal advocacy was the domain of producer groups, including trade unions, manufacturers and farmers, who encouraged government to establish public sector bodies, described as 'organs of syndical satisfaction', to advance their aims [98]. The tradition of sectional interests looking toward the administrative arm of the state, and the state providing them with agencies through which they could advance their claims, had a profound influence on Australian feminists. Most importantly, it encouraged them to look to this arena to have their demands met[99]. It was a conscious strategy on their part. As one former senior femocrat has stated:

> ...in a society which believes firmly in centralized wage fixation principles, and the role of the state, ...it is not at all surprising that Australian feminists have seen it as important to use state apparatus as one way of achieving feminist objectives...Were our society differently ordered then Australian feminists might be using other ...machinery [100]

The pattern of feminist's engagement with the bureaucracy did not replicate precisely that of producer groups. For instance, they did not attempt to gain a separate statutory agency, but rather entered the public service proper to work as 'inside agitators'. This meant that the government of the day has been able to become overtly involved in their actions, such as altering the structure and position of women's agencies. Nevertheless, the intention of feminists was similar to these other social actors: as Eisenstein notes, they 'developed a concept of women as a sectional interest, with a claim for state protection'[101]. There were original elements to the feminist strategy as well; it combined the traditional demand for a position within the bureaucracy 'with a modern, feminist-inspired ideology that directly challenged the patriarchal status quo'[102]. According to Eisenstein, the femocrat strategy was a

---

[95] Camilla Stivers, *Gender Images in Public Administration: Legitimacy and the Administrative State*, (California: Sage, 1993), 38.

[96] Ibid, 40.

[97] Ibid, 41.

[98] J.D.B Miller, *Australian Government and Politics 3rd Edition,* (London: Gerald Duckworth and Co. Ltd, 1964), 128.

[99] Marian Sawer 'Why has the Australian Women's Movement Had More Influence on Government in Australia than Elsewhere?' in Francis Castles ed. *Australia Compared.* (Sydney: Allen and Unwin, 1991).

[100] Marie Coleman quoted in Eisenstein, 'Inside', 81.

[101] Ibid, 81 also see Sawer 'Sisters', 23.

[102] Eisenstein, 'Inside' 82.

form of 'feminist judo' - an attempt by feminists to use the capitalist patriarchal state against itself[103].

The tolerance for advocates of sectional interests within the Australian public sector has presented those pursuing a femocrat strategy with a positive opportunity structure within the bureaucracy. It has legitimised their use of bureaucratic structures to pursue the interests of their 'syndicate' - ostensibly Australian women. Although, as Summers argues, government's may have regarded women's units with more suspicion than they did other 'client-driven' agencies, an acceptance of internal advocates has permitted femocrats to advance their claims and take public positions on issues[104]. Kathleen Townsend, former head of the key Commonwealth women's agency, the Office of the Status of Women (OSW), believes that the acceptance of 'inside agitators' within the Australian bureaucracy has been advantageous for women's agencies, including the OSW. In her view:

The OSW behaves differently in the bureaucracy and is expected to do so. It has a history of advocacy and because its constituency is half the population it can sometimes pull rank with other departments [105].

Canadian Bureaucratic Norms

Anglo-Canadian feminists wanting to pursue a femocrat strategy had to contend with a range of gender norms similar to their Australian counterparts. On entering the bureaucracy, women met with a highly masculine culture that had been reinforced through the preferential hiring of returned soldiers as well as restrictions on married women within the service until the end of the 1950s. At the beginning of the 1970s, when feminists first looked to these institutions, a military subculture was evident within the public service with the consequence that it was 'paternalistic, hierarchical and unsympathetic to women's advancement'[106]. An additional barrier for Canadian femocrats was that the ideal of neutrality remained as a central normative feature of the bureaucracy. Compared to Canberra, Ottawa can be seen to have follow more closely the pattern of 'the Whitehall model and the Weberian ideal' with emphasis given to the characteristics of 'anonymity, non-partisan neutrality, [and] a permanent career path'[107]. As Bourgault and Carroll state: 'The Whitehall model, as it has developed in Canada, seems to be one of the least affected by political partisanship than any of the Anglo-American countries' and this is a feature which is considered to be 'among the most important qualities of the ...public service of the future'[108].

The continuing potency of neutrality as a core bureaucratic value in Canada has presented a major obstacle to the femocrat project. By upholding neutrality as a central bureaucratic norm, Ottawa is asserting a claim to impartiality. However, from a gender perspective, we can argue that this neutral public servant model has operated to maintain entrenched gender values and practices. Neutrality has meant that within the bureaucracy there has been an

---

[103] Ibid, 81.
[104] Summers, 'The importance', 62.
[105] Interview with Kathleen Townsend, Director, Office of the Status of Women, Canberra 4 July 95.
[106] Canadian Council on the Status of Women, *The Equality Game: Women in the Public Service 1908-1987*, (Ottawa: CACSW, 1988), 16.
[107] Jacques Bourgault and Barbara Wake Carroll, 'The Canadian Public Service: The Last Vestiges of the Whitehall Model?' in Jacques Bourgault et al., *Public Administration and Public Management in Canada,* (Sainte-Foy, Quebec: Les Publications Du Quebec, 1997), 92.
[108] Ibid, 95; 100.

intolerance of advocates in general and of feminists in particular, who seek to unsettle existing gender norms.

The prejudice against internal 'feminist agitators' in Ottawa has been noted by former Canadian 'femocrats'. They talk of initiatives being stonewalled and trivialised, treated with indifference and impatience by senior managers or, met with a 'willful misunderstanding'[109]. According to Geller-Schwartz:

> Civil Servants are supposed to be the anonymous, efficient, unbiased administrators of the machinery of state... Even if the male-dominated bureaucracy had been prepared to recognize that certain policies (other than the obvious issues such as maternity leave) could have a differential impact on women, the idea that civil servants should adopt the role of internal lobbyists for women as a definable group was an anathema[110].

The recollections of Sue Findlay, who was the first head of the Women's Program in the 1970s reinforce this point. Findlay and the other officers in the Women's Program came closest to the Australian femocrat model, being drawn directly from the external women's movement and whose feminism could be seen to be a credential for their job. Findlay discusses the resistance of senior male managers in the public service to feminist projects, and argues that they made an effort to block connections between internal feminists and grassroots organisations, thereby hoping to disrupt the radical intent of the program[111]. Findlay also outlines the hostility directed toward her because of her feminism. Indeed, at one point her application for renewal in her position was rejected by an appointment committee on the grounds that: 'Her crusading may, on occasion, colour her judgement and objectivity and antagonize managers without her realizing it - thus limiting her effectiveness in this job'[112]. In the event, Findlay appealed the decision and was reinstated in the position. Nevertheless, the experience illustrated the extent of resistance to feminist advocates who were perceived as challenging the neutral public servant model.

From all accounts, the resistance to internal feminist advocates has been enduring. In an interview in 1995, Jacquie Claxton, head of the Women's Program, noted the difficulty women's agencies had in being heard within the bureaucracy. 'It's tougher for us because our position is seen to be imbued with a feminist ideology and does not fit within the traditional neutral mould'[113].

Strong neutrality norms are also evident within some Canadian provinces and have had a similar constraining effect on femocrats. In Ontario for example, the Women's Directorate's 'chief concern was maintaining institutional (bureaucratic) conformity to secure sufficient political and resource support to achieve feminist policy objectives'[114]. In Ontario in the early 1990s, under the New Democratic Party government, there was a short period when feminist advocates were drawn directly from the women's movement into the bureaucracy. However, the Directorate quickly became marginalised. As Malloy explains: 'No longer a 'safe'

---

[109] Sue Findlay 'Facing the State': The politics of the women's movement reconsidered' in Heather Maroney and Meg Luxton eds. *Feminism and Political economy* (Toronto: Methuen, 1987), 39; CACSW, 26; Geller-Schwartz, 'An Array' 57.

[110] Geller-Schwartz, 'An Array' 49.

[111] Findlay *Democracy*, 217; 231.

[112] Quoted in Findlay *Democracy,* 214.

[113] Interview, Ottawa, November 1995.

[114] Malloy, 'What makes' 279.

organization that conformed to the institutional environment of the bureaucracy, the OWD was avoided and bypassed by most economic ministries'[115]. It is interesting to note that in Quebec, feminists have had more success using the bureaucracy to advance their claims regardless of the party in office[116]. One possible explanation for this difference is that the bureaucracy in Quebec has a different normative base, as a result of its unique cultural heritage. Writing on French Canada and the 'bureaucratic phenomenon', Herman Bakvis tentatively suggests that French-Canadians have a different approach to bureaucracy than their Anglo counterparts[117]. Although Bakvis did not test whether neutrality norms operated in a different way, his work does suggest that this is a path worth exploring in the Quebec context.

UK Bureaucratic Norms

There are strong reasons to speculate that in the UK, home to the Westminster bureaucratic model, neutrality has also played a key role in shaping feminists engagement with the bureaucracy. As with Canada, neutrality has remained a central plank of the 'public service ethos'. According to Lovenduski and Randall:

> ...the national government is dependent both for advice and policy implementation on its ostensibly 'neutral' civil service, which is highly centralized and works under conditions of great secrecy [118].

The strength of commitment to neutrality as a bureaucratic norm was made very apparent in recent evidence given to a House of Lords Select Committee on the Public Service. For instance, one civil servant claimed that the central features of the ethos were 'integrity, political impartiality, [and] objectivity' while another emphasised 'subordination of private to Ministerial opinions; party political neutrality...resistance to take risks or experiment or innovate except within clearly authorised Ministerial authority' [119]. In sum, evidence to the committee clearly reflected an ongoing antipathy to the notion of having advocates operating within the ranks of the civil service.

As with Canada, such views can be seen to have operated as a constraint on the development of a UK femocrat strategy. Elizabeth Meehan made this point in 1985 in a comparative study of women's employment policy is the US and the UK. In her study Meehan suggested that the nature of the British bureaucratic culture - its secrecy, neutrality and rejection of partisanship - has made it extremely difficult for feminists to operate within the bureaucracy and especially to form networks with external feminist groups such as has occurred in the United States[120]. While the creation of the unit opens the possibility for the development of a sex or gender based approach in the future, it does not appear to have enhanced the presence of feminists in the bureaucracy to date.

---

[115] Ibid, 281.
[116] Arscott et al., 'Canadian Experiments'
[117] Herman Bakvis, 'French Canada and the 'Bureaucratic Phenomenon'. *Canadian Public Administration* 21, 1 (1978):101-24.
[118] Joni Lovenduski and Vicki Randall, 'Contemporary Feminist', 18.
[119] House of Lords, *Select Committee on Public Service Report* [online], London. UK Parliament Library 1997-98 [cited 1 August 2000] Available from World Wide Web: (http: www.parliament. the stationery-office.co.uk.pa/ld199798/ldselect/ldpub).
[120] Elizabeth Meehan, Women's Rights at Work: Campaigns and Policy in Britain and the United States (London: Macmillan, 1985).

CONCLUSIONS

Despite all operating in Westminster systems, feminist activists in Australia have had more success than their counterparts in Canada or the UK in creating women's policy making structures within the bureaucracy and influencing policy to take account of women's unique sex and gender differences. As this chapter has illustrated, these differences are not the result of something intrinsic to these feminist activists, but have been shaped by the different opportunity structure available to them within each bureaucracy. These opportunities have been influenced by three factors. The first relates to the configuration of federal structures in Australia and Canada and the operation of a unitary structure in the UK. In Australia, the presence of a multi-tiered system of government enabled femocrats to exploit a system of 'double democracy' entering the bureaucracy at the national and sub-national level. Such an opportunity was not available to feminist activists in either of the other polities. This was in small part because of the interaction between the national and sub-national system of power and in large part because of the role played by political parties in each system of government. Whereas in Australia, feminist opportunities were enhanced by the presence of a symmetrical progressive party, this option was not available in either of the other polities. In Canada, decentralisation in combination with an asymmetrical brokerage party system operated to stymie the femocrat project in most provinces and at the national level. In the UK, strong central government with the capacity to limit local government, combined with unsympathetic political parties, effectively closed off opportunities for a femocrat project.

In each country bureaucratic norms operated as another variable shaping the available political opportunity structure. Whereas in Australia, femocrats enjoyed a relatively favourable situation due to weak neutrality norms, the situation was markedly different for their contemporaries in Canada and the UK. In both of these countries, bureaucratic norms have made it difficult for any advocates to operate inside the public service, but even more so for those wanting to unsettle the existing masculine *status quo.*

The findings of this chapter make some contribution to both feminist analyses of the state as well as neo-institutionalism. In relation to the feminist literature, it points to the importance of adopting a comparative view of understanding the way political institutions influence feminist activists. It suggests that it assumptions should not be made about the obstacles or opportunities open to feminists in any particular institution, but rather, that it is necessary to consider these institutions in context to understand their influence. This chapter has offered one view of exactly when and where institutions can operate for this purpose, but there remain many other unexplored stories which need further research.

The argument presented in this chapter also provides some empirical grounding for certain neo-institutionalist claims. First, it has demonstrated the importance of disaggregating the state by looking at the role of individual institutions, rather than assuming that the state exists as a coherent entity. It has also shown the need for comparative institutional research, illustrating the extent to which similar institutions operate in different ways across polities. Although the bureaucracy in each country under review was based on Westminster principles, none was exactly alike. Within each bureaucracy different institutional norms were at play, shaping unique opportunities and obstacles for feminist activists. Moreover, the chapter drew attention to the importance of the interaction between the institutions within a given polity. It was the combination of bureaucracy and other key political institutions such as federal and unitary structures that shaped the opportunity structure open to feminist activists. The intervention of political parties was also crucial. This should not be taken to suggest that in these countries, feminists have not enjoyed opportunities or faced obstacles within other institutions. Indeed, these conclusions lead us to expect the opposite. However, which institutions these might be remains a question for another chapter.

In: Australia: Economic, Political and Social Issues
Editors: Lachlan J. Williams and Ethan N. Lee
ISBN: 978-1-60456-856-1

Chapter 5

AUSTRALIA'S TRADE RELATIONS WITH INDIA: PAST TRENDS AND FUTURE PROSPECTS*

M. A. B. Siddique
School of Economics & Commerce
Economics Program, Business School
The University of Western Australia

INTRODUCTION

Over the past few decades the direction of Australia's exports has moved away quite rapidly from its traditional trading partners to embrace Asia as an important export destination. Within Asia, South Asia has become an increasingly important destination for Australia's exports, and within South Asia, India has been the largest market in the region over the past two decades. During 1997, India was Australia's 12th largest export market, up from 24th in 1977. Bilateral trade with India reached A$2.33 billion in 1997 (with Australian exports valued at A$1.69 billion and imports at A$0.64 billion), an increase of 38.1 percent over the previous year. With few exceptions since 1977, the balance of trade has always been in Australia's favour. India is likely to be of special economic significance for Australia in the future, especially by serving as a market for Australia's exports, with the ability to supply its products at a comparative cost advantage to similar Indian products.

AUSTRALIA-INDIA TRADE CO-OPERATION: A BRIEF BACKGROUND

Official recognition from Canberra of India's importance as a trading partner has been of comparatively recent origin. Traditionally, Europe had been Australia's most important trading

* This chapter draws on work from a research program "Recent Trends in Australian-Indian Trade: Implications for Australia" funded by the Department of Economics at the University of Western Australia, whose support is gratefully acknowledged. I wish to thank Gina Yoon, Robin Wong and Ben Dyer for research assistance.

partner. However, the dominance of this region gradually declined during the first half of the twentieth century. With the emergence of the dynamic economies in the Asia-Pacific region since the end of the Second World War, Australia was becoming more and more dependent on this region for its trade. However, due to India's close links with the former Soviet blocs, Australia did not pay serious attention to improve bilateral relations with this country although it developed close economic links with two other important Asian countries namely, China and Japan. The first pragmatic approach to establish close economic links with India was taken by the Whitlam government, which included a 1973 visit to India. During his visit Whitlam openly admitted that Australia had paid more attention to developing relations with China and Japan than with India and indicated that India's importance as Australia's trading partner would receive due recognition in the future years.[1] Whitlam's visit was followed by the first formal trade agreement between these two countries in 1976. However, the agreement failed to leave any significant impact on the economic relations between the two countries. India maintained its image amongst Australians "as a land of poverty and problems"[2]; on the other hand, India looked upon Australia "as a country of open spaces and Kangaroos".[3] Bilateral contacts relating to various trade and economic issues intensified from the beginning of the 1980s. In 1983, the Agricultural Cooperation Agreement was signed in order to exchange scientific knowledge and technology for the development of agriculture in both the countries. Within three years the Australia-India Business Council was established and the Science and Technology Agreement which was initially signed in 1975 was updated. The year 1989 witnessed accelerated improvement in bilateral economic relations between these two countries: the Australia-India Joint Ministerial Commission was formed; a joint working group on trade, and another on coal was established; and the Development Cooperation Program and Treaty was signed.

The growing importance of India as a trading partner of Australia received further recognition in 1992 when the Australian government set up the Australian-Indian Council to promote bilateral trade. As a counterpart to this Council, an India-Australia Council was set up in March 1995. A six weeklong Australia-India New Horizons Promotion was also launched in India on October 22, 1996 by Alexander Downer to showcase Australia in India. The main objective of this promotional measure was to enhance Australian trade opportunities in India. New Horizon was followed up in 1997 by the Year of South Asia, which targeted potential commercial linkages between Australia and the other countries of South Asia, including India. Together with other countries, Australia and India co-operated to establish the Indian Ocean Rim Association for Regional Co-operation (IOR-ARC) which was launched by the Ministers from participating countries in March 1997. IOR-ARC aims to facilitate and promote economic co-operation among countries of the Indian Ocean rim.

Motivation and Organisation of the Paper

The main objective of this chapter is to examine the patterns and trends of trade between Australia and India since the signing of the Trade Agreement in 1976 with special emphasis on the possibilities of improving Australia's export performance in India. It will specifically

---

[1] Gurry, Meg (1993), p. 17.
[2] *Ibid*, p. 11.
[3] Frank, W W and Ghosh, R N (1981), p. 30.

investigate the relative competitive position of the two countries in the world market as well as in the market of each other in order to determine the scope for increases in trade. Given the recognition of the importance of these two countries to each other's long-term economic and commercial interests, the study has obvious policy implications for both Australia and India. The next section of the chapter focuses on the changes in the composition and direction of Australia's export trade during the last since 1977 with a view to establishing the importance of India as a trading partner of Australia. Past trends in trade between Australia and India and the international competitiveness of the two countries is discussed in sections 5 and 6 respectively. The prospects of increasing Australia's share of exports to the Indian market are discussed in section 7. As usual, the chapter finishes with some the concluding observations in the final section.

Structural Changes in Australia's Trade

Composition of Trade

Table 5.1 exhibits the structural changes that have taken place in the composition of export sectors of Australia between 1978 and 1997 based on 2 and 3-digit Trade Exports Classification (TREC).

Table 5.1. Change in Composition of Australia's Merchandise Exports to the World Based on Trade Exports Classification (TREC): 1978-97

TREC Description	Distribution of Exports (Percent)								
	1978	1980	1982	1985	1987	1990	1992	1995	1997
Primary Products	*69.3*	*67.3*	*69.5*	*68.9*	*61.6*	*53.4*	*53.8*	*43.1*	*43.7*
11 Unprocessed	47.6	46.6	50.2	56.8	48.9	39.5	38.5	28.7	29.9
12 Processed	21.7	20.7	19.4	12.0	12.7	13.8	15.3	14.4	13.8
Manufactured Products	*19.3*	*19.2*	*17.1*	*17.1*	*22.3*	*25.1*	*26.3*	*33.5*	*31.9*
23 Simply Transformed Manufactures (STMs)	8.8	8.4	5.8	7.3	8.8	9.9	9.4	10.0	8.7
24 Elaborately Transformed Manufactures ETMs)	10.5	10.8	11.3	9.7	13.5	15.2	16.9	23.6	23.3
Miscellaneous Products (NES)	*11.4*	*13.5*	*13.4*	*14.0*	*16.1*	*21.5*	*20.0*	*23.3*	*24.4*
Total Exports	*100*	*100*	*100*	*100*	*100*	*100*	*100*	*100*	*100*

Sources: Estimated from, Department of Foreign Affairs and Trade (DFAT), (1996), *Exports of Major Commodities Time Series, 1996,* Canberra: Commonwealth of Australia, pp.22-23 and 54-55); and Department of Foreign Affairs and Trade (DFAT), (1998), *Exports of Major Commodities Time Series, 1998,* Canberra: Commonwealth of Australia, pp.22-23 and 46-47.

Primary products have always accounted for the bulk of Australia's exports, although their share of total exports has declined from 69.3 percent in 1978 to 43.7 percent in 1997. The share of unprocessed products in total exports declined more rapidly (from 47.6 percent to 29.9 percent) as opposed to that of processed primary products (from 21.7 percent to 13.8 percent) during this period.

In contrast, the share of manufactured goods to total export earnings of Australia remarkably increased from 19.3 percent in 1978 to 31.9 percent in 1997. The main contribution came from the increase in the share of Elaborately Transformed Manufactures (ETMs) which increased from 10.5 percent to 23.3 percent. The share of Simply Transformed Manufactures (STMs) remained relatively steady during this period with some fluctuations.

Australia achieved these desirable changes in its export structures through movements in cost and price competitiveness; export oriented industry specific policies; and changes in business culture and attitude. International factors such as the acceleration in the growth of world ETM imports, also favoured Australia[4]. Australia also implemented a series of macroeconomic reforms from the beginning of the 1980s which contributed to its improved competitive position. Gradual removal of protective measures, large efforts to build bilateral relations with the dynamic regions of the world[5], and the introduction of a number of microeconomic reforms significantly improved Australia's relative competitive position over the years.

Direction of Trade

Table 5.2 clearly demonstrates that while Australia's share of exports to economic areas in Europe and America such as the EU[6], the EEA[7] and NAFTA[8] has declined between 1977 and 1997, the Asian countries have become increasingly important as the market for Australia's exports (as well as the most important sources of Australia's imports).

Table 5.2. Australia's Merchandise Exports to Major Economic Areas: 1977-1997 (Percentage Share)

Economic Areas	1977	1982	1987	1992	1997
APEC, of which	67.1	65.9	68.2	74.8	74.6
- ASEAN	6.7	8.4	6.8	14.4	15.2
- North-East Asia	41.8	38.1	40.8	43.2	41.8
- NAFTA	11.6	12.0	13.1	10.6	9.0
- Australasia	6.8	7.5	7.6	6.7	8.7
EEA, of which	16.9	14.2	16.4	13.4	10.4
- EU	16.5	14.1	16.3	13.2	10.2
SAARC	1.5	2.4	1.6	2.1	3.1
Industrialised and Developing					
OECD	67.4	62.1	66.4	61.7	55.2
Developing Countries	29.0	36.1	34.3	42.2	50.3

Source: Department of Foreign Affairs and Trade (1998a), *Direction of Trade Time Series 1977-1997,* Canberra: Commonwealth of Australia, p. 22.

4 Sheehan, P J et. al., (1994), p. ix.

5 Changes in Australia's bilateral trade relations with her important trading partners is discussed later.

6 European Union: Austria, Bulgaria, Czech Republic, Hungary, Poland, Romania, Slovak Republic, USSR (former), and Yugoslavia (former),

7 European Economic Areas: *EU*, Iceland, Norway.

8 North America Free Trade Agreement: Canada, Mexico, and the USA (including Puerto Rico and US Virgin Island).

For example, between 1977 and 1997, the share of the Asia-Pacific region (APEC)[9] in Australia's exports has increased from 67.1 percent to 74.6 percent most of which was contributed by an increase in the share of ASEAN[10] (from 6.7 percent to 15.2 percent). The share of SAARC[11] countries in Australia's exports doubled (from 1.5 percent to 3.1 percent) during 1977-97. Data in Table 5.2 also reveal that the relative importance of OECD (or industrially developed countries) as Australia's export destinations has been gradually declining over the years. Over 50 percent of Australia's exports are now (1997) directed to the developing countries.

However, as is evident from Table 5.3, industrialised countries have been the dominant source of Australia's imports although their relative importance has declined over the years. Australia's dependence on developing countries for its imports has gradually increased since 1977. Especially, the APEC countries have emerged as an important source of Australia's imports during the period under review. Its share rose from 58.7 percent in 1977 to 67.0 percent in 1997. SAARC countries share of Australia's imports however, has centred around only 1.1 percent for this period.

Table 5.3. Australia's Imports from Major Economic Areas 1977-1997 (Percentage Share)

Economic Areas	1977	1982	1987	1992	1997
APEC, of which	58.7	62.9	64.7	69.4	67.0
- ASEAN	4.8	7.5	5.9	8.5	11.0
- North-East Asia	26.2	27.9	30.7	30.2	27.3
- NAFTA	23.6	24.2	23.6	24.4	23.8
- Australasia	4.0	3.4	4.5	6.7	6.0
EEA, of which	28.8	23.7	27.2	23.1	24.5
- EU	28.5	23.5	26.8	22.9	24.3
SAARC	1.1	0.8	0.8	0.9	1.1
Industrialised and Developing					
OECD	76.2	73.3	78.4	73.9	71.0
Developing Countries	22.9	27.5	23.5	28.2	31.7

Source: Department of Foreign Affairs and Trade (1998a), *Direction of Trade Time Series 1977-1997*, Canberra: Commonwealth of Australia, p. 48.

The share of exports of Australia's top 20 trading partners (as judged by 1997 shares) is presented in Table 5.4. This ranking shows that Japan is the most important destination for Australian exports although its relative importance has been gradually declining over time. It also demonstrates that the US share in Australia's exports has rapidly declined between 1987 and 1997. Shares of Australia's European trading partners such as Germany, Italy, and United

[9] Asia Pacific Economic Co-operation: NAFTA, ASEAN6 (Brunei, Indonesia, Malaysia, the Philippines, Singapore and Thailand), China, Chile, Hong Kong, Japan, Korea and Taiwan)

[10] The Association of Southeast Asian Nations or ASEAN was established on 8 August 1967 in Bangkok by the five original Member Countries, namely, Indonesia, Malaysia, Philippines, Singapore, and Thailand. Brunei Darussalam joined on 8 January 1984, Vietnam on 28 July 1995, Laos and Myanmar on 23 July 1997, and Cambodia on 30 April 1999.

[11] South Asia Association for Regional Cooperation: Bangladesh, Bhutan, India, Maldives, Nepal, Pakistan and Sri Lanka.

Kingdom in Australia's exports have also declined over the years. Not surprisingly the dynamic regions of Asia (such as China, India, Indonesia, Hong Kong, Malaysia, the Republic of Korea, Taiwan, the Philippines, Singapore and Thailand) have increasingly emerged as important destinations for Australia's exports during 1977-97.

Table 5.4. Bilateral Share of Australia's Merchandise Exports by its Major Trading Partners: 1977-1997 (Percentage Share)

Country[a]	1977	1982	1987	1992	1997
1. Japan	33.6	26.7	25.5	25.3	19.8
2. Korea, Republic of	1.7	0.0	4.1	0.0	8.0
3. USA	9.1	10.3	11.4	8.8	7.5
4. New Zealand	5.0	5.2	5.6	5.3	7.3
5. Taiwan	1.3	2.4	3.3	4.4	4.8
6. China	3.5	3.6	4.0	3.2	4.7
7. Singapore	1.6	2.7	2.3	6.5	4.6
8. Hong Kong	1.4	1.9	3.8	4.0	4.5
9. Indonesia[b]	1.4	1.9	1.4	3.0	4.0
10. United Kingdom	4.2	4.3	4.3	3.9	2.9
11. Malaysia	1.7	2.0	1.6	2.0	2.8
12. India	0.8	1.7	1.2	1.4	2.0
13. Thailand	0.6	0.7	0.7	1.8	1.9
14. Italy	2.6	1.9	2.3	1.7	1.9
15. Philippines	1.2	1.0	0.7	0.9	1.6
16. Papua New Guinea	1.8	4.0	1.9	0.8	1.4
17. Canada	2.3	1.7	1.6	1.6	1.4
18. Germany[c]	3.5	2.7	2.9	1.9	1.3
19. South Africa	0.5	1.5	0.4	0.2	1.2
20. Belgium-Luxembourg	1.2	0.7	0.8	1.1	1.1

Source: Estimated from, Department of Foreign Affairs and Trade (1998a), *Direction of Trade Time Series 1977-1997*, Canberra: Commonwealth of Australia.

Notes:

[a] Ranked by DFAT in order exports in 1997.

[b] Includes Timor.

[c] Includes Federal Republic of Germany and Democratic Republic of Germany.

Data in Table 5.5 reveal that the United States of America and Japan have been the most important bilateral sources of Australia's imports although their relative importance declined between 1977 and 1997. India's relative importance as a source of Australia's imports improved slightly during the period under consideration but it still remained an insignificant source of Australia's imports. The EEA, EU, and NAFTA are economic areas with which Australia has a record of persistent bilateral trade deficits during most of the years between 1977 and 1997 (Table 5.6). By contrast, trade with ASEAN, North-East Asia and SAARC has yielded substantial surpluses. Overall, Asia-Pacific region has been contributing significantly to Australia's multilateral trade (Table 5.6).

Table 5.5. Bilateral Share of Australia's Imports by its Major Trading Partners: 1977-1997 (Percentage Share)

Country	1977	1982	1987	1992	1997
1. Japan	19.6	20.1	19.7	18.1	13.7
2. Korea, Republic of	1.0	1.4	2.6	2.7	3.6
3. United States of America	20.7	21.7	21.2	22.3	21.8
4. New Zealand	3.2	11.0	4.1	1.3	4.4
5.Taiwan	2.2	2.9	4.3	3.8	3.2
6. China	1.0	1.3	1.9	4.2	5.7
7. Singapore	2.4	2.8	2.1	2.9	3.0
8. Hong Kong	2.4	2.3	2.1	1.4	1.2
9. Indonesia[a]	0.6	3.1	1.3	2.2	2.7
10. United Kingdom	11.1	7.2	7.2	5.9	6.4
11. Malaysia	1.1	0.9	2.2	1.7	2.5
12. India	0.5	0.5	0.8	0.6	0.8
13. Thailand	0.3	0.3	0.8	1.3	1.6
14. Italy	2.7	2.3	3.2	2.4	2.8
15. Philippines	0.5	0.4	0.3	0.3	0.5
16. Papua New Guinea	0.8	0.3	0.4	2.0	1.1
17. Canada	2.7	2.3	2.0	1.6	1.5
18. Germany[b]	7.0	6.1	7.3	5.8	5.6
19. South Africa	0.6	0.3	0.3	0.3	0.6
20. Belgium-Luxembourg	0.9	0.6	0.8	0.8	0.9
World	100	100	100	100	100

Note: [a]Includes Timor.
[b]Includes Federal Republic of Germany and Democratic Republic of Germany.

Source: Estimated From: Department of Foreign Affairs and Trade (1998a), *Direction of Trade Time Series 1977-1997*, Canberra: Commonwealth of Australia, pp. 28-43 and 46-47.

Table 5.6. Australia's Merchandise Trade Balance with CountryGROUPS (A$ '000: 1977-1997)

Economic Areas	1977	1982	1987	1992	1997
APEC, of which	1,526,234	-784,138	959,981	5,150,730	7,306,037
- ASEAN	274,907	13,467	311,381	3,676,107	3,755,660
- North-East Asia	2,087,349	1,517,468	3,671,790	8,441,217	12,626,276
- NAFTA	1,210,340	-3,098,831	-4,106,527	-7,377,813	12,199,716
- Australasia	368,718	791,826	1,131,333	216,516	2,409,410
EEA, of which	1,146,812	-2,531,790	-4,225,496	-5,010,447	11,635,361
- EU	1,172,878	-2,499,603	-4,117,577	-4,987,523	11,618,209
- Other	26,066	-32,187	-107,919	-22,924	-17,152
Industrialised and Developing					
OECD	-360,086	-4,021,637	-5,009,132	-5,032,331	12,472,799
Developing Countries	925,458	1,178,679	3,943,569	9,993,944	16,202,580

Source: Department of Foreign Affairs and Trade (1998a), *Direction of Trade Time Series 1977-1997*, Canberra: Commonwealth of Australia, pp. 67- 68.

Australia's trade balance with its major trading partners demonstrates that Australia has enjoyed a prolonged bilateral trade surplus with Japan, Korea, Indonesia, Malaysia and India (Table 5.7).

Table 5.7. Australia's Merchandise Trade Balance with some of Its Major Trading Partners: 1977-1997 (A$'000)

Country	1977	1982	1987	1992	1997
Japan	1,841,040	945,740	2,076,117	4,711,427	5,398,198
Korea, Republic of	97,799	396,460	547,411	2,140,531	5,398,198
New Zealand	242,804	387,547	562,259	551,629	2,472,061
Taiwan	-80,649	-178,338	-389,473	470,752	1,403,752
Singapore	-66,608	-77,198	90,462	2,439,838	1,393,908
Hong Kong	-103,916	-123,311	599,707	1,552,457	2,797,309
Indonesia[a]	101,653	-341,527	8,951	479,497	1,106,855
Malaysia	80,552	225,275	129,408	172,211	258,704
India	9,540	237,610	236,918	518,995	1,054,987
Thailand	35,542	75,520	-51,651	361,575	319,964
Philippines	82,740	118,668	162,571	382,402	948,908
Papua New Guinea	125,914	404,729	568,073	-281,619	245,318
South Africa	-1,089	61,927	19,003	158,046	547,700
Belgium-Luxembourg	45,319	-1,661	-21,232	198,037	191,432
World	894,113	-2,252,789	-559,290	2,869,691	1,330,894

Note: [a]Includes Timor

Source: Department of Foreign Affairs and Trade (1998a), *Direction of Trade Time Series 1977-1997*, Canberra: Commonwealth of Australia, pp. 62-63.

Trade Intensities

The trade intensity index provides a useful analytical tool for measuring the relative importance of the bilateral trading relationship of a country with its trading partners. It measures the share of one country's trade with a selected trade partner as a proportion of the latter country's share of trade with the rest of the world. It is a simple measure, calculated in the following way with Australia as the reference country[12]:

Intensity Index of Australia's Exports (IIA_x) = $(A_{xj}/A_x)/M_j/(W_m - A_m)$

where

A_{xj} = Australia's exports to country j

A_x = Australia's total exports to the world

M_j = Country j's total imports from the world

W_m = Total world imports

A_m = Australia's total imports from the world

[12] For details on trade intensity indices see, Brown (1949), Kojima (1964), Drysdale and Gaurnaut (1982).

Likewise, the

Intensity Index of Australia's Imports (IIA_m) = $(Am_j/Am)/\ X_j/(W_x - A_x)$

where

A_{mj} = Australia's imports from country j
A_m = Australia's total imports from the world
X_j = Country j's total exports to the world
W_x = Total world exports
A_x = Australia's total exports to the world

An intensity index greater than unity implies that the trade (export/import) links between the countries in question are stronger than those with the rest of the world. Tables 5.8 and 5.9 present the estimated export and import intensity indices respectively for Australia's trade with up to twenty trade partners ranked in descending order of the magnitude of these indices in 1997, the latest year in the table.

Table 5.8 records that, over the twelve years from 1985, Australia's export intensity with New Zealand remained high and on an increasing trend. Apart from Papua New Guinea, which enjoys a special economic relationship with Australia, New Zealand has ranked consistently as Australia's most intensive exporting partner. The index, already high at nearly 15 in 1985, has risen to 27 in 1997, indicating that New Zealand's share of Australia's total exports is 27 times New Zealand's share of the rest of the world's total imports. For a small country, this is quite remarkable, and it demonstrates the contribution free trade, under the Closer Economic Relations (CER) agreement, makes to the two countries' trade relations. The Table also shows that most of Australia's significant export partners are in Asia, with the singular exception of South Africa, which has emerged in the 1990s as a partner of increasing significance. The intensity index has either remained stable or increased with most countries. The exception to this is Hong Kong with which export intensity seems to have been on a clearly declining trend; with Japan the trend has also been a declining one in the 1990s, even if the observed decline is rather mild.

Export trade intensity with the rest of the major partners is low as indicated by the index values of the six countries listed at the bottom of the Table 5.8. These are all large industrialized countries, but they obviously take, as imports, a smaller share of Australia's total exports relative to their share of the rest of the world's total imports. Over the period under consideration, the magnitude of the index has fluctuated around a declining trend in the case of countries such as Germany, France and the USA, and around an increasing trend against other countries such as Italy, the UK and Canada. The decline has been noticeable particularly in the 1990s, a decade in which the Asian countries had been emerging as Australia's stronger export partners.

Table 5.8. Intensity Index of Australia's Exports by Destination: 1985-97 (1997 Basis)

	1985	1986	1987	1988	1989	1990	1991	1992	1993	1994	1995	1996	1997
1. Papua New Guinea	34.49	36.5	36.64	36.88	33.7	38.78	39.6	37.99	37.55	40.7	45	44.58	41.33
2. New Zealand	14.74	15.54	18.75	18.45	17.12	18.16	20.48	22.13	22.55	23.7	26.68	25.87	27.48
3. Indonesia	2.58	3.14	2.57	2.97	3.6	4.21	3.58	4.15	3.72	4.31	4.15	5.01	5.35
4. Japan	3.98	4.29	4.06	3.96	3.72	3.87	4.17	4.18	3.81	3.81	3.48	3.03	3.24
5. Korea, Republic of	2.29	2.64	2.37	2.49	2.51	2.82	2.83	2.95	3.17	3.01	3.18	3.35	3.03
6. India	1.31	1.65	1.62	1.98	1.72	1.82	2.3	2.29	2.57	2.23	2.26	2.32	2.84
7. Taiwan	2.87	2.78	2.31	1.92	2.05	2.22	2.45	2.35	2.13	2.13	2.24	2.31	2.3
8. South Africa	0.82	0.68	0.62	0.46	0.49	0.43	0.62	0.67	1.03	1.16	1.57	2.18	2.12
9. Singapore	1.95	1.56	1.77	1.98	2.18	2.64	2.94	3.4	2.32	2.2	2.19	1.64	1.92
10. Malaysia	2.6	3.07	3.01	2.71	2.36	2.21	1.95	1.76	2.04	2.13	2.02	1.92	1.91
11. China	1.68	2.23	2.23	1.31	1.26	1.58	1.57	1.52	1.31	1.59	1.67	1.92	1.81
12. Philippines	2.11	2.06	2.59	2.43	2.5	2.41	2.48	2.52	2.15	2.07	2.51	2.2	1.79
13. Thailand	1.09	1.27	1.26	1.23	1.34	1.18	1.21	1.74	1.61	1.64	1.65	1.56	1.72
14. Hong Kong	1.59	1.31	1.81	2.16	1.48	1.08	1.28	1.25	1.16	1.06	1.04	1.03	1.17
15. UK	0.59	0.59	0.67	0.51	0.53	0.56	0.55	0.68	0.82	0.68	0.67	0.66	0.52
16. Italy	0.43	0.44	0.44	0.54	0.42	0.36	0.34	0.35	0.37	0.45	0.45	0.41	0.51
17. USA	0.53	0.56	0.64	0.64	0.64	0.74	0.7	0.62	0.5	0.43	0.42	0.41	0.46
18. Canada	0.26	0.39	0.42	0.45	0.32	0.44	0.43	0.46	0.49	0.43	0.47	0.48	0.35
19. France	0.36	0.38	0.39	0.35	0.31	0.23	0.25	0.27	0.23	0.22	0.19	0.17	0.22
20. Germany	0.3	0.32	0.3	0.28	0.27	0.22	0.17	0.18	0.17	0.18	0.18	0.16	0.17

Source: Estimated from: International Monetary Fund, *Direction of Trade Statistics Yearbook*, 1992 and 1998.

Table 5.9 records Australia's import intensity indices with the top 18 import sources. Once again, New Zealand ranks as the country with which Australia has the most intensive import trade links; and the index value has been on an increasing trend over the period. Most of the other top trade partners with a high import intensity index are, again, Asian countries. The exceptions are the USA and the UK, both of which economies have an index value greater than one, indicating that their share in Australia's global imports is larger than their share in the exports of the rest of the world. The other import partners listed in the Table are all non-Asian economies, with the sole exception of Hong Kong which has experienced a declining import intensity vis-à-vis Australia over the period.

Table 5.9. Intensity Indices of Australia's Imports by Source: 1985-97 (1997 Basis)

	1985	1987	1989	1991	1993	1994	1995	1996	1997
1. New Zealand	11.56	12.22	12	14.95	15.58	15.84	15.46	15.44	15.79
2. Indonesia	0.67	1.69	1.14	1.95	1.76	1.52	1.8	2.07	2.57
3. Japan	2.12	1.83	1.94	1.75	1.76	1.71	1.59	1.5	1.61
4. USA	1.7	1.82	1.63	1.82	1.55	1.64	1.71	1.78	1.6
5. Malaysia	1.06	1.45	1.51	1.42	1.18	1.17	1.25	1.32	1.59
6. China	0.74	0.97	1.17	1.54	1.71	1.56	1.53	1.65	1.54
7. Thailand	1.22	1.52	1.21	1.28	1.1	1.08	1.05	1.17	1.38
8. Taiwan	1.78	1.78	1.61	1.54	1.44	1.47	1.36	1.33	1.3
9. Korea, Republic of	0.81	1.17	1.13	1.11	1.22	1.03	1.06	1.1	1.26
10. Singapore	1.75	1.55	1.44	1.41	1.16	1.2	1.13	1.29	1.19
11. UK	1.13	1.18	1.15	1.05	1.06	1.11	1.15	1.18	1.14
12. Philippines	1.29	1.18	1.16	0.98	0.88	0.97	0.79	0.83	0.78
13. Italy	0.65	0.59	0.56	0.48	0.46	0.54	0.55	0.56	0.59
14. Germany	0.6	0.53	0.48	0.48	0.53	0.54	0.6	0.56	0.54
15. France	0.33	0.31	0.36	0.38	0.38	0.39	0.39	0.41	0.39
16. Canada	0.36	0.45	0.52	0.43	0.39	0.38	0.46	0.44	0.35
17. Hong Kong	1.09	0.96	0.62	0.48	0.3	0.31	0.34	0.3	0.32
18. Belgium-Luxembourg	0.23	0.22	0.22	0.19	0.23	0.21	0.26	0.26	0.26

Source: Estimated from: International Monetary Fund, *Direction of Trade Statistics Yearbook*, 1992, and 1998.

It is an interesting coincidence that, over the period under study, Australia's trade intensities (both export and import) with Hong Kong have steadily declined, but its trade intensities with China have steadily increased. As China gradually opened up to the rest of the world in the 1980s, its trade with most countries has increased significantly. It is entirely possible therefore that, in respect to many of the items that Australia traded with Hong Kong, China has gradually become the preferred trade partner. In 1998, Hong Kong was returned to the Peoples' Republic of China (PRC); but its economic links with PRC had been growing stronger over the period since the early 1980s. The changes to the structure of the two countries' trade with Australia are perhaps reflective of that.

New Zealand's top rank in both tables is again a testimony to the success of the CER agreement in promoting mutual trade in both directions between two small economies located in a remote part of the world.

Growth

Average annual growth rates of Australian exports by various economic areas fluctuated over the years as shown in Table 5.10. It is interesting to note that in spite of gradual decline in the rate of growth of Australia's total exports to the world during the periods of 1982-87, and 1987-97, the corresponding rate to SAARC countries has gradually increased during these periods. During the entire period of 1977-97, rate of growth of Australia's exports to ASEAN countries has been the highest (15.2 percent) and well above the average of total exports of Australia (10.1 percent). The average annual rate of growth of Australian exports to South Asia has been the second highest (12.8 percent) during the same period, again, this growth rate has been higher than the average of total exports. The rate of growth of exports to the EEA (8.2%) and the OECD (9.5%) has been lower than the average of total exports during the period under consideration. It is not therefore surprising to note that developing countries have emerged as important destinations for Australia's exports as opposed to the OECD[13] or industrialised countries. Overall, the average rate of growth of Australia's exports to developing countries (12.8 percent) has been higher than that of its total exports to the world (10.1 percent) during 1977-97.

Table 5.10. Average Annual Rates of Growth of Australia's Merchandise *Exports to Country Groups: 1977-1997*

Economic Areas	1977-97	1982-97	1987-97	1992-97
APEC, of which	11.2	10.7	9.0	7.6
- ASEAN	15.2	16.3	16.6	9.5
- North-East Asia	11.0	10.4	8.3	6.9
- NAFTA	8.0	6.5	2.5	3.0
- Australasia	11.2	10.8	10.8	13.7
EEA, of which	8.2	6.8	3.4	3.0
- EU	8.3	6.8	3.2	3.0
- Other	7.1	19.5	21.6	6.5
Industrialised and Developing				
OECD	9.5	8.6	5.8	5.4
Developing Countries	12.8	12.5	12.4	11.7
World	10.1	10.0	8.8	7.9

Source: Department of Foreign Affairs and Trade (1998a), Direction of Trade Time Series 1977-1997, Canberra: Commonwealth of Australia, p. 26.

Most recent (1992-1997) average annual growth rates of Australian exports by various geographic regions reveal that North Asia and South-East Asia have lost their relative importance as Australia's export destinations and Sub-Saharan Africa (26.6 percent), South Asia (15.8 percent), the Middle-East and North Africa (14.4 percent) and Oceania (13.0 percent) have emerged as Australia's dominant trading partners (Table 8.10). Growth rates of Australia's exports to these regions have been much higher than the average growth rate of Australia's total exports (7.9 percent) for this period. The average rate of growth of

[13] Organisation for Economic Co-operation and Development: EU, Australia, Canada, Czech Republic, Hungary, Iceland, Japan, Republic of Korea, Mexico, India, Norway, Poland, Switzerland, Turkey, and the USA.

Australia's exports to developing countries (11.7 percent) has been much higher than that of its total exports to the world (7.9 percent) during 1992-1997. It can therefore be concluded that Australia is gradually becoming increasingly dependent on developing countries for its exports.

Significant inter-country variations are also noticed in the growth rates of Australia's exports to its important trading partners (Table 5.11). Particularly, the average annual growth rate of Australian merchandise exports to most of its Southeast and North Asian countries such as Thailand (18.5 percent), the Republic of Korea (18.3 percent), Singapore (17 percent), Hong Kong (16.7 percent) and Indonesia (15.7 percent) has been well above the average rate of growth of total exports. The average rate of growth of Australia's export to India has been 15 percent. By contrast, exports to Japan (Australia's largest export destination), the USA, the UK, Italy, Canada and Germany have grown at a lesser rate than the average rate of growth of total exports.

Table 5.11. Rates of Growth of Australia's Merchandise Exports to Its top 20 Trading Partners: 1977-1997

Country	1977-97	1982-97	1987-97	1992-97
1. Japan	8.5	7.6	4.9	2.0
2. Korea, Republic of	18.3	16.9	16.0	14.9
3. United States of America	7.7	5.6	1.4	2.9
4. New Zealand	12.2	12.1	12.4	15.0
5. Taiwan	16.6	14.2	11.8	9.2
6. China	11.3	12.2	14.4	16.8
7. Singapore	17.0	16.0	13.7	0.5
8. Hong Kong	16.7	15.0	9.2	8.2
9. Indonesia[b]	15.7	17.3	19.3	15.8
10. United Kingdom	9.0	7.9	6.3	0.8
11. Malaysia	12.0	13.2	15.7	14.7
12. India	15.0	14.0	12.5	14.0
13. Thailand	18.5	20.6	20.7	9.7
14. Italy	8.5	8.0	4.2	10.5
15. Philippines	12.2	15.2	15.8	20.2
16. Papua New Guinea	7.9	6.4	5.0	8.0
17. Canada	9.2	11.0	7.5	3.6
18. Germany[c]	5.7	3.6	-0.6	1.5
19. South Africa	11.9	13.3	25.2	31.0
20. Belgium-Luxembourg	10.1	11.6	8.9	9.4
World	10.1	10.0	8.8	7.9

Source: Estimated from, Department of Foreign Affairs and Trade (1998a), *Direction of Trade Time Series 1977-1997*, Canberra: Commonwealth of Australia, p. 24.

Notes: Ranked by DFAT in order exports in 1997.

[b]Includes Timor.

[c]Includes Federal Republic of Germany and Democratic Republic of Germany.

Growth of Australia's merchandise exports to its top 20 partners for the period of 1992-97 demonstrates that South Africa has been emerging as an important trading partner for Australia - the annual average rate of growth of exports to this country has been 31 percent (the highest) during this period (Table 5.11). The other countries with impressive rates of growth of Australian exports during 1992-97 have been: the Philippines (20.2 percent), China (16.8 percent), India (15.0 percent), and the Republic of Korea (14.9 percent). Exports to Japan have grown by almost one quarter of the average rate of growth of Australia's total exports during the same period. Exports to the UK, Canada and Germany have grown at a lower rate than that of the total exports. There has been very little growth of exports to Singapore (0.5 percent) during 1992-97.

India As A Destination for Australia's Exports

Total Trade

Direction of Australia's merchandise trade between 1977 and 1997 (in 1990 constant prices) are shown in Table 5.12. It is observed that during 1977, Australia-India's trade was in the order of A$357.4 million. Since then the bilateral trade has increased steadily. Australia-India's trade for 1997 was worth A$1608.7 million. The value of Australia's total merchandise exports to India has increased by about 7 times during the period under consideration (from A$170.9 million in 1977 to A$1,207.9 million in 1997). In contrast, Australia's merchandise imports from India increased by only two-fold (from 186.5 million in 1977 to 400.6 million in 1997). Data in Table 5.13 demonstrates that with few exceptions since 1977, the balance of trade has always been in Australia's favour which implies that India is likely to be of special economic significance for Australia in the future, especially by serving as a market for Australia's exports, with the ability to supply its products at a comparative cost advantage.

Again, it has been shown in Table 5.1, while Australia's earnings from exports of unprocessed primary products declined from 47.6 percent in 1978 to 29.9 percent in 1997, an opposite trend is noticed with respect to Australia's exports of primary products to India. The contribution of these products of Australia's total export earnings from India increased from 44.0 percent in 1978 to 63.4 percent in 1997 (Table 5.14). The trend in Australia's exports of processed products to India is in line with changes in composition in the structure of Australia's exports over the years.

It has already been shown in Table 5.1 that the contribution of processed products of Australia's total export earnings declined from 21.7 percent in 1978 to 13.8 percent in 1997. The contribution of this class of products to total export earnings of Australia from India also decreased from 13.6 percent in 1978 to almost zero (0.8 percent) in 1997 (Table 5.12).

Table 5.12. Direction of Australia's Merchandise Trade with India: 1977-1997 (at 1990 Prices in A$ '000)

	Australia's Total merchandise Exports to the world	Australia's Total merchandise Imports from the world	Australia's Total merchandise trade with the world	Australia's Total merchandise exports to India	Australia's Total merchandise imports from India	Total trade between Australia and India
1	2	3	4(=2+3)	5	6	7(=5+6)
1977	21,446,136	24,061,489	45,507,625	170,940	186,489	357,429
1978	21,790,732	24,626,079	46,416,811	123,331	191,984	315,315
1979	23,601,678	23,929,710	47,531,387	213,622	185,248	398,870
1980	24,909,352	23,960,929	48,870,281	232,543	155,529	388,072
1981	22,735,341	25,788,649	48,523,990	205,691	144,534	350,225
1982	24,120,946	27,052,728	51,173,674	418,490	147,876	566,365
1983	25,733,079	23,558,288	49,291,367	167,514	142,453	309,967
1984	27,314,839	26,347,675	53,662,514	152,073	151,236	303,309
1985	30,907,948	29,372,442	60,280,390	370,566	151,020	521,586
1986	32,363,119	29,547,125	61,910,244	395,686	159,921	555,607
1987	36,406,705	31,186,477	67,593,182	418,800	161,640	580,441
1988	38,561,077	37,331,760	75,892,837	525,029	212,266	737,295
1989	37,111,904	42,099,026	79,210,930	413,469	220,685	634,154
1990	39,355,057	38,515,236	77,870,293	496,161	215,817	711,978
1991	44,754,683	37,442,302	82,196,985	552,253	195,070	747,323
1992	45,837,068	38,492,485	84,329,553	659,736	222,768	882,504
1993	51,616,290	42,507,655	94,123,945	758,232	277,171	1,035,403
1994	58,509,133	50,718,374	109,227,507	789,533	354,563	1,144,096
1995	57,045,508	52,658,953	109,704,461	876,424	376,058	1,252,483
1996	64,750,645	57,035,255	121,785,900	1,029,907	410,308	1,440,215
1997	60,533,411	52,515,781	113,049,192	1,207,991	400,689	1,608,680

Source: Estimated from Department of Foreign Affairs and Trade (1998a), *Direction of Trade Time Series 1977-1997*, Canberra: Commonwealth of Australia, June, pp.16-17, 42-43, 56-57, 8-9, 34-35, 54-55.

Exports of Manufactured Products

Although exports of Australia's manufactured products to India increased from A$29.5 million in 1977 to A$191 million in 1997,[14] India has not emerged as one of major destinations for exports of Australia's manufactured products. The share of manufactured products in Australia's total exports to India declined from 42.0 percent in 1977 to 11.3 percent in 1997 with wide fluctuations in the share of ETMs (Table 5.14). The share of STM also gradually declined throughout the entire period.

[14] DFAT (1996), *Exports of Major Commodities Time Series 1978 to 1995*, p.54 and DFAT (1998), *Exports of Major Commodities Time Series 1980 to 1997*, p.47.

Table 5.13. Value of Australia's Merchandise Trade Balance with India: 1977-1997

Year	Australia's Total merchandise exports to India	Australia's Total merchandise imports from India	Trade balance (1-2)
1977	170,940	186,489	-15,549
1978	123,331	191,984	-68,653
1979	213,622	185,248	28,374
1980	232,543	155,529	77,014
1981	205,691	144,534	61,157
1982	418,490	147,876	270,614
1983	167,514	142,453	25,061
1984	152,073	151,236	837
1985	370,566	151,020	219,546
1986	395,686	159,921	235,765
1987	418,800	161,640	257,160
1988	525,029	212,266	312,763
1989	413,469	220,685	192,784
1990	496,161	215,817	280,344
1991	552,253	195,070	357,183
1992	659,736	222,768	436,968
1993	758,232	277,171	481,061
1994	789,533	354,563	434,970
1995	876,424	376,058	500,366
1996	1,029,907	410,308	619,599
1997	1,207,991	400,689	807,302

Source: Estimated from Table 5.12

Table 5.14. Change in Composition of Australia's Merchandise Exports to India Based on Trade Exports Classification (TREC) 1978-1997

TREC description	Distribution of exports (percent)								
	1978	1980	1982	1985	1987	1990	1992	1995	1997
Primary Products	57.6	53.1	78.9	78.5	71.6	33.1	71.0	71.4	64.2
11 Unprocessed	44.0	33.9	72.0	68.3	69.7	26.7	69.6	70.5	63.4
12 Processed	13.6	19.1	6.9	10.3	1.9	6.5	1.4	0.8	0.8
Manufactured Products	42.0	45.7	18.9	19.9	24.7	16.0	17.6	26.2	11.3
23 Simply Transformed Manufactures (STMs)	29.2	27.3	14.9	15.6	11.2	9.5	4.3	6.3	4.0
24 Elaborately Transformed Manufactures (ETMs)	12.8	18.3	4.0	4.3	13.5	6.5	13.3	19.9	7.3
Miscellaneous Products (NES)	0.4	1.3	2.2	1.6	3.7	50.9	11.4	2.4	24.5
Total Exports	100	100	100	100	100	100	100	100	100

Source: Estimated from: DFAT (1996), *Exports of Major Commodities Time Series 1978 to 1995*, Canberra: Commonwealth of Australia, (pp.22-23 and 54-55), and DFAT (1998), *Exports of Major Commodities Time Series 1980 to 1997,* Canberra: Commonwealth of Australia, (pp.22-23 and 46-47).

Recent (1992 to 1997) average annual growth rates of Australia's merchandise exports to India are provided in Table 5.15. The growth rate of exports of manufactured products to India has been lower than the world average. However, Australia's exports of ETMs to India grew at a much higher rate than the world average.

The average annual growth rate of Australia's exports of primary products to the world has been 4.9 percent in contrast to 13.7 percent to India. Similarly, the growth rate of exports of unprocessed primary products to the world has been 3.7 percent in comparison to 13.7 percent to India. Processed primary products also recorded similar relative growth rates.

Table 5.15. Average Annual Growth Rates of Australian Merchandise Exports Based on TREC: 1992-1997

TREC Description	Percentage Distribution of exports to:	
	World	India
Primary Products (a)	*4.1*	*13.7*
11 Unprocessed	3.7	13.7
12 Processed	4.8	14.9
Manufactured Products (a)	*10.8*	*8.9*
23 Simply Transformed Manufactures (STMs)	6.3	15.2
24 Elaborately Transformed Manufactures (ETMs)	12.7	6.6
30 Miscellaneous Products, nes (b)	*11.2*	*7.4*
Total Exports	*7.7*	*14.0*

Source: Department of Foreign Affairs and Trade (1998), Exports of Major Commodities Time Series 1980-1997, Canberra: Commonwealth of Australia, pp. 23 and 47.

Note: (a) Excludes commodities subject to a confidentiality restriction.
(b) Includes commodities subject to a confidentiality restriction.

Growth

It has already been shown in Table 5.11 that Australia's exports to India have grown at an average annual growth rate of 15.0 percent per annum during 1977-97. It has grown at 14 percent between 1992 and 1997. India has been the 12th most important export destination for Australia during 1997[15]. Australia's exports to India have grown at a much higher rate (15 percent) than the rate of growth of total exports (10.1 percent) throughout the entire period.

Australia's imports from India grew at 10.5 percent during 1977. The growth rate of Australia's imports from India accelerated during 1992-97 (13.9 percent). India was the 25th largest importing nation of Australia during 1997[16]. Average annual growth rate of imports

[15] During 1997 Australia's top 20 export destination were 1. Japan, 2. Korea, Republic of, 3. the United States of America, 4. India, 5.Taiwan, 6. China, 7. Singapore, 8. Hong Kong, 9. Indonesia, 10. United Kingdom, 11. Malaysia, 12. India, 13. Thailand, 14. Italy, 15. Philippines, 16. Papua New Guinea, 17. Canada, 18. Germany, 19. South Africa and 20. Belgium-Luxembourg. Department of Foreign Affairs and Trade (1998a), *Direction of Trade Time Series 1977-1997*, Canberra: Commonwealth of Australia, p. 24.

[16] *Ibid*, p. 46.

from India have exceeded the average rate of growth of total imports of Australia during 1977-97[17].

Trade Intensities and Share of Trade with India

It has already been demonstrated that Australia's export intensity and import trade indices with respect to India have increased steadily since 1985 (Tables 5.8 and 5.9). The bilateral share of India of Australia's exports has increased from 0.8 percent to 2.0 percent during 1977-97 (Table 5.16). Similarly, Australia's share of imports from India has increased from 0.79 percent in 1977 to 1.4 percent in 1997.

The bilateral share of Australia's imports from India has remained below 1.0 percent although it steadily declined between 1977 and 1992 with some minor fluctuations. However, this began to increase from 1993 (Table 5.16). As mentioned earlier, the balance of trade has always been heavily in favour of Australia.

Table 5.16. Australia's Share of Trade with India (Percentage Share)

Year	Exports	Imports	Total
1977	0.80	0.78	0.79
1978	0.57	0.78	0.67
1979	0.91	0.77	0.84
1980	0.93	0.65	0.80
1981	0.90	0.56	0.72
1982	1.73	0.55	1.11
1983	0.65	0.60	0.63
1984	0.56	0.57	0.57
1985	1.20	0.51	0.85
1986	1.22	0.54	0.87
1987	1.15	0.52	0.83
1988	1.36	0.57	0.96
1989	1.11	0.52	0.81
1990	1.26	0.56	0.91
1991	1.23	0.52	0.89
1992	1.44	0.58	1.02
1993	1.47	0.65	1.06
1994	1.35	0.70	1.02
1995	1.54	0.71	1.11
1996	1.59	0.72	1.15
1997	2.00	0.76	1.38

Source: Estimated from Department of Foreign Affairs and Trade (1998a), *Direction of Trade Time Series 1977-1997*, Canberra: Commonwealth of Australia.

[17] *Ibid*, p. 50.

INTRA-INDUSTRY TRADE BETWEEN AUSTRALIA AND INDIA

Intra-industry trade (IIT) refers to trade involving similar, even identical, products between two countries. As is well known, much of traditional trade theory, a la Ricardo and Heckscher-Ohlin, explains inter-industry trade, i.e. trade involving different products. Explanations for such trade usually run in terms of pre-trade relative price differences between countries. Global trade patterns however have evolved in such a way that trade between developed countries in particular is more preference-based than cost-based, i.e. demand side factors would explain such trade better. Growth in inter-industry trade is also linked to the rapid increase in recent decades of international integration of production structures. Such integration of production structures, in turn, has been assisted by the proliferation of regional trading agreements (RTAs), such as the CER agreement between Australia and New Zealand, in recent times. Horizontally and vertically integrated multinational companies engage in intra-firm import and export trade which can show up as intra-industry trade between countries, depending on the level of aggregation of products used in the measurement of IIT.

Measures of intra-industry (IIT) trade attempt to capture the extent of such trade. The purpose here is to simply touch on the nature of such trade between the two countries. We measure IIT at only the one-digit level. There are other studies on both Australia and New Zealand that go into this issue in greater detail. The interested reader is referred to Menon and Dixon (1994), Menon (1994), Bano and Lane (1987). A simple measure of IIT was developed by Grubel and Lloyd (1975) as follows:

$$\text{Intra-Industry Trade Index} = [1-(abs(X_{ij}-M_{ij}))/(X_{ij}+M_{ij})]*100$$

where

X_{ij} = Country i's exports of product j to its trading partner;

M_{ij} = Country j's imports of product j from the same trading partner.

"abs" indicates that it is only the magnitudes (absolute values) of the parameters within the brackets, and not their signs, that are of relevance to the calculations.

It varies between 0 and 100. When it is zero, it indicates complete absence of intra-industry trade; and when 100, the values of exports and imports of a given product between the trading partners are exactly the same, i.e. there is "perfect" intra-industry trade.

It has been noted above that Australia has experienced a remarkable shift in its export trade - the dominance of primary sector has been declining while the manufacturing sector has been increasing. Consequently, intra-industry trade (the value of exports of a group of industrial products in exchange for imports of similar products from the trading partner of a particular country) flows between Australia and India, for a number of industrial products have increased over the years.

Australia's intra-industry trade indices of a number of commodity groups such as SITC0, SITC5, SITC6, SITC67, SITC7, SITC74 and SITC8) have considerably increased between 1980 and 2000 with some minor fluctuations (Table 8.17). Particularly, the intra-industry indexes of commodity groups 7 and 74 are quite high and have been close to 100 in 2000, indicating that the value of exports of these groups of products from Australia to India are almost equal to the value of imports of similar products from India.

Table 5.17. Australia India Intra-Industry Trade Index: 1980-2000

SITC	1980	1985	1990	1995	2000
0	6.43	41.75	69.98	51.11	71.49
1	78.60	19.31	32.89	-	-
2	14.49	18.76	39.93	22.02	10.79
5	59.89	70.32	82.91	94.94	61.84
67	13.93	0.38	78.62	84.17	73.97
6	88.54	50.89	53.95	60.44	58.58
74	92.86	69.33	65.68	74.76	89.34
7	96.13	86.42	90.18	73.97	94.73
8	7.05	30.11	27.83	0.07	45.63
988	-	-	-	19.99	24.80
9	81.47	83.05	1.56	-	-

Source: For data between 1980 and 1990, IIT index estimated from ABS, Foreign Trade Australia: Comparative and Summary Tables, Catalog. No. 5410.0, various issues. For data between 1995 and 2000, IIT index estimated from DFAT, Composition of Trade Australia, various issues.

It can also be deduced from the intra-industry index with respect to the commodity groups of SITC0, SITC5, SITC67, SITC7 and SITC74 that Australian markets have been gradually opened up to the goods produced in India (Table 5.17). It is difficult to isolate the impact of New Horizon on gradual opening of Australian markets to the goods of India. However, it is impossible to deny that policies, which were introduced both in Australia and India as a consequence of New Horizon, partly contributed to Australia's higher intra-industry index with India.

Aspects of International Competitiveness of Australia and India

The Revealed Comparative Advantage

To measure the international competitiveness of a country, usually the Revealed Comparative Advantage Index (RCAI) for that country is estimated. The RCAI for a country can be measured with the help of the net export ratio, the export performance ratio and the export specialisation ratio[18]. The most common measure of RCAI is the export specialisation ratio. It involves three steps: (i) measuring the share of a particular commodity group in a country's total exports; (ii) measuring the share of that commodity group in the world exports; (iii) divide (i) by (ii).

[18] For details, see, Mohammed Ariff (1991:78-86)

Symbolically,

$$RCAI = \{X_{ij}/X_i\}/(W_j/W)$$

where

X_{ij} = Country i's export of product j;
X_i = Country i's total merchandise exports;
W_j = World exports of product j; and
W = World total merchandise exports.

If the RCAI of a particular commodity group is greater than unity, the export share of the commodity group in a country exceeds the world average export share of that commodity group, implying that the country tends to have relatively high comparative advantage in that commodity group. On the contrary, an RCAI of less than unity indicates that the county has a lower comparative advantage in that commodity group than the world average level.

The RCAI has been calculated for Australia and India for a number of commodity groups and are reported in Tables 5.18 and 5.19. Australia has comparative advantages in a number of food and mineral products, as well as in some manufactured products (Table 5.18). It has strong comparative advantages in producing food and live animals, beverages and tobacco, crude materials, mineral fuels and non-ferrous metals. Its comparative advantage over mineral fuels has increased over the years; an opposite average annual trend is also noticed with respect to animal oil, vegetable oil, and fat. It should be noted here that Australia's higher comparative advantage still lies in primary and resource based commodities. India has a strong comparative advantage in basic and miscellaneous manufactured goods, although, its comparative advantage has fluctuated over the years (Table 5.17). Its comparative advantage in food and live animals, beverages, tobacco and crude materials has decreased since 1980. However, its comparative advantage over basic and miscellaneous goods increased during 1980-1994 and then decreased slightly.

Table 5.18. Australia: Revealed Comparative Advantage Index (RCAI): 1980 – 1997

	1980	**1985**	**1990**	**1995**	**1996**	**1997**
Food & Live Animals, Beverages & Tobacco	3.36	2.58	2.10	2.34	2.61	2.74
Crude materials, excluding fuels	4.50	5.22	3.69	3.99	4.12	4.35
Mineral Fuels etc	0.46	1.41	1.62	2.23	2.00	2.27
Animal and vegetable oil, fat	0.96	0.65	0.30	0.69	0.67	0.66
Chemicals, related products (nes)	0.31	0.21	0.25	0.42	0.41	0.39
Iron & steel	0.81	0.51	0.57	0.82	0.79	0.74
Non-ferrous Metals	2.30	3.33	3.51	3.43	3.11	2.78
Machines and transport equipment	0.21	0.11	0.16	0.33	0.33	0.34
Basic & Misc. manufacturing Goods	0.55	0.48	0.47	0.62	0.59	0.56

Source: Estimated from UN, (1999), pp.30-35 and various other issues.

Table 5.19. India: Revealed Comparative Advantage Index (RCAI): 1980 – 1996*

	1980	1985	1990	1994	1995	1996
Food & Live Animal, Beverages and Tobacco	2.72	2.67	1.73	1.73	2.13	2.11
Crude materials, excluding fuels	1.99	1.90	2.08	0.98	1.02	1.36
Mineral fuels etc.	0.02	0.32	0.27	0.24	0.22	0.18
Animal & vegetable oil, fat	0.80	0.68	0.67	1.20	1.56	1.24
Chemicals, related products (nes)	0.59	0.46	0.84	0.88	0.86	0.96
Iron & steel	0.30	0.14	0.50	1.01	1.04	1.13
Non-ferrous Metals	0.10	0.21	0.26	0.36	0.24	0.35
Machines & Transport equipment	0.32	0.21	0.21	0.19	0.20	0.21
Basic & Misc. Manufacturing Goods	1.93	1.99	1.96	2.12	2.02	1.97

Source: Estimated from UN, (1999) and UN (1996), various issues.

*Figure for 1997 onwards were not available at the time of calculation (Oct 2001)

Thus, there are a number of commodities in which Australia has comparative advantage over India and vice versa. Therefore, there is significant scope for increasing trade of these commodities between the two countries. Australia and India can possibly develop a common marketing strategy (without violating the WTO[19] regulations) in areas where these two countries have relatively high comparative advantages

The Constant Market Share (CMS) Analysis

India and Australia's bilateral trade performance, relative to their competitors can be evaluated using the constant market share analysis (CMS). The methodology used for this analysis is based on the methodology used by Tyers and Phillips (1984).

Export growth is decomposed into 3 components; the standard growth effect, the commodity composition effect and the competitiveness residual.[20]

The **Standard Growth** term indicates the general growth of imports in the destination country and reflects the export growth performance of the focus country's competitors. The standard growth term is the "standard" to which the exporter can compare its export performance with. A high standard growth term relative to their export growth indicates that the focus country is not as competitive as its competitors.

In our analysis, the focus country's competitors will be the world, thus standard growth is measured as the growth of world imports in the destination country.

The **commodity composition** component measures the amount of export growth that was attributable to the exports of commodities that had strong demand in the exporting destination. If a country demands a particular commodity, then naturally it is expected that the focus exporter should perform well with that commodity. A positive commodity composition term will mean that the exporter's composition of exports will consist mainly of those goods that have achieved strong import demand in the focus destination. A large commodity

[19] World Trade Organisation.

[20] The market distribution effect does not enter into our analysis.

composition effect implies that export growth is reliant on the demand for certain commodities in the export destination.

Finally, the **competitiveness residual** component is the net gain in market share by the focus exporter in the export destination. A positive term implies that the focus exporter is a strong competitor in terms of relative prices. Caution should be used when interpreting this term since the residual does not take into account trade barriers and trade is measured in values rather than volume.

Table 5.20. CMS Analysis of Australian Exports to India 1988-97 (Percentage)

	Growth of Australia's exports to India	Growth of India's imports from the rest of the world (standard growth)	Commodity composition effect	Competitiveness Residual
1988-91	14.91	0.82	12.42	1.67
1992-94	4.03	18.79	46.15	-60.92
1995-97	53.67	11.68	61.56	-19.57

Source: Data used was provided by the Department of Foreign Affairs and Trade and were extracted from the STARS database. For details of data, see Appendix 1.

Table 5.21. CMS Analysis of Indian Exports to Australia 1988-97 (Percentage)

	Growth of India's Exports to Australia	Growth of Australia's imports from the rest of the world (standard growth)	Commodity Composition effect	Competitiveness Residual
1988-91	7.31	26.79	35.85	-55.33
1992-94	48.19	10.96	61.56	-24.33
1995-97	15.05	18.30	12.16	-15.42

Source: Data used was provided by the Department of Foreign Affairs and Trade and were extracted from the STARS database. For details of data, see Appendix 1.

The CMS analysis was applied to Australia and India for the period 1988-1997[21]. In total, six CMS analyses were conducted in Australia as the focus exporting country and India as the destination country (Table 5.20) and ii) India as the focus exporting country and Australia as the destination country (Table 5.21). The data was also divided into three intervals in which CMS analyses were conducted, 1988-91, 1992-94 and 1995-97.

From Tables 5.20 and 5.21 we can compare each country's export growth rate (to each others market) to the standard growth rate to see how well Australia and India performed against their competitors (the world). Australia seemed to perform well in India's market as its export growth rate was higher than the standard growth rate in two of the three periods analysed. On the other hand, India's exports to Australia only performed better than the standard growth rate in one of the three periods.

In 1992-94 Australia's export growth to India can be explained largely by the commodity composition effect which was relatively high in 1992-94 (46.1 percent). The commodity groups that had the largest share of Australian exports to India were coal, coke and briquettes (55.6 percent), and wool (10.7 percent) in 1994. As expected, Indian imports of coal, coke

[21] Details of the calculations are outlined in the Appendix 1.

and briquettes and wool grew by 28.9 and 4.6 percent respectively in the period 1995-97, thus resulting in a larger commodity composition effect.

In the other two periods, 1988-91 and 1995-97, Australia experienced positive competitiveness residuals. This implies that on average Australia's export market share had increased for that period.

The performance of India's exports into Australia in terms of "competitiveness" has been poor for the entire period of 1988-97 with negative residual components for each of the three periods analysed. These negative terms indicate that on average, India had lost its export market share in Australia.

Future Trade Prospects

Merchandise Trade

India is emerging as one of Australia's most important trading partners in recent years. One of the most striking features of the market is the sheer number of consumers which is of direct interest to countries selling consumer goods. The size of the consumer market is between 100 and 300 million people depending on type of product[22].

Australia's merchandise exports to India grew over 50 percent faster than total growth of 8 percent per year in the 1990s[23]. Primary commodities such as coking coal, wool and pulses, still account for the bulk of exports, and will probably do so for many years to come. The most rapidly growing area of exports is in ETMs. With the introduction of initial trade liberalisation measures in India in 1991, Australian ETM exports to India increased by three-fold between 1991 and 1992[24]. There exists opportunities to further enhance the exports of ETMs to India. The Department of Foreign Affairs and Trade is of the view, that with further trade liberalisation in India, exports of the following ETMs to India will increase in the coming years:[25]

- Mining, earth moving and bulldozing equipment;
- Heating and cooling equipment, pumps for gas and liquids, conveyors and associated parts;
- Electrical machinery, photographical and optical apparatus

From Australia's point of view, the major opportunities in the Indian markets arise from its massive development needs in the fields high technology manufactures such as power, energy and mineral resources, telecommunications, infrastructure (roads and ports), food processing and services. India's need to rapidly expand the power and steel industries presents opportunities for a significant expansion in exports of both coking and thermal coal.

---

[22] Department of Foreign Affairs and Trade (1994), p.30
[23] Department of Foreign Affairs and Trade (2001), p. 72
[24] *Ibid*, p. 82.
[25] *Ibid*, p. 83.

Services

Exports of Australian services to India have been growing quite considerably, with tourism and education being two of the major services exports to India. Arrivals from India to Australia grew at an impressive rate of 12 percent per year since the beginning of the 1990s.[26] Over 39,000 Indian tourists visited Australia compared during 2000 compared to 32,183 in 1999.[27] There are indications that with proper marketing strategy adopted by the Australian Tourist Commission, this number will gradually increase in the future given the fact that there are a growing number of Indians who can afford to travel abroad. In 2001, approximately 60 to 70 million people fell into the "high income" households in India[28] with the capacity to travel to long haul destinations such as Australia. Visa International estimates that there are 40 million Indians living with annual household incomes over US$30,000[29]. Thus the outbound travel market holds considerable promise for growth, and as such there is considerable potential for the expansion of tourism to Australia. Another striking feature of the Indian tourists is that they spend more than other overseas visitors while visiting Australia. According to the estimates of the Department of Foreign Affairs and Trade, Indian tourists spend an average of A$3,034 per visit in Australia as opposed to the overall visitor average of A$2,152 per visit[30].

With considerable growth in the size of middle and upper middle class of people in India, demand for overseas education has increased over the years and is expected to continue to grow in the future. Historically, UK has been the most popular destination for receiving overseas education by the Indian students because of the past colonial connections between these two countries. The USA, Germany and the Soviet Union also receive a considerable number of students from India. Australia's penetration to the Indian market for exporting education has been of recent origin; and since the beginning of the 1990s, India has emerged as one of Australia's top five overseas education markets[31]. Demand for overseas education in India will increase in the years due the growth in income, as well as the limited availability of quality domestic education in some areas such as vocational, educational and professional training, which are in great demand. The Australian education providers should take these opportunities, and attempts must be made to promote the excellent educational opportunities in Australia amongst the prospective students in India.

Conclusion

Bilateral trade relations between Australia and India have improved quite considerably since the 1990s. But the trade between Australia and India has not yet reached at its optimum level. It has been shown in this chapter that in recent years the average annual rate of growth of Australia's merchandise exports to North and South-East Asian regions has slowed down.

---

[26] *Ibid*, p. 84.

[27] During 1994 approximately, 14,000 passengers or less than 1% of the Indian outbound market travels to Australia, Department of Foreign Affairs and Trade (1994), p. 32.

[28] Department of Foreign Affairs and Trade (2001), p. 5.

[29] Department of Foreign Affairs and Trade (1994), p. 33.

[30] Department of Foreign Affairs and Trade (2001), p. 84.

[31] *Ibid*, p. 85.

It can therefore be argued that demand for Australia's exports in these regions will continue to decline. By contrast, the rate of growth of Australia's exports to SAARC countries and particularly to India has increased considerably in recent years. Most of the SAARC countries, including India, have not been seriously affected by the Asian economic crisis. It is therefore expected that the demand for Australian products in this region will continue to grow; subsequently Australia can no longer afford to neglect India as a strategic trading partner. Fortunately, Canberra has now recognised this and trade relations between Australia and India are expected to improve in future years.

References

ABS, (1981), Foreign Trade Australia: Comparative and Summary Tables 1969-70 to 1979-80, *Catalog. No. 5410.0*

Bano, S. and Lane, P. (1987), "New Zealand - Australia Intra-industry Trade", in A. Bollard and M.A. Thompson (eds.) *Trans-Tasman Trade and Investment*, Wellington: New Zealand Institute of Economic Research, and Victoria University of Wellington Institute of Policy Studies, pp. 28-36.

Brown, A.J. (1949), *Applied Economics: Aspects of World Economy in War and Peace*, London: George Allen and Unwin.

Department of Foreign Affairs and Trade (DFAT), - (1976), *Trade Agreement Between the Government of Australia and the Government of India* (2 August 1976, Canberra), Australian Treaty Series, No. 2

______ (1990), *Agreement Between the Government of Australia and the Government of the Republic of India on Development Co-operation*, (25 October 1990, Canberra), Australian Treaty Series, 190. No. 38.

______ (1994), *India's Economy at the Midnight Hour: Australia's India Strategy,* Canberra: Commonwealth of Australia

______ (1996), *Exports of Major Commodities Time Series, 1996*, Canberra: Commonwealth of Australia.

______ (1996a), *Integrated Country Promotion - Australia-India and New Horizons*, Canberra: Commonwealth of Australia

______ (1998) *Exports of Major Commodities Time Series, 1998*, Canberra, Commonwealth of Australia.

______ (1998a), *Direction of Trade Time Series 1977-1997,* Canberra, Commonwealth of Australia.

______ (2001), *India – New Economy Old Economy,* Canberra: Commonwealth of Australia

Drysdale, P. and Garnaut, R. (1982), "Trade Intensities and the Analysis of Bilateral Trade-flows in a Many-country World", *Hitotsubashi Journal of Economics*, 22(2), pp. 62-84.

Frank, W.T. and Ghosh, R.N., (1981), "Some Aspects of Economic Relations Between Australia and South and Southeast Asia" in A. Kerr (ed.) *The Indian Ocean Region: Resources and Development*, Western Australia: University of Western Australia Press

Garnaut, Ross (1991), "Australia Revolutionises: the New Trade Commitments", *International Economic Insights*, Vol. 2, No. 4, pp. 2-5.

Grubel, H G and Lloyd, P J (1975), *Inter-industry Trade: The Theory and Measurement of International Trade in Differentiated Products*, London: Macmillan

Gurry, Meg, (1993), "A Tale of Missed Opportunities: Australia's Relations with India since 1947", in M. Vicziany (ed.), *Australia-India Economic Links: Past, Present and Future,* pp. 10-23

International Monetary Fund (IMF), (1992), *Direction of Trade Statistics Yearbook 1992,* Washington, D.C: International Monetary Fund

______ (1998), *Direction of Trade Statistics Yearbook 1998,* Washington, D.C: International Monetary Fund

______ (1987), *Direction of Trade Statistics Yearbook,* Washington, D.C: International Monetary Fund

______ (2000), *Direction of Trade Statistics Yearbook,* Washington, D.C: International Monetary Fund

______ (2001), *Direction of Trade Statistics Quarterly,* (June 2001), Washington, D.C: International Monetary Fund

Kojima, K. (1964), "The Pattern of International Trade among Advanced Countries", *Hitotsubashi Journal of Economics*, 5(1), pp. 16-36.

Lloyd, P. J. (1994), " The Future of the CER Agreement: A Single Market for Australia and New Zealand", in R. Garnaut and P. Drysdale (eds.) *Asia Pacific Regionalism: Readings in International Economic Relations*, Pymble, NSW: Harper Educational, pp. 341-362.

Menon, J. (1994), "Trade Liberalisation, Closer Economic Relations, and Intra-industry Specialisation", *Australian Economic Review*, 106, pp. 31-42.

Menon, P. and Dixon, P.B. (1994), "How Important is Intra-industry Trade in Trade Growth?" *General Paper*, 109, Melbourne: Centre for Policy Studies and IMPACT Project, Monash University.

Mohamed Ariff, K A (1991), *The Malaysian Economy: Pacific Connections*, Singapore; New York: Oxford University Press

Sheenhan, P.J., Pappas, N. and Cheng, E., (1994), *The rebirth of Australian industry: Australian trade in elaborately transformed manufactures, 1979-1993* Melbourne, Vic.: Centre for Strategic Economic Studies, Victoria University of Technology

Tyers, R and P. Phillips (1984) "AESA Merchandise Trade with the Pacific Basin: Factor Composition and Performance", *Pacific Economic Papers,* No. 116. Australia-Japan Research Centre, Australian National University.

United Nations (UN), *International Trade Statistics Yearbook,* New York: United Nations, *various issues.*

APPENDIX 1. METHODOLOGY FOR DERIVING THE CONSTANT MARKET SHARE

The CMS analysis decomposes a county's export growth into four components:

Export Growth = Standard Growth + Commodity Composition
+ Market Distribution Effect and Competitiveness.

In our analysis, we will only be focusing on the export growth performance of two sectors, namely Australian exports into India and India's exports into Australia. The model can be simplified into the following equation:

$$\underbrace{\frac{E_t - E_{t-1}}{E_{t-1}}}_{\text{Export growth of focus country}} = \underbrace{r}_{\text{Standard Growth}} + \underbrace{\frac{\sum_i (r_i - r)E_{i,t}}{E_{t-1}}}_{\text{Market Distribution Effect}} + \text{competitiveness residual.}$$

where

$$r = \frac{W_t - W_{t-1}}{W_t} = \text{Growth of world imports in destination country.}$$

$$r_i = \frac{W_{i,t} - W_{i,t-1}}{W_{i,t}} = \text{Growth of imports of commodity i in destination country.}$$

E_t = the total value of the focus country's exports to the destination country during period t.

$E_{i,t}$ = the total value of the focus country's exports of commodity i to the destination country during period t.

W_t = the total value of exports from the world to the destination country during period t.

$W_{i,t}$ = the total value of exports of commodity i from the world to the destination country during period t.

The data used in the analysis for the period 1988-97 analysis are:

- The value ($A) of Australian exports to India classified into 3 digit SITC (r.3) commodities.
- The value ($A) of Australian imports from India (or India's exports to Australia) classified into 3 digit SITC (r.3) commodities.
- The value ($A) of imports from the world to Australia classified into 3 digit SITC (r.3) commodities
- The value ($A) of imports from the world to India classified into 3 digit SITC (r.3) commodities.

Data used was provided by the Department of Foreign Affairs and Trade and were extracted from the STARS database.

In: Australia: Economics, Political and Social Issues
Editors: Lachlan J. Williams and Ethan N. Lee
ISBN: 978-1-60456-856-1

Chapter 6

A VIEW FROM THE GROUND: LIFE-WORLD EXPERIENCES OF FOUR ABORIGINAL CHILDREN IN A WESTERN AUSTRALIAN DESERT COMMUNITY

Ian Edmondson

INTRODUCTION

Broome occupies a tiny portion of coastline in the Kimberley region of far North Western Australia (Figure 1). From an aerial perspective, the town spreads seductively below, clusters of single story buildings partially hidden amongst vigorous leafy green. Broome lies vulnerably sandwiched between the deep milky aqua of salt-laden Roebuck Bay to the West and the encroaching creep of ochre desert to the East, where horizontal terrain stretches hundreds of kilometres and melts into hazy horizon. During the wet months, this inland desert country is abundant with flora and carries a tropical guise. A prehistoric river cuts through this desert, a raging, cleansing flood for some months of the year gouging gorges of awesome proportions. In the dry season, the Fitzroy River forms placid, dark pools. It eventually empties into the shallows of King Sound, near Derby, to the North of Broome. This river has sustained human existence far longer than the pearls, palm trees, exotic attractions, cattle stations and promise of desert adventure that draws tourists to the modern Kimberly region.

The Australian Aboriginal children featured in this chapter live in the inland desert region, several hundred kilometres East of Broome, within a tiny community eighty kilometres off the main highway. The area is undeniably beautiful, with a deep, glowing redness of sand reflected in layered hues of the surrounding rocky hills. Dominant colours change from soft, dusky pinks of morning to a deep glowing rust preceding a sub-tropical downpour, when the greens of wet season growth complement the sand. The guarding hills, crowned with balls of spinifex, feature distinctly even plateaus as if some mythical giant has passed over with a lawnmower. Temperatures range from oppressive, steamy hot during the wet season to warm sunny days and cool nights over the dry months. The children's home location will be hereafter referred to as "The Community".

My connection with The Community is from working there in my first year as a teacher a few years ago.

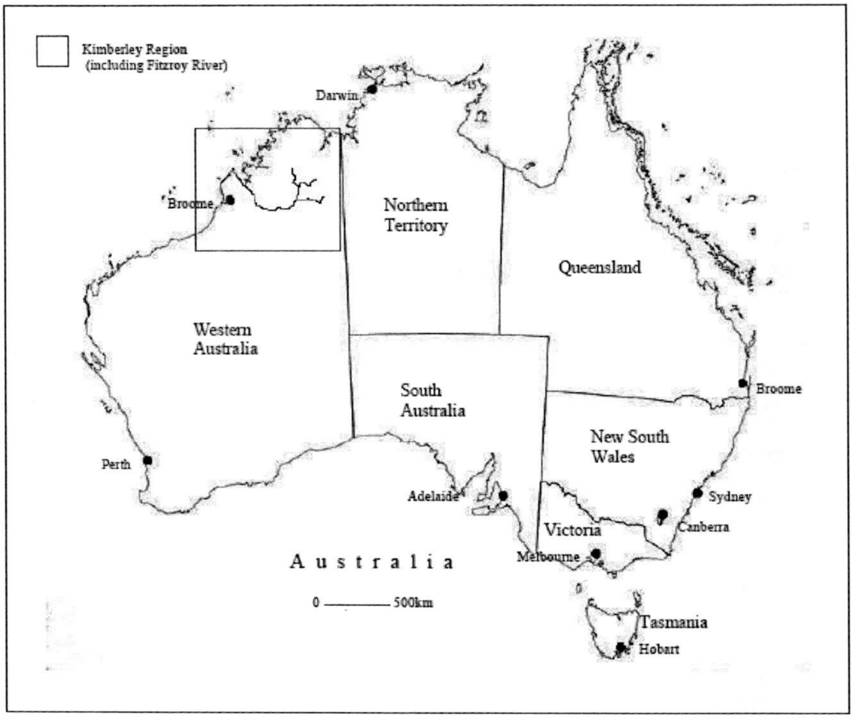

Figure 1. General location map adapted with permission from Geoscience basic outline map: *Copyright Commonwealth of Australia, Geoscience Australia (2006).*

Blinded by early career enthusiasm and culture shock I spent too much time floundering with emerging teaching philosophy. Perhaps, the potential value of life-world knowledge was overshadowed by focus on curricular detail and striving for personal satisfaction as a teacher.

METHODOLOGY

This chapter is a record of my (non-indigenous) observations and interpretations of life-world experiences of four children, collated following a recent return visit. It is also a vehicle for reflection, containing reference to my former experience living in The Community. During this return visit, information was gathered over a seven day period. The children became active, empowered participants in the research process, gathering their own photographic evidence of daily life which contributed to ongoing discussions and interviews, supplemented by my own photographs. Interviews could be better described as collaborative conversation, with photographic images stimulating dialogue, rather than being controlled by researcher-directed questions. This collaborative, two-way method of building shared meaning is supported by Harper (1998) who describes a "new ethnography" redefining the researcher/ subject relationship where: "the researcher becomes a listener and one who encourages the dialogue to continue." (p.35). This method moves forward from its roots in "photo elicitation" (Collier and Collier, 1986), which Pink (2001) defines as problematic in that it relies on the image *itself* to draw out information, and where photographs tended to be used in illustrative or documentary fashion (Emmison and Smith, 2000). My process utilized photographs as a companion to interviews, accompanied by other visual images (family and community maps), supported by conversation and by reference to events and other knowledge shared during the week. In conducting these interviews, my role was primarily in listening and seeking clarification. This collaborative conversational approach acknowledges the "multivocality" of photographic images, where different viewers bring quite different interpretations to an image presented (Banks, 2001, p.144). True meaning in this context is collectively and carefully moulded rather than assumed.

Questioning is inherently problematic with Aboriginal children as I experienced when teaching in The Community, and research supports this: "In Aboriginal society there is no obligation to answer [questions] and indirect methods of obtaining information are preferred over more direct questions" (Berry and Hudson, 1997, p.6). In my work in the field, a preferred method was to only ask questions in clarification once sufficient information had been offered through general conversation. This became a more drawn out process, but worked in the context of the loose time structures that typified each day I spent with the children. This method supported the likelihood of the passing of more real, honest and relevant information. A risk with questioning is the potential for children to simply supply the answer they think you want to hear. Questions can interfere in research processes and serve to organise and influence the perceptions of those interviewed (Sanoff, 1991).

To shift the locus of control and power as much as possible, closing interviews were conducted in an informal spatial setting, away from The Community in a place of personal significance to the children. The outdoor setting of the "Rock-hole" was selected as this interview location. By this time (day six) we had collected and printed a number of digital photographic images and shared much knowledge through informal conversation. Productive, trusting relationships were deeply established. It became clear that the children were more at ease away from the formal setting of my lodging, where a room with tables and chairs was used as a base and a place to conduct the more structured mapping activities earlier in the week.

My positions as cultural 'outsider', adult, former teacher and driver of information sharing created inevitable power differentials of researcher and subject (Prosser and Schwartz, 1998) which may have influenced the outcomes of this chapter. Being already known to The Community and to the families of the children helped enormously, and research was conducted with the full support of community elders, parents and the children themselves. Banks (2001) advocates social research approaches that build trust with indigenous people, making ethical issues more "manageable" (p.119).

Over the course of the week, we progressed from a focus on immediate surroundings and the events, people and places therein, to a collaborative exploration of places beyond the community, sharing knowledge of deeper personal meaning. Through this spatial transition, the lives of the children expanded before me.

The children of this chapter have been given fictional names, which will be used hereafter. The names were similarly adopted for the research process, where children chose a name of a favourite native animal. The two boys ("Kangaroo" and "Barramundi") were aged 10 and 12 years respectively. The two girls ("Turkey" and "Brolga") were both aged 12 years. Similarly, for privacy reasons, place names have been altered or omitted, and the children's home location will be referred to simply as "The Community".

This particular community is small, with approximately 130 Aboriginal inhabitants. Teachers and administration staff make up the 5-7 non-indigenous inhabitants. Community infrastructure comprises 24 Indigenous houses and 5 teacher houses, a school, including library, music room and adult education buildings, a store, powerhouse, water tanks and garage. Recent Government focus on health funding is reflected in a clinic and new airstrip currently under construction. Historically, health funding has been predominantly channelled into housing. Community statistics show living density has been lowered from 15-20 indigenous inhabitants per house, to 5-10 people, (variation due to extended family members moving between communities), and that the general health of the people of The Community has improved in parallel to this change.

The influence of *history*, the children's connectedness to *place* and the binding, unifying qualities of their *social networks* emerge as interlinked foundations for the children's life-worlds, and form the basis of this chapter.

This chapter then explores *places* special to the children, examining how they interact with, and make meaning of, their physical environment and make sense of their own lives. Finally, the *social setting* of the community is explored through several facets of life-world experience, including family structures, food, language, risk and education.

History: The Making of Place

Written and oral accounts of history reveal periods of huge upheaval, dislocation and relocation, with profound effect on the people of The Community and directly involving many older people still alive today. The following section highlights critical components of history that give grounding to The Community as the ancestral home to these children and their kin, forging a sense of place and belonging, maintaining connectedness to spiritual and cultural domains. This account of history can be viewed through four distinct periods: the period prior to colonial invasion of 1788; the gradual move from desert to station living (i.e. living on a large cattle station or ranch) in the early 1900's; the exodus to towns in the early 1970's; and eventual relocation to traditional lands in subsequent years.

Prior to the invasion of Australia by European explorers in the late 1700's, the ancestors of The Community lived a tribal life in the Great Sandy Desert area of the Kimberley region. This traditional tribal life is beautifully preserved for modern interpretation in the paintings and illustrations of deceased Aboriginal artist Jimmy Pike, supported in writing by his partner Pat Lowe, (see Lowe and Pike, 1990, 1992, 1997, 1999). It was a life typified by an intimate relationship with the land, a tradition of respect and caring for people and places, strong family networks and a nomadic existence demanded by seasonal change, hunting and gathering, kinship links and the interconnectedness of neighbouring tribal groups (Richards, Hudson and Lowe, 2002).

In the broader context of non-Indigenous colonisation of the country, it is widely acknowledged that Europeans invaded Australia in 1788, initially establishing a settlement in the Botany Bay area of New South Wales in the South East of the country, and rapidly claiming any areas of land along the East coast. Patterns of settlement were largely dictated by a search for sources of permanent water and land areas suitable for agriculture. Aboriginal people were systematically displaced, dispersed and killed in large numbers. Populations declined enormously and rapidly through conflict and the introduction of disease. Richard Broome (1994 : 65) refers to Aboriginal populations in the Southern State of Victoria declining by eighty percent in eighteen years up to 1853. Various maps depict Aboriginal tribal boundaries constructed over the last century. For example, the Macquarie Atlas of Australia includes maps from Horton, 1996; Tindale, 1974; and Thompson, 1956, showing that Indigenous territory covered the entire country, not only the fertile, temperate zones coveted by colonial settlers.

The eventual and inevitable settlement of pastoralists represented the greatest disruption to traditional life of Indigenous people Australia-wide. In comparison to the extreme levels of devastation and dislocation experienced at the more temperate end of the country, environmental conditions of the North West and isolation from the rest of the country offered some initial immunity from more destructive settlement (Richards, Hudson and Lowe, 2002). There are, however, many accounts of conflict and violence largely the result of miscommunication, misunderstanding, fear of, and lack of respect for, indigenous populations (see: KALACC, 1996; Pederson, 1995; Crawford, 2001; Jebb, 2002; Milnes and Truscott, 2002; Smith, 2004).

The pastoralists who did eventually settle in this region, mostly in the early 1900's, came in small numbers, and with little understanding of the natural environment. Aboriginal people were forcibly taken as workers on the stations. Their knowledge of the land, seasonal cycles of change and understanding of the locations of waterholes and food sources were vital to the efficient running of the stations. Eric Lawford recalls Aboriginal drovers moving cattle, on foot, hundreds of kilometres from station to coast for shipping (in Marshall, 1989, p.19). He later describes the practice of "taking" women and girls to work as "house girls" in station homesteads (Marshall, 1989, p.24). Other Aboriginal tribal groups remained out in desert country, but were inevitably lured to the fringes of the stations with the prospect of food, tobacco and clothing: scant offerings in return for hard labour, but tempting to a people used to harsh desert living and unpredictable food supplies.

In this manner the gradual relocation of "home" eventuated, and the forbears of The Community (including some of the older people still alive) set up camp just beyond the boundary of The Station (name altered) homestead. By the 1940's and 50's the last of the desert people had succumbed to the pressures of family relocation and the relative ease of station life, and joined the new communities thus formed (Richards, Hudson and Lowe, 2002).

There was some controlled allowance by station bosses to sustain culture and ceremony, as described by Barnes: "they let people go to ceremonies during the wet" (Marshall, 1989). As Broome (1994, p.56) states: "...most Aborigines, even while floundering to work out some means of survival amid the new political realities, clung tenaciously to their culture". Most importantly, communities maintained the passing of traditional knowledge to their children.

In line with Government 'assimilation' policies (see Smith, 2004; HREOC, 2005) equal pay legislation and alcohol law changes of the late nineteen sixties caused enormous social and physical disruption to Aboriginal people in Northern Australia. They typified this period of control of Aboriginal people's lives. As a result of this policy Aboriginal people were evicted from station communities across the Kimberley region in huge numbers. Station owners chose to keep and pay only the most skilled stockmen. People of The Community, accustomed now to an easier existence, could not simply return to desert life. Instead, they migrated eighty kilometres North to the tiny township of Fitzroy Crossing, creating a virtual overnight, long-term welfare and housing crisis, with issues of declining health, a lack of education (The town had only one small school) negative tribal mixing and degradation of traditional languages. Fitzroy Crossing (and Halls Creek, two hundred and fifty kilometres East) did not have the infrastructure to cope with the situation, which continued well into the 1980s. The people of The Community became further removed from their traditional home country and cultural roots.

In the most positive and recent historical shift, Aboriginal people embarked on proactive and persistent efforts to change this situation. They made repeated claims for government to acquire pastoral land, on their behalf. Claims were based on a need to reconnect with tribal land and customs, claim for recognition of the enormous, unpaid contribution that Aboriginal people had made in initial establishment of these stations and concern for the environmental degradation of station properties (Hawke and Gallagher, 1989). This overriding and intimate symbiotic connection of land and people suggested that without the presence of Aboriginal people, the land suffered: "When the people leave…the waters all dry up" (Lewis, 2000, p.101).

As a result of these claims, three run-down stations in this area were purchased by government, on behalf of Aboriginal people. Other smaller "outstation" communities sprang up across the north of Australia over the next 20 years. Claire Smith, referring to similar moves in the Northern Territory describes these settlements as "places of independence, power and cultural renewal…statements of affiliation to country" (2004, p.114).

Elders of The Community persistently lodged claims over a number of years. They did not succeed in gaining ownership of a station property as intended, but eventually secured a lease of one square kilometre of land to establish an independent community. This piece of land on the outer fringes of The Station forms the modern day community, surrounded by traditionally familiar defining landmarks, water and food sources. The move back represents a return to traditional place, an opportunity to maintain, and in some sense rebuild, cultural heritage in the context of modern Australia.

PLACE: THE COMMUNITY TODAY

A unique relationship to place exists as a formative element of the children's life-worlds. The children identified special places; powerful spatial settings within which they willingly, at times fervently, shared understandings, skills and knowledge. Social interactions and daily events occurring within these special places nurture epistemological foundations of community and cultural belonging.

When questioned: *"So, what are the really special places around The Community, not just around here* [within community boundaries] *because I want you to take me to these places in the next few days?"* the children were quick to answer, and four key places emerged: The Rock, The Spring, The Rock Hole and The Station (names changed, see Figure 2 for locations).

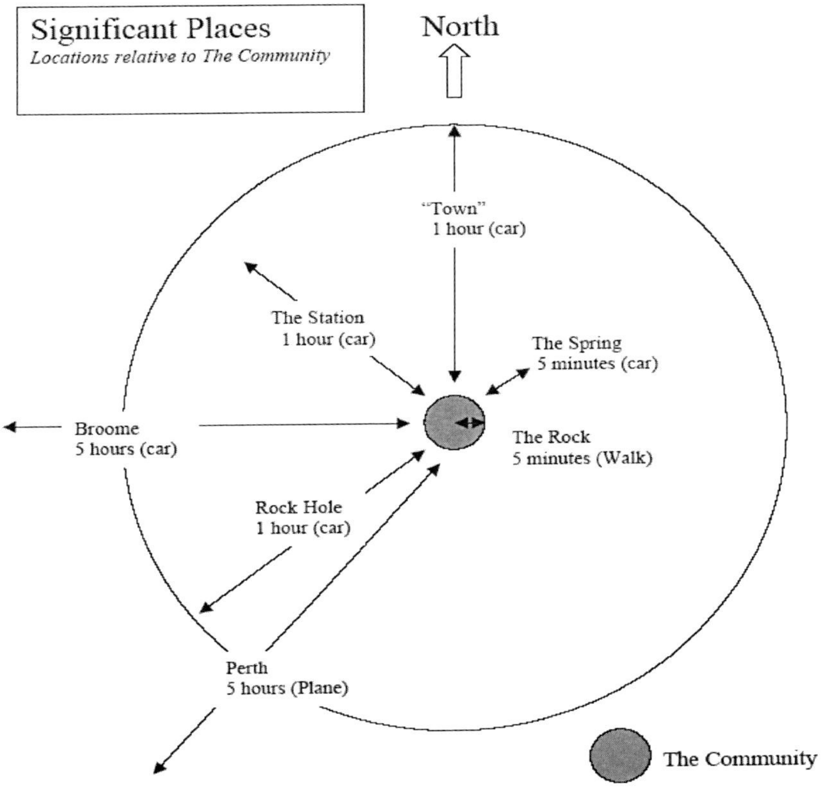

Figure 2. Map of Special Places, Travel Times and Directions in The Community.

The Rock forms a backdrop to The Community. This rock sits around forty meters high like an anchor to the people here, a traditional monument, bearing a story of a female traveller.

> We drive to The Rock, which is the first place the children identify as '*special'*. It is located just beyond the community boundary, but visually defines The Community's location, with water-streaked stains and deep red tones similar to central Australia's Ayers Rock.
>
> Turkey: *That's Women's land*
> Brolga: *She* [uses her name] *travelled here a long time ago...she's bending down* [demonstrates by leaning forward with arms folded over her head].

Like many traditional Aboriginal stories, the detailed telling of this story is limited to certain people. The children clearly understand and respect the true significance of the place and talk of it with reverence, describing, for example, the shape of the rock as a female form and it's matriarchal importance; that women can "ask" The Rock for babies.

The Spring is located about two kilometres beyond the fenced community boundary.

> The children react with great excitement when I produce a photo of one area of The Spring from five years ago in its previous state as a clear pool:
>
> Kangaroo: [over top] *M! M! M!* [recognises The Spring]
> Brolga: *Oh, let me look, he's got M!* [reaches immediately and grabs]
> Brolga: [wistfully, with feeling] *It's green!*
> Ian: *It's green... Looks like wet time does it?* [more affirming comment than question]
> Brolga: *'Es all dried up, that bit, you know?*
>
> I note Brolga's tones of sadness and longing in this explanation, justifying their excitement at seeing this place in its former state.

Another area of the spring, once tapped with a pipe at *"Station time"* now spouts water continuously. The children comment that the spring has been there *"long time, you know?"* with the implication that it predates pastoral settlement. Questions about time confuse the children, who place more importance on 'meaning' of places, stories and events. Kangaroo describes The Spring using the traditional definition of *"living water"* referring to its permanent status (Natural landforms subject to seasonal change, such as water holes, carry many different names in the Walmajarri language.). In a visit to this location the children reveal an abundance of bush foods and share extensive knowledge of gathering and processing the same. They talk of regular visits here to supplement store-bought food.

The diversity of the children's knowledge of places, and the dichotomous meanings of places is demonstrated in a profound shift when they lead me a short distance to a low hill:

> White fragments scatter across the burnt red sandy surface. Turkey bends down and gathers some of the fragments in her hand, separating pieces carefully:
>
> Turkey: *You can touch, but don't squeeze.*
> Brolga: *They shot 'em, even women and little babies, made them stand like this* [she turns and faces away].
> The children, after carefully placed steps, charge up the sand hill and are soon rolling down the slopes with squeals of delight.

Accounts of massacres in these remote regions of Australia are rarely recorded in 'official'.

Historical documents, but more recent evidences have been collected and published in stories told by older people of this region (e.g. collated stories of violence in the Kimberley region are found in sources such as Jebb, 2002; Marshall, 1989; and Richards, Hudson and Lowe, 2002). Like many stories of people of The Community, memories are *real* for children and adults alike. Time is compressed, and seemingly unimportant as factual history, legend, stories and events contribute to collaborative understanding and collective meaning.

The Rock Hole is the third natural landform of traditional importance, located about 10km away in the rocky foothills south of the community. The Rock Hole is another spring fed water source and a tranquil oasis of unrivalled beauty. Here, the children swim and play, fish, gather mussels, find a snake skin, a white frog, and explore. Barramundi and Kangaroo find their own private space in a rock crevice and play there for some time. The children describe attributes of flora and fauna, and name specific rock formations for catching water. Brolga warns of the presence of a spiritual snake in the waters, I am reminded of a school trip here where I was instructed to wipe a stone under my armpit and throw it into the water before swimming.

After our visit to The Rock Hole, Barramundi's father, a community elder, reflects on a time, possibly during his childhood, when the Rock Hole dried up:

He was all dried up one time...A big rock [had] *moved away from the hole...you know? All the water ran out...and the moon...he pulled that stone back again*

The Station comprises the ruins of the former station homestead (now relocated a day's drive away) sited on the banks of a vast river.

To the children, The Station is a place of importance on different levels: as a place of shared meaning through memories and stories passed down from adults who lived here once, and as a place they come regularly for fishing, swimming and relaxation.

On our car journey to The Station we pass 'Crocodile Dam'. Barramundi explains the name: *He had a crocodile in 'im once.* Brolga's sister questions the kids on what they do there:

Brolga: [excitedly] *We make a mud slide...a big mob* [lot] *of mud...and you slide down into the water...and you can swim, and fish...for Jarrampa, or Cherrabin* [large fresh water shrimp]*...with a throw net...P.* [Barramundi's father] *he teach us to throw the net... and we get...what you call it...? Punta* [small fish] *and big mob of catfish!*

Brolga's older sister tells a story of making dolls with a grandmother from the gnarled roots of a riverbank tree, or playing a *"shop game"* using the yellow flowers from the *"twisty tree"* as pretend food. They all join in excitedly to relay stories of a game called *"predator"* a form of chases along the river banks *"...then we hunt him...you know...like Arnold Schwarzenegger!"*

Beyond The Station homestead boundary, less obvious in terms of architectural remnants, but far more significant for the Aboriginal people of The Community, there is a large expanse of flat plain with subtle features defining their former home location.

Barramundi's father walks me amidst the site of his former camp, reading the seemingly bare ground like a map, adding life and meaning through identification of long-gone shelter structures, toilets, fire places with rocks for *"...cooking meat on"*. He recalls with chuckles childhood stories of crawling into pens at night to drink milk straight from the goats, and reflects on the two white boys who grew up on the station but were eventually sent to boarding school: *"That boss man...he didn't like those kids losing their language you know?* [chuckling] *they were talking Aboriginal language!"* He identifies a midden pile of old bones. Bullamen (cow) bones, and evidence of other station provisions like meat tins lie mixed with native animal bones like kangaroo and goanna. He then spots a lone rock partially buried: [stopping suddenly, pointing down] *"That rock...doesn't belong here...from somewhere else...*[I question what he means]*...used for grinding seeds".*

The historical and social significance of these places is encapsulated in the sharing of knowledge and perpetuated in children's games and stories they tell. Memory and knowledge is similarly attached to natural forms and constructed objects.

> We drive through a gate into the area of the ruins of the former station homestead. There is a sense of its former significance in the variety of architectural remnants, with evidences of isolation in the huge water storage tanks and caged meat drying room. Beyond the surrounding desert, there is a clear sense of 'oasis' and feeling of home with the backdrop of The River, abundance of growth, larger trees and screeching cockatoos. We pass a pair of rooms in one building:
>
> Brolga: *That's where my Grandmother used to live...right there* [points to a room]
> Ian: *Oh, why did she live here?*
> Brolga: *A cleaner...at the big house.*
>
> The children photograph the building, and I note at least two of their names etched in charcoal graffiti on the walls.

Gerber (2001) refers to children making sense of their world through exploration and curiosity. He also describes a shared, participatory sense of place developed within enduring relationships. This essentially social, dynamic, interactive and continually evolving view of space, supports Massey's notion of space as a "product of interrelations; as constituted through interactions…a sphere of coexisting heterogeneity…always under construction". (2005, p.9) and echoes Lefebvre's concept of space as a "social product" defined and redefined by "spatial practice" (1997, p. 26). The children make meaning of places through play. The children visit The Station often, either with different family members, other families, or on school trips with non-indigenous and indigenous teaching staff. Massey proposes there are "…multiple meanings of places, held by different social groups" (1994, p. 141).The children's understanding of place, and of themselves, continually changes and expands as they visit these places at different times with different people, adding new layers of meaning. Their reactions and responses provided repeated illustrations of this conclusion.

Place: Mapping, Way-Finding and Tracking

The children's way-finding abilities are supported by heightened spatial awareness and intricate relationship to their country. Much of their daily life is governed by acute abilities to 'read' the physical landscape, locating or recognising clues, signs, signposts and guides.

As a relationship building and orientation task, I conducted a formal mapping exercise. The children sat at individual tables in a room of my lodging set up as a formal workspace, with three tables for the children and one set up with my computer, digital photo printer and associated gear. The children had varieties of drawing tools on their tables, and sheets of A3 paper. The activity was introduced to the children as follows:

Within fifteen minutes, the children had produced maps demonstrating expansive cognitive mapping abilities and remarkable spatial awareness of a complicated, non-linear environment (see Figures 2-5 and associated notes). Rikkinen connects "regional identity" and "attachment to space and place" to childhood experiences:

Ian: *I want you to draw something for me, so that I can learn more about this special place where you live.* [All nod] *I want you to be a bird, imagine you are a bird flying over your community looking down. Think about what you might see. I want you to draw me a picture that shows just what that bird might see. Do you know what I mean?*
All: *Yeah, yeah* [nod knowingly and seem clear on this instruction]
Ian: [after handing out paper] *So this is where you really need to work by yourself, because there's no 'right" way to do this, it's just your way...just the way you might see your community, so all the things that are important to you will come out in this picture.*
Turkey: [murmurs something in background to Brolga]
Brolga: *Got to do a map, like we're looking down from there* [holds hand above head]
Turkey: *Yeah, yeah I know.*

"The possibility and freedom to explore, to investigate and learn about the structure of the environment definitely develops the child's spatial acuity..." (In Robertson and Gerber, 2000, p. 88). Sanoff (2001) equates orientation to feelings of well-being within environments, generating a sense of "ease and enjoyment [allowing] us to appreciate new and unexpected features" (p.73). In conducting research into visual recall and mapping abilities of Aboriginal children compared to semi-urban non-indigenous children in the late nineteen seventies, Kearins (1976, 1981; see also Harris, 1991, p. 34) found that there was evidence supporting superior spatial understandings. Recent studies in mathematics education lend further support and refer to aspects of daily life similar to children of The Community:

> Aboriginal children (urban and rural) generally excel at spatial aspects of maths such as drawing aerial views or plans of their homes. Their ability may reflect differences in child raising methods where Aboriginal children are generally given more freedom to explore space and to take risks than non-Aboriginal children; they are allowed to observe their environment more closely and may travel more than average, eg visiting relatives in distant communities.
> (DECS, 2005, p. 9)

Brolga began with roads as an organising element. Here she is making early comment about her planning process, about 4 minutes into the activity. Like Kangaroo, she talks as if there, with little difficulty in comprehending the task.

'I'm gonna put all the roads, then all the houses, gonna put the school, then that road, then the store here then top camp here and bottom camp there, and then the oval [other indecipherable references to particular 'camps' (peoples homes) and connecting roads] then all the roads around' [very fast speech, sweeping motions, and finger directions over a near blank page (some roads sketched in) indicating that she was planning how she might fit things, in great detail, into the whole page before committing.

Turkey became frustrated with details and insisted on starting again. Like the others, she recognised the significance of the powerhouse, store, school, basketball court, football oval and her own house as points of reference, linked by networks of foot and road tracks.

Kangaroo chose to map from a closer viewpoint, stemming from the building we were in (marked " ian" on his map) Kangaroo describes his map in animated detail, visualising the processes of getting from place to place: *...this is this home right now* [drawing in a road] *this road goes right round here like that....this is Barra's house* [friend] *and this is the playground...school road.*

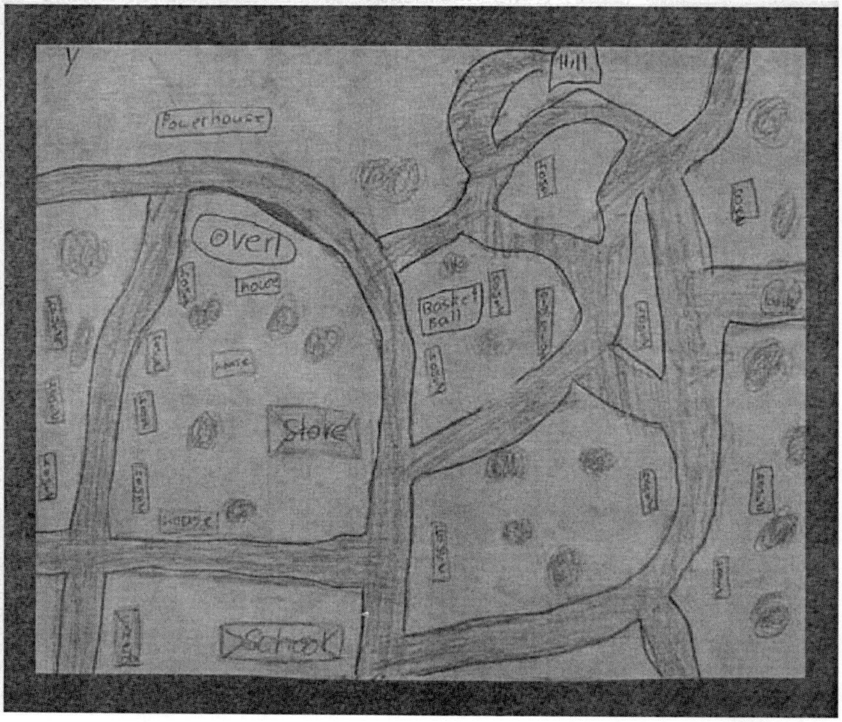

Figure 3. Brolga's Map.

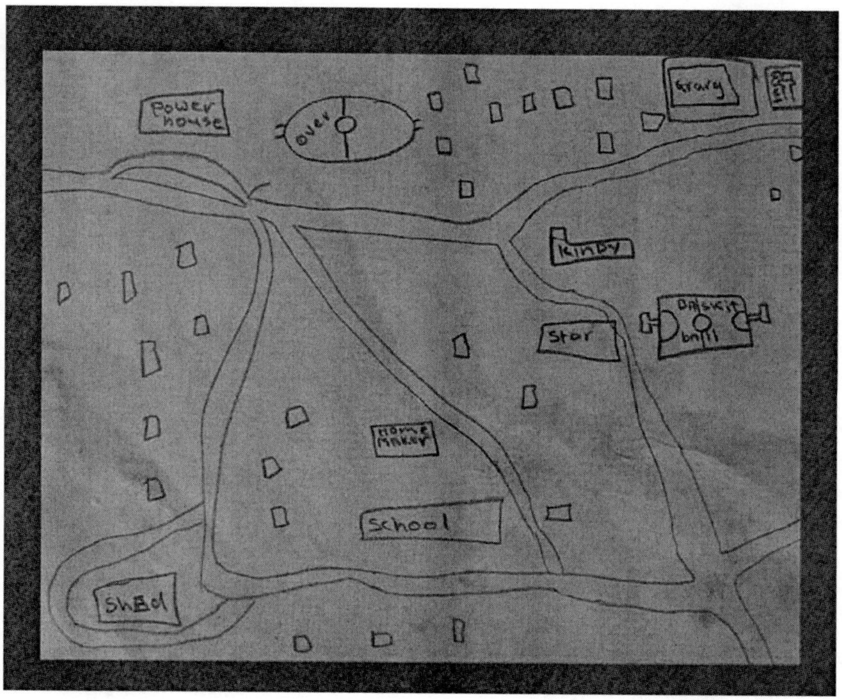

Figure 4. Turkey's Map.

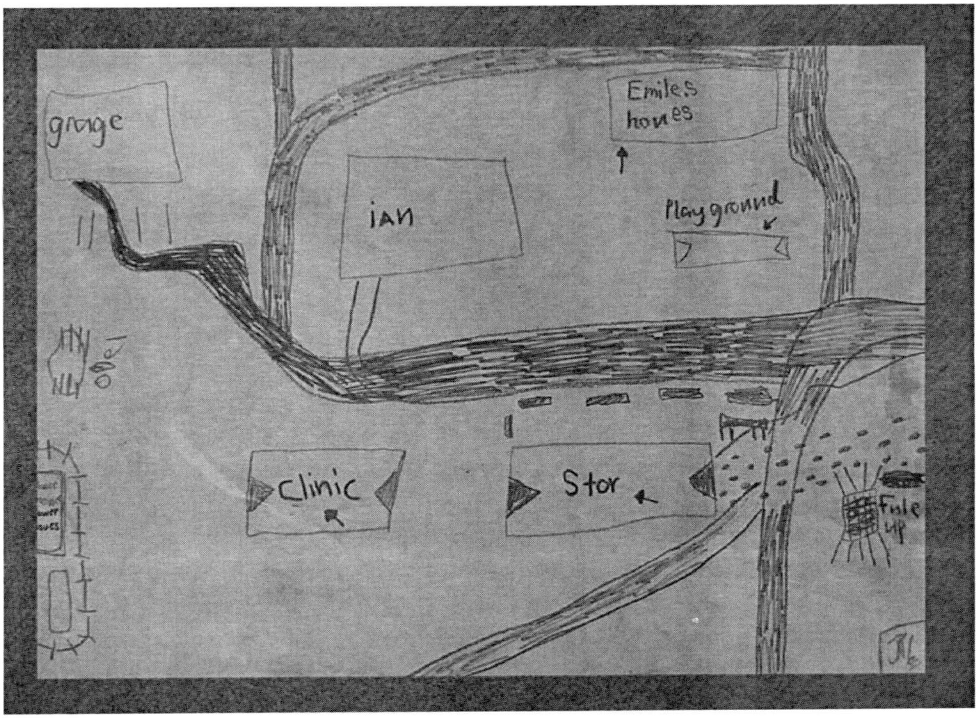

Figure 5. Kangaroo's Map.

And they always go with the bike and grab food at the store, and they walk back like that... for tracks [following with pencil the bike track and footprints going to and from the school...*this is the fuel part, you know... when they fill up the Toyota.*

When travelling beyond the immediate community boundaries the children demonstrated remarkable directional knowledge. They used reference points of place names and familiar landmarks as simple visual cues and peripheral signposts. Landmarks, places and built objects carry unofficial names such as 'double-gate' 'boundary' 'gap bore' 'big hole' and 'crocodile rock'. Other places connect to stories, like 'crocodile dam' and 'devil tree' a roadside tree associated with a scary story told by relatives on the way home in the dark, and relayed by Brolga's older sister: *"Don't look back or the devil will get you!"* .

Tracking is another key visual way-finding method used for different purposes by children of The Community. On one occasion we had travelled a distance of fifteen kilometres with an enormous number of twists and turns. Kangaroo, when asked to: "*Show me the way home*" used a stick to draw a map on the ground explaining guiding points of rivers, fence lines and gates, only some of which I could recall from the journey there.

This capacity for directional orientation seems similar to that identified by Lewis (1976, 2003) who transferred an interest in sea navigation to study of the way-finding abilities of central Australian desert Aboriginal people in the 1970s. Lewis found remarkable evidence that Aboriginal hunters could pursue quarry at speed following haphazard and irregular paths, then return in direct lines to unseen vehicles with pinpoint accuracy. He determined that there was an innate ability to mentally absorb spatial information as they went, constantly, but subconsciously realigning mental note of direction of base and objective, the angle of the sun and wind direction, instinctively knowing the way back as a result (2000, p.103). Such innate ability is supported by Tuan's (1979, pp.78-79) discussion of a keenly developed "spatial-geometric vocabulary" relating to Carpenter's (1955) study of Arctic Canadian Eskimo people who, despite a bleak and seemingly featureless landscape, possess refined perceptual and spatial skills necessitated by a need to survive in a harsh environment. Traditional Walmajarri language of The Community (and modern Aboriginal Kriol) carries a number of words relating to direction finding, similar to compass points, which are part of everyday descriptive language of location of places, people and even objects (Lowe, 2002).

When leaving The Station, the children helped track one of their dads, who had *"gone looking for turkey"* in his car. As a non-Aboriginal observer the road was *alive* with tracks, but Barramundi, despite the pace of the car, height above the ground, and the fact that our target had left the road at several points was able to casually report the route he'd taken. Every time I hesitated he stated: *"Na... 'e right...straight on!"*

All four children participate in regular hunting and gathering trips with family. I recall a notable incident from my time as a teacher on a hunting trip with one family, where a fifteen year old boy used a CD to reflect sunlight to a junction at the back of a goanna hole to determine the hapless lizard's direction of travel: *" ...He went that way!"*. Lowe (2003, p. 26) includes a pictorial depiction of the same method, but using a tobacco tin. Brolga was able to easily identify two kids of the community from photographs I'd taken one morning of footprints in the sand. Kangaroo included foot and bike tracks in his community map to depict a connection, and major human traffic route, between the school and store. The state of the sand at different times of the day, or in different seasons, or different weather conditions, provides additional indication of time, or the age of tracks. It is common practice for community elders to use tracking skills to identify offenders in minor community crimes. Brolga claimed she used tracking mostly to find out where her friends were.

SOCIAL INTERACTIONS: FAMILY STRUCTURES

Special places and historical events provide foundational structure of knowledge for the children of The Community. Social interactions of daily life continually mould, shape and define meaning.

Family structures of The Community are complex to an outsider. As Turkey announced: *"I think I'm related to everybody in The Community!"*. Perplexed, she declared that she would only map her *"Community family"*. Her *"family map"* as I referred to it in instruction, again demonstrated superior skills in spatial organization of information (see Figure 6). Turkey explained that some members were *"blood family"* others were *"family"* and others *"skin family"* She also explained that there were *"23 pages of family"* with her Aunt in a nearby town, implying the compilation of a family tree. Turkey's brother Kangaroo produced an entirely different version of the same family, adopting an immediate family perspective, preferring detail in the same way he approached his community map (see Figure 7). His younger age perhaps accounts for his more introspective view. A baby in the family was drawn at one end of a line. Connection to the mother (line and arrow) was made in explanation to me about who the baby *"belonged to"*. Questions about this belonging caused much confusion. Younger children are often the shared responsibility of many family members. Brolga produced a wonderful photograph of three women all with outstretched arms to an infant child: "[laughing] *they're fighting over the baby!*" admitting that if she didn't have the camera, she would have been doing the same. Both girls produced family representations with grandparents at the top and strong female representation (see Figures 6 and 8). The boys favoured more immediate family with parents a central feature. Hierarchies were represented in these maps, and in conversation children invariably placed grandparents in high esteem. Conversations on other occasions consistently pointed to significant older people passing knowledge. Both girls repeatedly referred to cultural knowledge such as learning about food sources, location and preparation coming from more than one person, on the female side, like mother, aunties, or grandmother. Boys referred to male counterparts on similar occasions such as knowledge about hunting and tracking.

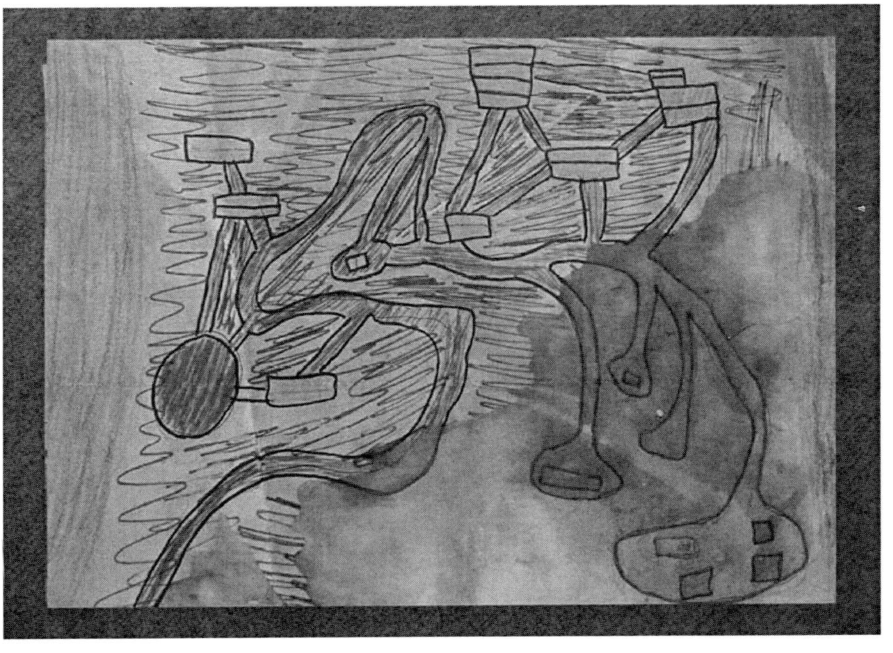

Figure 6. Barramundi's Map.

Barramundi began from his own 'camp' (home) perspective, drawing significant roads radiating out from his home. He showed particular interest in recent sightings of swans *...five, you know, I've never seen swans there before...* at the sewerage settlement ponds beyond the community tip, with further reference to a dead pelican found some time in the past. Like the others, he adopted a strong "living" approach in describing places through significant events.

Turkey adopted a standard format in consideration of a family tree (she remembered the existence of an official version with an aunt in a nearby town). She laughed at the daunting nature of the scope of her task, and chose only to map *...my community family.*

Kangaroo adopted a pictorial model of "family" linking members more by familiarity to each other rather than thoughts of descendent linkage. "Ownership" of the baby (my own misguided question) was settled by the arrow.

There is much diversity in family relationships and evidence of shared ancestry between communities hundreds of kilometres apart in this region.

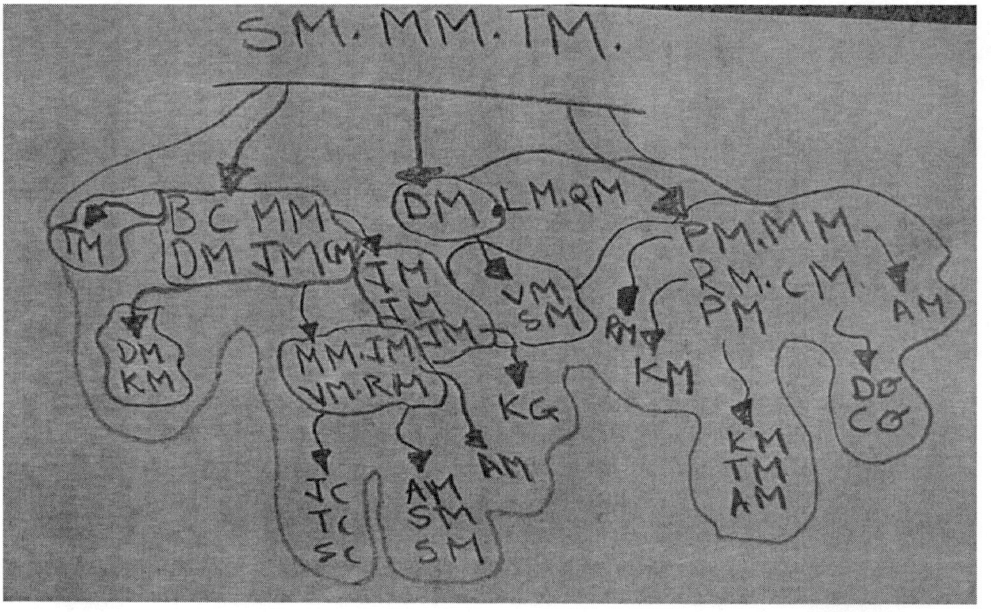

Figure 7. Turkey's Family Tree.

Figure 8. Kangaroo's Pictorial Family model.

Arguably, in comparison to Aboriginal groups in southern regions of Australia, family groups have remained more connected in this North Western region, where the destructive forces of settlement were less devastating. Racial variation in the community can be attributed to other factors such as migration of Japanese people to work as pearl divers in Broome. Brolga declared part-descendency from a Mexican pastoralist who settled in the area, whilst Barramundi has a white mother and Aboriginal father. To reflect his inter-racial parentage,

Barramundi stated: *"I need a white pen and a black pen!"* Suggestion of a pink pen produced the desired result for his *"Aboriginal family"* and his *"white family"* as he put it (see Figures 9 and 10). He represents himself and his sister as Aboriginal.

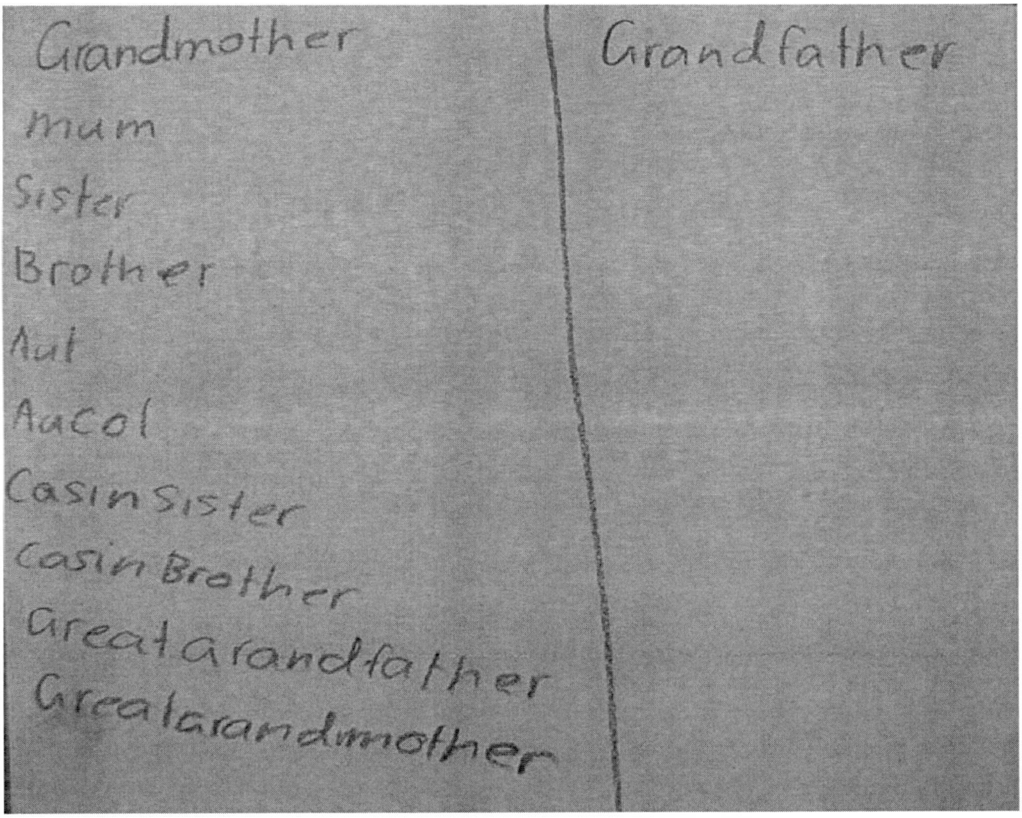

Figure 9. Brolga's Family Map.

Kangaroo adopted a pictorial model of "family" linking members more by familiarity to each other rather than thoughts of descendent linkage. "Ownership" of the baby (my own misguided question) was settled by the arrow.

Figure 10. Barramundi's Family Map.

Barramundi sat perplexed for some time when faced with the instruction to produce a family map. *I need a black pen and a white pen!* He declared before settling to the task, beginning with his Aboriginal father and white mother, representing himself and his sister as Aboriginal.

Reflecting the high value of social networks, all the children favoured people in the photographs they took. Turkey's personal photographs were all of people, primarily family. However, older people were noticeably absent from the children's pictures. Turkey stated: *"the old people are shy, and don't like their photos taken much"*. Brolga indicated that her photographs were missing pictures of her grandmother as she was: *"out hunting...for Turkey and Jurnta (Bush Onions) and stuff....with my sister...and my aunty...mum's older sister"*.

Social Interactions: Food

Food, and the settings and circumstances of procuring and eating, forms a significant part of the identity of the children of The Community, and serves as a link between people and cultural tradition. The Community has a store, sited in a central location. It is a meeting place as much as it is a shop. The store supplies basic food and grocery needs, trucked in during the dry season, often flown in during the wet. Families purchase through a credit system known as 'book-down'. Houses of The Community have stoves, but cooking often takes place outside on open fires, with food shared amongst larger family groups, sometimes involving people from different houses. Brolga's pictures revealed one such night, where eating takes place alongside talking: *"telling stories...funny stories, scary stories and stories from a long time ago"* and singing and playing guitar. *"Only the little kids dance...*[why?]*...we* [bigger kids] *get shame* [overcome with shyness]*"*. Another photograph depicted her mother preparing a large piece of meat *"Killer"* that she *"marinated... the night before...and chopped it up into a stew"*. The people of The Community are permitted to kill a certain number of cattle (*Killer*) for their own consumption. They hunt for a suitable animal and process the meat, which is then shared among different family groups.

Bush food forms an irregular, but common part of people's diets. *Jilji* by Pat Lowe and Jimmy Pike (1990) offers a detailed description of bush food, its preparation and its traditional significance to people in this region.

> At The Spring, I question Brolga and Turkey about food gathering:
>
> Ian: *How often do you come out here?*
> Brolga: [in thought for a moment] *Oh...quite a lot...and sometimes when we run out of book-down* [store credit]
> Ian: *So who do you come here with then?*
> Brolga: *My mum, my aunties...*

Bush food varies from multiple plant-based varieties to fauna of all sizes, from insects to Kangaroos and rare Emu. River areas in particular are abundant with life:

At The Station, the children work together washing handfuls of native mussels plucked from the weedy edges of the river.

Turkey: *We should have put 'em in water for a while, you know, so they'd spit out the mud.*

We later cook these in the coals of a fire before lying them open on a bed of broad leaves to cool before eating.

Children readily demonstrate their intricate knowledge of food preparation, but more significantly their understanding of location, connections with landforms and place in natural cycles, legends and stories. One such example of this interconnectivity and integral understanding of their country is revealed in the following conversation, in relation to gathering *Jurnta* (or 'Bush Onion' in its popular English nomenclature):

We're sitting in the middle of an open plain, cross-legged on a warm pile of sand. It's pleasantly hot with a cooling breeze. I watch Turkey rake the sand towards herself with open fingers, occasionally I see a *Jurnta*, a bulb about the size of a small peanut with a straggly dried grassy remnant, fall through her fingers onto the sand. She picks it up quickly and drops it into a cup. I find the taste mildly nutty and pleasant.

Ian: *How do you know they* [the Jurnta] *are here…who makes the sand pit?*
Turkey: *You see the cows... dance on the ground and make it soft, and Brolga…every time you see that, you see Brolga flying around, making a big noise… 'that's our spot' they're saying.*
Ian: *Who shows you how to do that?* [Brolga finds Jurnta, rubs skin off between thumb and forefinger and eats]
Brolga: *The old people, my grandmother, my aunties…Sometimes when you got a big tin like that* [shows coffee-tin size with hands] *you can fill it right up to the top.*
Ian: *Wow, that must take a long time!*
Brolga: *Yeah….but a lot of people just like to sit…just like doing it, you know?*

In this last line Brolga pointedly placed the act of gathering in a distinctly social context, steering away from my implications that time and quantity mattered more!

That same day we also eat *jargootagoota*, a tiny greenish berry growing on a parasitic vine. Brolga hands me a semi-transparent one *"He's a cooked* [ripe] *one"*. Turkey squeals with delight and calls me to another area, where she has already loaded her shirt front with yellowish *kampabaga* (Bush Tomato). Brolga shows me how to work her thumb under the spiky crown to remove it, then Kangaroo demonstrates and explains how to squeeze and split them into two halves, scooping out the black pith within. Black seeds fall back to the sand. He hands me the skin and flesh to eat, and I enjoy its mild sweetness. We are in the same area of sand hills as the spring and the location of the bones. This abundance of food, shelter from the hills and associated growth and the presence of flint-like stones *Jalypa* (traditionally used as cutting tools), scattered on the sand, collectively suggest that this is a site of huge significance.

SOCIAL INTERACTIONS: LANGUAGE

Traditional language of The Community is Walmajarri. It is one of many Aboriginal Language systems of Western Australia, several within this region. The children speak Aboriginal Kriol, a complex language system in itself borrowing from traditional language and English. Hudson, Carr and Reid (1996) attribute the loss of traditional languages and the development of Kriol to historical events like the mixing of races amongst children sent away from their homes, or the scattering of people during the Second World War. Sudden occurrences like the closing of Aboriginal missions meant that larger groups of children, with established Kriol acquired through racial mixing and emphasis on English acquisition, were returned to towns like Fitzroy Crossing where they mixed with children speaking mainly traditional languages. (1996). The Children's Kriol preserves traditional elements of language connecting to deep cultural knowledge. Much effort has been made in the Kimberley region to preserve and record traditional languages as well as recognising the value of Kriol, (e.g. Richards and Hudson, 1990; Hudson, Carr and Reid, 1996).

SOCIAL INTERACTIONS: RISK, RECREATION AND PLAY

Risk, and the tenuous nature of life in The Community, looms large as we pass three rolled car bodies along the way to The Station- a legacy of poor road quality (mostly seasonal, unsealed bush tracks of variable surface) and also testament to late night returns from town where alcohol may have been consumed. I found a former student of the school had recently died in a car accident at age seventeen. For a more positive slant on risk, Gerber (2001) writes of the notion of "wild places", of children being allowed more freedom to explore environments beyond their immediate home, and "develop a sense for the geography of wild places" (p.68). At The Station, Barramundi, with bare feet, climbs to the top of an enormous windmill, and leans out waving, hanging on with one hand. The teacher within me is horrified; the father next to me says nothing. The photographs he takes from up there are spectacular!

Children's photographs revealed a life of play and activity not dissimilar to children's after school lives in other parts of Australia. Climate, and the structure of the school day, tend to dictate the nature of activity and the times children engage in activity and play. School starts at 7 a.m. and concludes by 1 p.m.. In the hot season, children are inclined towards rest after school, wandering to other locations in the community beyond sundown. Groups of children of all ages, some in nappies, or older teenagers, meet until late at night on the basketball court, playing basketball, chasing or just sitting and talking, attracted, like the thousands of insects, to the floodlit setting. The cold season sees children spending more time wandering and playing after school, but coming home earlier as evenings are often breezy and hover around ten degrees centigrade (*cold* in comparison to balmy temperatures over twenty degrees celsius for hot season evenings!). During the cold season, children are more reluctant to get out of bed in the mornings. The girls of this chapter indicated a preference for the children's playground with Turkey's own photographs revealed clusters of girls round the public telephone. She declared that they spent a lot of time there *"just hanging round, or talking to friends in Fitzroy* [Crossing]*"*. Kangaroo indicated he liked to *"Go to Barramundi's house"*.

> I sit with Kangaroo and we discuss his collection of photographs taken the day before. He has five photographs of his bike:
>
> Kangaroo: *This is my bike*
> Ian: *Wow, five photographs, you seem to like this bike. Where do you go on your bike?*
> Kangaroo: *To friends house…it's got a flat tyre, you know, so I have to pump it up and go really really fast then it goes down.*
> Ian: *Do you ever fix the tyre?*
> Kangaroo: *Yeah, my dad helps me. My dad, he learns me everything.*
> Ian: *Oh? What else does dad teach you?*
> Kangaroo: *Lots of thing, fixing things…he teaches me to play guitar. He's a good guitar player.*
> [Dad is a well known local musician, but doesn't perform publicly now.]

Music, mostly country genre, features largely in the lives of people of the community. The school has a new band room, built a couple of years ago. Annual visits from Broome musicians in a residential teaching program support a vital part of the curriculum. A former community band experienced success and occasionally performed beyond the community. Aboriginal people in this region favour country music. They effectively use the story-telling capacity of the genre to capture significant aspects of life and history, stories of loss, alienation, hardship and discrimination (Walker, 2000). Most houses have an electronic music system of some form, and the children idolize black musicians in particular with posters on bedroom walls. Occasional discos run by local police and staged in the open on the basketball court, bring people out in large numbers. Kids of all ages gyrate and twist, mimicking dance videos with incredible rhythm and flexibility, whilst older people sit on the ground watching, talking and laughing.

SOCIAL INTERACTIONS: EDUCATION

School teachers are predominantly non-Indigenous, on one or two year contracts with high teacher turnover. More Aboriginal people of the community are training to become teachers, but most support comes from Aboriginal Education Workers (AEW's –Aboriginal teacher aides). Education here is geared towards learning to read and write, and communicate effectively in mainstream Australian society. It follows principles of "two-way" education (Teasdale and Teasdale, 1993). Functional literacies prevail and a specialized literacy program is taught across the school (see *Scaffolding Literacy,* Gray and Cowey, 2003). Self-determination ideals (Article 1 on the *International Covenant on Civil and Political Rights*) are a driving force behind adult education programs offered in the areas of education and business skills. Children appear to recognise some value and status attached to paid work, and recognize education as a link to this kind of employment. However, like most kids their age their answers in relation to questions and discussion about future jobs seem to echo adult sentiment rather than any drive or interest in work.

Ian: *Why is the school an important place?* [Brolga had just described it as important]
Brolga: *so you can learn...get an education*
Ian: *Why is an education important to you?*
Brolga: *So you can get a job...*
Ian: *What kind of job?*
Brolga: *Like...in the office* [referring to the community office]
Kangaroo: *Yeah...*[nods agreement, other two seem distracted]

The school Principal indicated that change and progress is slow, and educational futures are marred by retention difficulties at college level, beyond high school. Further education beyond high schooling is only offered in Perth, or Darwin, an extremely long way from close-knit family circumstances of The Community. Perth introduces a cold season like none these kids have ever known (ten to fifteen degrees centigrade cooler) and the temptation to stay back home during the mid-year break is often overwhelming. The adult education programs offer a chance for community members to move back into education at a later stage, whilst maintaining young families. The children's own thoughts about "future" place greatest emphasis on living in the community and *"being with family*".

For Aboriginal people living in this community, the move back to living in the desert, within traditional home country has had positive personal and cultural impact. History is drawn into the present through shared knowledge, stories, legends and memories. Deep understanding and learning is "situated" and "distributed" (Lave and Wenger, 1991), arising from social interactions of everyday life, integrated into social practice and emerging from joint perspectives (Gardner, 2000). In this way, for these children, events of history, importance of special places and social interactions all contribute to the life-world construct.

CONCLUSIONS

As they push and jostle in the back of the car, laughing, fighting, farting and picking on each other's personal differences, I'm reminded of the commonalities of childhood.

Their life-worlds exist at a complex junction of rich and turbulent histories and an interplay of cultures occurring through relationships with different people in different settings of place. It is within this vortex of colliding cultures that children make daily decisions, form opinions, build knowledge systems and forge self-identity. Children balance critical cultural knowledge and knowledge of the world beyond the community in the course of their everyday living. They learn skills vital to survival, promoting harmonious coexistence with the natural environment. It is no wonder, given the communication difficulties faced by older people of The Community and their *lived* experience of atrocities, that the indigenous children of The Community have become the interpreters, protectors and defenders of multiple cultures. In their future life-worlds these children will be the custodians of this expansive, multi-layered and collaborative knowledge, but for now, like any other children, they live for the moment.

Australian Aboriginal people are often wrongly considered as one homogeneous group. In reality, there is enormous geographical, social and historical diversity of Aboriginal culture covering thousands of kilometres from one end of Australia to the other. This chapter captures *one* glimpse of life as an Aboriginal child in Australia, unique to the context described here. Many Aboriginal children in other parts of Australia grow up removed from extended family networks and geographically disconnected from their cultural roots. There is no single life-world that encapsulates the wealth and diversity of these people and this account must be viewed in this light: a mere snippet of life, a view from the outside looking in, that might inspire thought and generate an interest in finding out more.

REFERENCES

Arthur, B. and Morphy, F. (eds.). (2005). *Macquarie atlas of indigenous Australia.* N.S.W.: Macquarie.

Banks, M. (2001). *Visual methods in social research.* London: Sage Publications.

Broome, R. (1982). *Aboriginal Australians, black responses to white dominance, 1788-2001.* NSW: Allen and Unwin.

Collier, J. and Collier, M. (1986). *Visual anthropology: photography as a research method.* Albuquerque: University of New Mexico Press.

Crawford, I. (2001). *We won the victory.* W.A.: Freemantle Arts Center Press

DECS, (n.d.). *Aboriginal culture and mathematics.* A handout from DECS Aboriginal Education, found at www.aboriginaleducation.sa.edu.au October 2005.

Edgar, I. (2004). Imagework in ethnographic research. In S.Pink, L. Kurti, and A.I. Afonso, (eds.), (2004). *Working images.* London: Routledge.

Emmison, M. and Smith, P. (2004). *Researching the visual.* London: Sage.

Gardner, H. (2000). *The Disciplined Mind.* New York: Penguin.

Gerber. R. (2001). Developing a sense of community and place in different cultural settings and environments. In M. Robertson, and R. Gerber, (eds.), *Children's ways of knowing.* (pp.62-78) Victoria: ACER.

Gray, B. and Cowey, W. (2003). *Key elements of scaffolding literacy.* Canberra: University of Canberra.

Harris, P. (1991). *Mathematics in a cultural context: aboriginal perspectives on space, time and money.* Geelong: Deakin University Press

Harper, D. (1998). An argument for visual sociology, in J. Prosser, (ed.). (1998). *Image based research,* London: Falmer Press. ch4 pp.24-41.

Hawke, S. and Gallagher, M. (1989). *Noonkanbah, whose land, whose law?* Fremantle, WA: Freemantle Arts Centre Press.

HREOC (n.d.). Article 1 on the *international covenant on civil and political rights* found at: www.hreoc.gov.au 4th January 2006.

Hudson, J., Carr, T. and Reid, M. (1996). *Languages of the kimberley region.* Broome: Catholic Education Office.

Jebb, M. (2002). *Blood, sweat and welfare - a history of white bosses and aboriginal pastoral workers.* Crawley, WA: University of Western Australia Press.

Kearins, J. (1981). *Visual spatial memory in australian aboriginal children of desert regions.* Cognitive Psychology, 13, 436-460.

Kearins, J. (1976). Skills of desert aboriginal children, in G. Kearney, and D. McElwaine, (eds.), *Aboriginal cognition*. New Jersey, USA: Humanities Press.
Kimberley Aboriginal Law and Culture Office. (1996). *Yirra, land, law and language.* Fitzroy Crossing, WA: KALACC.
Lewis, D. (2000). *Shapes on the wind*. Australia: Harper Collins.
Lewis, D. (1976). *Observations on route finding and spatial orientation among the aboriginal people of the western desert region of central Australia*. Oceania, Vol. 46, 4, 249-282.
Lave, J. and Wenger, E. (1991). *Situated learning, legitimate peripheral participation.* Cambridge, UK: Cambridge University Press.
Lefebvre, H. (1997). *The production of space*. Oxford, UK: Blackwell Publishers Ltd.
Lowe, P. and Pike, J. (1990). *Jilji, life in the great sandy desert*. Broome: Magaballa Books.
Lowe, P. and Pike, J. (1992). *Yinti*, Broome: Magaballa Books.
Lowe, P. and Pike, J. (1997). *Desert dog.* Broome: Magaballa Books.
Lowe, P. and Pike, J. (1999). *Jimmy and pat meet the queen*. Australia: Backroom Press.
Lowe, P. (2002) *Hunters and trackers of the Australian desert.* NSW: Rosenberg.
Marshall, P. ed. (1998) *Raparapa, stories from the fitzroy river drovers*. Broome: Magaballa Books.
Massey, D. (2005). *For space*. London: SAGE.
Massey, D. (1994). *Space, place and gender.* Cambridge, UK: Polity Press.
Milnes, P. and Truscott, K. (2002). *Teaching to the difference*. Western Australian Journal of Educational Research.
Pederson, H., Woorunmurra, B. (1995). *Jandamarra and the bunuba resistance*, Broome: Magaballa Books.
Pink, S. (2001). *Doing visual ethnography: images, media and representation in research.* London: SAGE.
Prosser, J. and Schwartz, D. (1998). Photographs within the sociological research process. In J. Prosser, (ed.), (1998). *Image-Based Research*, London: Falmer Press.
Richards, E. and Hudson, J. (1990). *Walmajarri-English Dictionary*, Darwin: SIL.
Rikkinen, H. (2000). Children's life-worlds. In M. Robertson, and R. Gerber, (Eds.). *The child's world, triggers for learning.* (pp.87-108). Victoria, Australia: ACER.
Rose, G. (2001). *Visual methodologies*. London: Sage.
Sanoff, H. (1991). *Visual research methods in design.* New York: Van Nostrand Reinhold.
Smith, C. (2004). *Country, kin and culture*, South Australia: Wakefield Press.
Tuan, Y.F. (1977). *Space and place: the perspective of experience.* London: Edward Arnold.
Teasdale, B. and Teasdale, J. (1993). Culture and schooling in aboriginal Australia. In E. Thomas, (ed.), *International perspectives on Culture and Schooling: A symposium of Proceedings.* (pp.174-196). London: Institute of Education.
Walker, C. (2000). *Buried country: the story of aboriginal country music*. Australia: Pluto Press.

In: Australia: Economics, Political and Social Issues
Editors: Lachlan J. Williams and Ethan N. Lee
ISBN: 978-1-60456-856-1

Chapter 7

Australian Citizenship: A Continuing State of Becoming

Margaret Robertson

Learning to be an Australian Citizen

In 2001 Australia celebrated one hundred years of Federation. Separate colonies and territories marked the previous one hundred years of European occupation, during which time each established a clear identity and separate set of ruling legislative bodies. Nationhood was slow to arrive and finally took place on January 1st 1901. The Proclamation of the Commonwealth of Australia was held in Centennial Park, Sydney and the first Federal Parliament sitting took place on May 9th, 1901. At the time Aboriginal Australians were denied the vote and were not recognised as full Australian citizens. They had to wait for this right until 1967. Women fared better. By contrast with most other Western nations, women already had the vote in some States at the time of Federation, and voting rights federally came shortly after in time for the 1902 elections. In so doing, white Australian women, who were among the first in the Western world to gain voting citizenship rights, provided inspiration for suffragettes in other nations. The history of Australia since this significant period has been one of changing population profile and ongoing expansion of the citizenship base.

Significant changes in the demographic profile of Australians and the ethnic origins of its people have occurred since Federation. However, the political structures remain as they were constituted in 1901, with clear demarcation between Commonwealth and States' rights. Funded by Commonwealth taxation, States have their own education, health, policing and transport systems. Hence, civic responsibilities vary between States. Each State takes pride in its identity with its own State and local government bodies developing and implementing policy.

Understanding Australian citizenship is embedded in this State and Commonwealth structure. Intersecting spaces of power, knowledge and policy are part of the complex place collectively recognised as Australia. For instance, there is no national curriculum for education. There are agreed goals for States to direct their policy towards (Australian

Education Council, 1989), and there are ways in which the Commonwealth can exert pressure on States through targeted funds and resource allocation. Illustrative of these power plays are the ways in which the Nation's Centenary of Federation was celebrated in schools around the country. All schools were recipients of teaching and learning materials designed to raise awareness of our heritage, our ideals for democracy, and what freedom and responsibility mean for individuals. Titled *Discovering Democracy* they are available in package form and linked to a well-maintained and ongoing web site (http://www.curriculum.edu.au/democracy/aboutdd.htm). Centralised curriculum teams in States have viewed these materials as important resources for classroom teachers with active promotion through professional development programs. In the 'Welcome page' to the web site the statement of the Commonwealth Minister of Education, Science and Training, Dr. Brendan Nelson, makes a number of significant points of relevance to this Australian study. He states,

> Civics and citizenship education is an important national priority. Our democracy depends on informed participation. Schools play a crucial role in helping to foster such participation. Young people need to understand the workings of our political and legal system and our history as a democratic nation so they can take their place as confident and open-minded citizens in a twenty-first century Australia.

He then goes on to establish the ground rules for dissemination of the materials and alludes to the responsibilities which States have for education. Allocated to States for implementation, Commonwealth moneys fund provision of buildings and staffing as well as the design, implementation and maintenance of the separate and independent States' curricula. He states,

> ...I am delighted that the high quality *Discovering Democracy* curriculum resources already provided free of charge to all schools have won such widespread acclaim in the education community. I am also pleased that the extensive *Discovering Democracy* professional development activities in States and Territories are helping teachers become increasingly more confident in handling civics and citizenship education.

The next part of the statement emphasises the importance of the State's role to ensure maintenance of active citizenship and participation of all Australians in the civic and democratic processes of the country. Accountability measures, implemented through reporting mechanisms between the relevant States and the Commonwealth departments, are designed to promote aligned outcomes. They are reflected in these statements:

> ...All education authorities agree that effective civics and citizenship education is central to contemporary schooling. The National Goals for Schooling in the Twenty-first Century agreed by all Education Ministers [1989], include an emphasis on educating students to understand their role in Australia's democracy. The National Goals state that students, when they leave school, should 'be active and informed citizens with an understanding and appreciation of Australia's system of government and civic life.' (Goal 1.4). In addition students are expected to 'have the capacity to exercise judgement and responsibility in matters of morality, ethics and social justice, and the capacity to make sense of their world, to think about how things got to be the way they are, to make rational and informed decisions about their own lives, and to accept responsibility for their own action' (Goal 1.3).

The statement then focuses on the ongoing tension between the traditional colonial heritage linked with British systems and traditions and the emerging Australian identity with its much broader cultural base. References to the changing population highlight the evolving profile of the Australian population and in so doing challenge the population to be reflective and reconsider past values and their currency in the current and predicted future contexts.

> *Discovering Democracy* helps students to learn about Australia's democratic heritage and the values underpinning it, including equality, liberty, fairness, trust, mutual respect and social co-operation. *Discovering Democracy* also helps students to learn how the Australian system of government and law operates and to explore what it means to be an Australian today. Students can discover how Australian national identity has changed over time and how it has come to encompass both cultural diversity and social cohesion. For example, students can analyse both how Federation in 1901 was followed by the White Australia policy and how our democracy has been immeasurably strengthened since then by the contributions of migrants from all over the world with their diverse heritages and cultures (See http://www.curriculum.edu.au/democracy/aboutdd.htm).

Part of this ability to be reflective and ready to embrace change is linked to past contributions of forward thinking political leaders who established the social and cultural climate for reform without violence. As the Minister observes,

> ...Australia has a rich democratic history. The secret ballot, for example, a nineteenth-century Australian invention, was once known around the world as 'the Australian ballot'. Australia was a world leader in payment of Members of Parliament and votes for women. The Australian practice of holding elections on Saturdays made voting easier. Our nation-building process, Federation, came about not through violence or civil war, but through the thoughtful democratic involvement of ordinary Australians. They literally constituted the nation by attending mass meetings, sending delegates to Conventions, and voting in referendums.

These ideals of 'ordinary' Australians formed a sound basis for cultural inclusion – a condition that has been sorely tested in the twenty-first century with the arrival in Australian waters of large numbers of Muslim refugees. Known as the 'boat people,' images of women and children clinging to rusty, old, barely seaworthy vessels from South East Asian ports has troubled many Australians. Some citizens have reacted to a perceived cultural crisis of increasing Islamic numbers in much the same way as the earlier generation of the World War Two era reacted to Asian immigration through the White Australia Policy. The re-emergence of right wing conservative politics has renewed significance in the Liberal government at the time of writing (2003) led by arch-conservative and long term politician John Howard. Current strong alignment with the U.S. Presidency of George Bush makes the positioning of Australia's future seem at a crossroads for many of its new citizens.

With global politics set to divide the West and the East at the time of writing, and post-Iraq War settlement still underway (2003) in the Middle East, domestic politics seem submerged by the international scene. However, the political alignment of Australia in the global arena does not reflect the views of more moderate and humanitarian minded Australians. These are the Australian citizens who have celebrated the arrival of refugees from war-torn Middle Eastern nations such as Afghanistan and Iraq. They condemn authorities for their harsh handling of refugees in remote and climatically harsh 'holding' centres while processing asylum applications. Marches for peace and fair treatment of refugees along with newspaper and media protests have drawn people into the open from all political backgrounds and ages. By so doing, they reflect that very precious element of democracy expressed in the Minister's statement for schools and education of young Australians:

> As Australians we have rights with which also come responsibilities. We should not exercise one without understanding the other. We live in a free, independent and democratic country which enables us to express our views while respecting and listening to those of others.

In brief, the nation of Australia born out of colonial times has a short and colourful history of emerging citizenship with roots in multiple national identities.

Herein lies the dilemma of perceived community antagonisms. To appreciate the complexity of the recent context and associated social change processes requires a look back at the way in which the demography has evolved. The next section of this chapter provides a brief overview of a nation in population transition. This is followed by some comment on the issues for Australian identity including references to the International Civic Education Study comparing views of fourteen-year-olds in twenty-eight countries. The chapter concludes with examples of the rhetoric in action.

Australia's Changing Population Profile

Until recent years, the United Kingdom remained the largest contributor to new settlers in Australia. Other European countries, especially Italy and Greece, formed the major component of the remaining group of settlers – until the dismantling of the White Australia Policy in 1958. Liberation from this policy, that positioned Australia in 'profound isolation' within the Asian-Pacific Region (Powell, 1988), made possible an 'Australianness' built on new alliances and cultural connections. In his Population Centenary Article published in the *Australia Year Book*, Hugo (2002) notes:

> ...the twentieth century saw a transformation of Australia from an overwhelmingly Anglo-Celtic, homogeneous population in which 95.2% had been born in Australia, the United Kingdom or Ireland, to one of the world's most multicultural societies by 1996 when 16.2% had been born elsewhere. Moreover, 19% were Australia-born persons with at least one parent born overseas and 8% had at least one parent born in a country in which English is not the main language. ... while the country remains Christian, the proportion of the population with no religious affiliation increased substantially, as did the proportion of the population with non-Christian religions.

Hugo's sources estimate 'the Asian origin population has increased from 0.3% in 1947 to 6.4% in 1999 and is anticipated to increase to around 10% in 2030 if trends in the late 1990s are continued'. This shifting migration influences Australian life in social, cultural, and economic terms. It also changes the demographic profile. Similar demographic trends to most Western nations followed during the twentieth century with significant population aging and fertility rates following the inter-war decline and post-war baby boom. However, recent waves of immigration have resulted in an increase in women compared with earlier years of European population. This feature as well as the longer life expectancy of women has led to a closing in the gap of males outnumbering women.

The other dimension of population characteristics that is relevant to a discussion of the meaning of Australian citizenship is the increasing concentration of people into the major cities. Hugo observes: 'At the 1933 Census 37.4% of Australians lived in rural areas, but by 1961 this proportion had halved, and in 1976 only 13.9% of the population was classified as rural'. The concentration of two-thirds of the nation's population in the major metropolitan areas notably, Sydney, Melbourne, Brisbane, and Perth creates a dynamic that can be seen to exclude 'ruralness' and in so doing a major part of Australia's nation building folklore.

Once a nation of farmers and miners in which wealth was strongly linked with the land and its resources, the newcomers help emphasise the emergent gap between urban and rural lifestyles. Further adding to this estrangement with the land has been the growing strength of the environmental movement and the greening of politics in industry and commerce. Nowadays, lifestyles firmly linked with cities and employment in industry and commerce result in diminished contact with the rural lifestyle. Traditional ideals of rural Australia associate with strong community ties, mateship, and strong camaraderie often linked with the Anzac (Australian and New Zealand Army Corps) legend. Albeit at the cost of Aboriginal Australians, the early pioneering farmers and miners were applauded for their courage in adversity – overcoming drought and floods and fluctuating global markets. Over the vast distances that characterise much of Australian settlement away from the coasts, there appeared to develop a bond of mutual dependency. Fuelled by the deliberately protectionist and racist White Australia Policy that seemed in part a response to the expanding number of Chinese, Melanesian and Japanese migrants in the north of the country and associated gold rushes of the southern States during the nineteenth century (Reynolds, 1999), a fear of invasion helped sustain a way of thinking that repelled difference.

In the 'new' era of ethnic diversity, multiple identities, inclusivity of faiths and values, the highly regarded exclusionary politics of the nineteenth and early twentieth-century Australian seem lost, or at least suppressed. What are emerging are authoritative voices that celebrate difference and celebrate indigenous Australians. Even modern day sporting heroes, who seem to preserve many of the pioneering shared views on working together and team play, are themselves under the lens of cultural and political correctness to observe tolerant behaviours towards difference both with spoken and non-verbal conduct.

Expanding Ethnicity, Human Rights and Education

The ascendancy of individualism over community values with lifestyles governed by materialism is central to the 'new' Australian identity (Wark, 1999). Embracing widely divergent cultural and ethnic origins has challenged the processes of assimilation evident during the period of strong European migration. There is the view that 'older' Australians see Asian migration introducing an 'otherness' and 'differentness' that seems too distinct for immediate culturally cohesive processes to take place – at least in the first generation.

However, this time around there is no protectionist policy for preserving past values and practices. Globalisation and issues of human rights bring nationalism under the microscope, as Australia has experienced with its policy of providing aid to small remote Pacific Island populations in return for 'solving' its immediate problem of providing refuge for asylum seekers. Farmers are subject to the laws of agribusiness, and industrial policy is largely governed by transnationals. In other words, national governments are no longer able to manipulate contexts in isolation from world opinion and trade practices. Even the United States of America – indisputably the most powerful nation on earth – has been forced to listen to international opinion regarding its views on what President Bush has described as the 'axis of evil' surrounding weapons of mass destruction in Iraq, North Korea and Iran.

Ultimately, understanding the significance of a modern democracy and its impact on everyday life depends on the quality and ongoing status of education. As Wark (1999: 310) states of civic life: 'Suburbia tolerates differences, but a more urbane culture actually encourages differences'. Arguing in favour of education as a major element likely to aid the emergence of a new Australian identity, which embraces difference, Wark notes the already observed link with growing individualism (1999: 310),

> An enlightening education is one that enhances differences. This enhanced difference is one of the reasons people feel that 'individualism' is on the rise, and that there is more alienation and less community. Learning weakens obedience to cultural authorities, including church and party. It weakens compulsory community based on sameness and encourages free association based on difference.

In other words inter-cultural learning and education help lift the fears in a nation, eliminate ignorance and promote shared understandings. Bellicose views can be diffused through talking and listening.

Writing on educational citizenship, Hogan (2000) distinguishes the 'particular' and 'common' interests of citizens that come under scrutiny when arguing the case for a republican version of a liberal democracy. How do we best develop 'individual' 'civic' virtue? He argues:

> ...it requires a form of education that is committed to the development of those social practices and forms of agency that promote an understanding of, and commitment to, republican and liberal democratic principles, strong but pluralistic forms of civic identity, and active and deliberative forms of civic agency. These objectives are recursively linked (171).

Implicit in Hogan's analysis is a reflection of the need for Australian citizenship education and the important role of agency in achieving that purpose. The changed profile of the population means that to be Australian in the twenty-first century is not so easily explained as it appeared in the first century of European settlement – except for the principles of underlying democracy and freedom to choose, along with rights and responsibilities, such as those emphasised in the Minister's statement quoted in the earlier section of this chapter. The following account of Australian students' knowledge and beliefs would appear to support the view of Hogan regarding the role of agency and should please the minister and his political colleagues.

Australian Fourteen-Year-Olds and the Civic Education Study

Conducted in twenty-eight countries, The Civic Education Study (Mellor et al., 2002) provides insights to the political thinking of fourteen-year-olds. Young Australians were included in the 1999 snapshot of opinion on their civic knowledge, attitudes and behaviour and the results indicate they 'already know a good deal about their democracy' (Mellor et al., 2002: xxii). Given that the survey occurred before the distribution of the *Discovering Democracy* (See: http://www.curriculum.edu.au/democracy) kit to schools, this conclusion is a positive reflection on schools and community agencies.

One aspect of citizenship in Australia helps the process of political awareness. Participation in the political process includes compulsory voting. This has always been a strong incentive for both the federal and state governments to be active education agents through provision of curriculum materials to all schools. They provide a rich collection of print, audio-visual and interactive materials that are both online and freely available and designed for primary and secondary age groups. Supported by expert curriculum staff, these resource materials strive for the following qualities:

- Modelling educational and pedagogical best practice.
- Informing teachers and providing scope for learners at different stages and readiness for new knowledge about civic responsibility and democratic processes.
- Providing ways of introducing knowledge about the cultural ways of an ethnically diverse society.
- Allowing for extended engagement as well as differing learning styles.
- Providing teachers and learners in schools throughout the country with professional quality materials at no real cost apart from making the time to include the content in the curriculum.

This review would suggest that Commonwealth and State government education authorities could believe that their materials are providing the 'right' kinds of materials to suit the perceived desirable lifelong citizenship learning in schools.

However, teachers surveyed in the Civic Education Study (Mellor et al., 2002: xxii) provided evidence of a different reality in their classrooms. Teachers indicated little support for 'imposed' materials: they like to choose materials with an 'open agenda' of topics. The following were the teaching approaches reported in the study:

- The key learning outcomes for teachers of civics education are certain values. (For example: teachers most want their students to learn to develop consciousness about the needs of the whole world, to develop honesty, to stand up for one's opinion, to ensure opportunities for minorities to express their own culture and to recognise the value of Australia as a nation.) Over ninety percent of teachers viewed each of these goals as important.
- Ninety-eight percent of teachers thought that 'teaching civic education makes a difference for students' political and civic development'.

- Ninety-eight percent of teachers thought that schools had a very important role in developing student attitudes and opinions.

This last comment is the crucial one. Human agency in the classroom relies on processes generated by local State's systems and Commonwealth government initiatives. However, the school's culture and most importantly the classroom itself are the contexts for learning. To make change work towards a more inclusive society that celebrates difference, the real target for promoting lifelong learning may need to be the teachers and a critical review of their teacher training and ongoing professional development.

The following data illustrate this point. In choice of topics which students have the 'opportunity to learn', teachers in the Civic Education Study responded 'considerable' or 'very much' at 40 percent or more to only 7 of the 20 Civics topics listed in the survey. The data show a strong emphasis on 'environmental issues (70 percent), important events in the nation's history (70 percent), cultural differences and minorities (56 percent), media (54 percent), citizens' rights and obligations (48 percent), human and civil rights (42 percent) and equal opportunities for men and women (41 percent)' (Mellor *et al.*, 2002: 115). Topics avoided according to teachers are economic issues, international organisations and comparative politics. By contrast, more than 80 percent of teachers indicated that more emphasis should be placed on 'knowledge about society' (112).

Teacher profiles and curriculum status help reveal why the topics may be narrowly selected. In the Australian context the most likely curriculum location for Civics Education is Studies of Society and Environment or subjects related to the social sciences. This curriculum strand has its origins in Social Studies and the 'Hobart Declaration of Schooling' in 1989 (Australian Education Council, 1989). A further factor is the non-compulsory status of this curriculum strand for Year 9 education, which most closely relates to the sampled fourteen year-old cohort.

In terms of background, half the teachers indicated that they held a major in history, a quarter had a major in geography, fourteen percent had an economics major and twelve percent had a major in politics. Their strengths were reflected in their choices of Civics topics. Of subjects taught in 1999, the study year, twenty-eight percent had taught geography, thirty-eight percent had taught Studies of Society and Environment and forty-two percent claimed to have taught History. Furthermore, most were teaching in non-government (private) schools where the trend has gone against decisions of the government sector to make Studies of Society and Environment non-compulsory after year 9 of schooling (fourteen years old). This means that the teaching of Civics Education is likely to be even more restricted than the figures would tend to indicate.

Online Case Study – Moving Towards Lifelong Learning

In Australia children no longer live in singular worlds of home, school and local neighbourhoods (Robertson and Gerber, 2001). Our research in Tasmanian schools (See: http://www.educ.utas.edu.au/users/ilwebb/Research) indicates the diversity of young people's experiences. They live in multiple worlds with varied value systems, accessing online information and communication at several different places. Home online access can be separate places for both parents, including parents' place of work; then there are the grandparents' places, local community access through libraries and net cafes, and friends' places. The skills are portable to wherever the Information Technology access may be present. Schools benefit from these self-motivated young people. They build personal networks of place and space and cope with multiple value systems with the apparent natural ease or spontaneity that often separates youthful worlds from adults. Our view is that central to managing these diverse worlds of young people are the pedagogical processes employed. Teachers producing the best outcomes work in partnerships with the children (Robertson and Fluck, 2002). They provide opportunities for children to contribute to the content of the classroom from skills and knowledge gained outside the classroom. The enrichment of this approach within classrooms is obvious. Children feel valued; members of the class learn from one another through expressions of diverse value systems, and opportunities exist for the teacher to lead their understandings into more meaningful and outward looking ways – and become good citizens in the process.

The clear message from these practitioner approaches appears to be that educational outcomes are best served in contexts where the teacher is provided sufficient latitude to reflect the ongoing change that characterises the worlds of young people. Not easily regulated by policy, popular culture moves at a pace that requires responsiveness and constructed realities.

My argument is that the contribution of the internet and Information and Communication Technologies to intercultural learning and expanded constructs of citizenship should not be underestimated. In Australia, young people embrace multiple realities in their day-to-day experiences of other lives and other places. These experiences contribute to their personal identities and with any luck enable harmonious living in neighbourhoods increasingly enriched by immigration and characterised by 'differentness' and 'otherness'. Approaching citizenship holistically and eclectically is at the core of successful teaching and learning within this great country of geographic and social contrasts.

With so many 'new' Australians, older citizens may well cling to their country of origin. However, rather than isolating their cultural practices to the privacy of home and neighbourhoods there are now active change agencies through community organizations and multicultural celebrations designed to share customs with others. Indeed the passing on of cultural traditions from such diverse sources is part of the emerging identity. Driven by globalisation and partly attributable to heightened media and educational awareness, there is a new sense of valuing 'otherness' and 'differentness'. Intercultural contact in the past may well have met with suspicion: now there is sharing and dialogue. Acceptance of different dress codes, religious practices, social interactions and eating habits are all surface features that are now commonplace within Australian society. At these simplest levels this may mean simple breaks with long held preferences/prejudices. At the same time, and to balance these positive observations, it must be stated that in this early period of the new century the wider community does not always welcome these 'different' claims to Australian citizenship. Patently evident of the transitional state of Australian citizenship have been reactions to international responsibilities for Middle East asylum seekers and refugees since widespread boat arrivals on our shores in the late 1990s. The hard line view taken by the Australian government to the processing of applications from these stateless families has been simultaneously greeted by horror and widespread condemnation as well as applause. Clearly, there is need for much more education about the global community in which we live. The inclusive society, which we espouse, may not yet have arrived in all quarters of the country.

Being an Australian Citizen in a Context of Difference: A Final Word

Many Australians struggle to articulate their identity in clear-cut terms. Nevertheless, they wear the badge of citizenship proudly and have a sense of belonging that seems unquestioned. They also display nationalism with great enthusiasm whenever the opportunity presents, such as at the 2000 Olympics held in Sydney or sporting events like cricket's World Cup. The difficulty in 'answering the question' of Australian citizenship seems to occur because of the continuing pioneering status of its population profile. There always seems to be a new frontier to negotiate. Since European settlement just over two hundred years ago the population has been continually re-profiling. The gradual shift from European dominance to embrace more aspects of its geographic positioning in the world has not diminished the 'old world' links so much as embellished them. The nation's people are still writing the script for Australian identity. Perhaps the difficulty of finding appropriate descriptors is best deflected by the personal qualities that are more clearly identifiable in Australian citizenship. Strongly embedded in the ideals of democracy, being an Australian in the twenty-first century brings expectations of a good life; a just life with access to high quality resources that protect personal freedoms and choice. The environment exists for these to happen. Learning to be an Australian citizen is about making the 'right' decisions.

References

[1] Australian Education Council (1989) *Common and Agreed Goals for Australian Schooling*, Hobart: Australian Education Council.

[2] Hogan, D. (2000) Educational citizenship. In W. Hudson and J. Kane (eds.) *Rethinking Australian Citizenship*, pp. 158-173, Cambridge: Cambridge University Press.

[3] Hugo, G. (2002) A century of population change in Australia, *Australian Bureau of Statistics,* Online at http://www.abs.gov.au

[4] Mellor, S., Kennedy, K. and Greenwood, L. (2002) *Citizenship and Democracy Australian Students' Knowledge and Beliefs. The IEA Civic Education Study of Fourteen Year Olds,* Camberwell: ACER Press.

[5] Powell, J. (1988) *An Historical Geography of Modern Australia. The Restive Fringe,* Cambridge: Cambridge University Press.

[6] Reynolds, H. (1999) *Why Weren't We Told*, Ringwood: Viking Penguin Books Australia.

[7] Robertson, M. and Fluck, A. (2002) *Children, On-Line Learning and Authentic Teaching Skills in Primary Education.* Refereed paper presented at the Australian Association for Research in Education Conference, Brisbane, December, published online at www.aare.com.au

[8] Robertson, M.E. and Gerber, R. (eds.) (2001) *Children's Ways of Knowing: Learning through Experience,* Camberwell: ACER Press.

[9] Wark, M. (1999) *Celebrities, Culture and Cyberspace*, Annandale: Pluto Press Australia.

In: Australia: Economics, Political and Social Issues
Editors: Lachlan J. Williams and Ethan N. Lee
ISBN: 978-1-60456-856-1

Chapter 8

EFFECTIVENESS: A CONTRIBUTION FROM AUSTRALIAN NON-GOVERNMENT ORGANIZATIONS

Linda Kelly

ABSTRACT

Australian NGOs have in recent years attempted to engage with the aid effectiveness debate through joint research and publication of the NGO Effectiveness Framework. At the same time the wider aid world has begun to approach aid effectiveness more broadly, with an emerging agreement that aid effectiveness is the result of a complex set of processes and interrelationships. This is in line with the findings from the Australian research. In response to these emerging themes some Australian NGOs are now experimenting with alternative organizational forms and different ways of doing development in order to try to promote more effective aid. Some challenges remain however, including the questions of how to assess effectiveness from the perspective of the beneficiaries of aid, how to best measure effective aid and what reliable evidence we have about the effectiveness of one aid interventions over another? As NGOs in Australian continue to contract with the Australian Government and other donors for aid delivery they continue to have to find space to address these debates and to challenge the more restricted views of those donors.

INTRODUCTION

Non-Government Organizations (NGOs) working in international aid and development have been concerned with the effectiveness of their interventions for some years now. This has resulted in several stages or phases of activity. Prior to 2000 the NGOs were more concerned with ***'identifying'*** their unique effectiveness (Fowler, 1997). Discussions focused on the specific contribution of NGOs and what they offered that could not be duplicated by the official aid donors. Alongside that debate emerged the concern with how to demonstrate and ***'measure'*** the effectiveness of NGOs (Oakley, 1999; Roche, 1999; Madon, 2000). More recently NGOs, certainly in Australia, have been concerned with ***'proving'*** their effectiveness. There has been considerable engagement with the Australian Government around assessment of NGO interventions (AusAID 1995; Crooke, 1996; Australian National Audit Office, 1996; AusAID, 2002). In recent years a conservative political climate has only heightened this scrutiny, with NGOs spending increased time and resources responding to requests related to accountability. Currently NGOs and the wider donor and official aid sectors, appear to be engaged in discussion about ***'defining'*** what effectiveness means. It appears that the debates have now moved to a more fundamental and essential level. And at this level there appears to be some emerging challenges and ideas which may pave the way for better identification, measurement and proof of effective aid and development.

This chapter will explore some of those emerging understandings through a review of the research that has been undertaken in Australia among the NGO community about effective development work and the emerging new forms of practice that have developed from this research. Considering some other relevant research and findings from the intentional aid community more generally, it will conclude with examination of the remaining challenges in this ongoing exploration of effective aid delivery, for NGOs in Australia and beyond.

Effective Aid among Australian NGOs

Spurred by the regular inquiry from government and elsewhere about the effectiveness of their aid and development interventions, in 2002 Australian NGOs, under the leadership of the Australian Council for International Development (ACFID)[1] committed themselves to research about what made for effective NGO practice in development. How could this be assessed across organizations for the purposes of accountability, and therefore how that practice could be improved?

The methodology for this research has been described in detail elsewhere (Kelly & Chapman, 2003; ACFID, 2002). It started with a process of appreciative inquiry or a focus upon best practice examples. It then expanded to field based and other studies to verify and expand the original findings. The findings have proven themselves surprisingly reliable and valid over a range of organizations and development situations. Several Australian NGOs committed resources to the process and the Australian NGO community committed itself to the results of the research.

The key findings were captured in a document titled the Australian NGO Effectiveness Framework (ACFID 2003). The Framework listed agreed principles, program strategies and field based standards that the Australian NGOs agreed promoted the most effective practice across the sector. In addition to the development of this Framework, the research identified two important conclusions:

> Australian NGO effectiveness is more than the result of implementation of designs and plans or other areas of program engagement. It is also a product of the organizational principles, policies and strategies of development. There are a number of practice standards that Australian NGOs agree should apply to field programs or other forms of engagement, in order to promote effective outcomes. However these standards alone are insufficient to describe and explain effectiveness in Australian NGO work, and must be

[1] ACFID is the peak body for non-government organisations in Australia. It was formerly known as the Australian Council for Overseas Aid (ACFOA).

> understood in light of the aforementioned principles, policies and strategies (ACFOA, 2003)

The results indicated that Australian NGOs are part of an established sector, with shared principles, features and standards and that they are working towards common outcomes. At the same time, each Australian NGO is an autonomous organization, operating from a particular philosophy and value base and with particular approaches and contributions to make to development. The critical finding of the research was that Australian NGO effectiveness can only be understood as a combination of such factors. These include what NGOs do, their field and program work and their advocacy and other influencing work. It also includes who they are, their values and principles and their approaches to engaging and working with people and other organizations. The research concluded that

> The more synergistic all these features, the more effective the overall outcomes of the agency for poor people and communities (ACFOA, 2003).

The more typical approach to measuring the performance of NGOs, and by extension other aid delivery mechanisms relies on the assumption that organisations are simply what they do, that is, that an aggregation of activity assessments is a good enough proxy for a judgement of organisational performance. However this research suggested that effective outcomes require that the program and influencing work of an organisation is congruent with the identity of the organisation, the values it represents and its approach to intervention.

The Broader Environment

As Australian NGOs have grappled with this notion of effectiveness in their development work, related and complementary ideas have emerged from other parts of the aid world. The emerging discussions seem to confirm the view that aid effectiveness is the result of a complex set of processes and interrelationships (Carlson et al, 2005; Smillie & Hailey, 2001; Moore et al, 2001; Acharya & Thomas, 1999).

More than the Sum of the Whole

There now seems to be some agreement among donors and NGOs that assessment of effectiveness has to go beyond the outcomes (however well measured) of single activities, projects or programs (Lehtinen, 2002; UNDP, 2003; Hofmann et al, 2004; Interaction, 2006) and that the focus should be on outcomes that bring together results of numerous development activities. Increasingly the assessments being undertaken of the work of donors and multilateral organisations are pointing to the need to examine their field based achievement and also the synergy and calibre of internal systems and the values and approaches underlying their work (Scott, 2004; Stewart, 2003; DFID 2003). In particular some of the examination that has been made of effective public service reform and effective improvement in governance points to critical features of the donor partner relationship which, in part, are about the values and program strategies of the donor agency (DFID, 2003; Schacter, 2001).

Process and Approach May Be More Important than Activity

International donors are increasingly focusing on "how' things are being done as much as 'what' is achieved. The World Bank and the Development Assistance Committee of the OECD now both speak of the importance of donor harmonization, partner government ownership and partner government capacity as being critical aspects of the effectiveness and quality of aid (World Bank, 2005). There are various contributions to this area from different sectors, with the humanitarian and micro finance areas having developed their own focus on process alongside outcomes as a measure of aid effectiveness (Helms & Latortue, 2004; Hofmann, et al, 2004). There appears to be greater agreement that processes and relationships may be as important, indeed may even be more important, than the technical quality and nature of the intervention that is made (Eyben, 2005). A report by the peak body for British NGOs that researched effective work among those organizations concludes that the *"Quality of an NGO's work is primarily determined by the quality of its relationships with its intended beneficiaries" (BOND 2006).*

Effective from Whose Perspective?

Recent studies suggest that assessment of effective aid depends to some degree who is defining the notion of effectiveness (Masud & Yontcheva, 2005; Fielding et al, 2006; Nancy & Yontcheva, 2006). For example, the economic literature concludes that aid has been of limited effectiveness in contributing to stable economic growth in poor countries. However others conclude that that same aid has been highly effective in achievement of key social development gains such as improvements in health, education and well-being (Fielding et al, 2006). What is currently missing from this aspect of the debate is the perspective of the beneficiaries. The discussion remains dominated by those doing the intervening. If partner organizations, recipient governments or beneficiary communities were given the opportunity to define effective aid, this may lead to very different assessments (Adong, 2005; Kilby, 2006). Yet these voices are largely silent in the current aid effectiveness dialogue.

How Should Effectiveness Be Measured?

In line with the above debates, there has been considerable discussion about how to assess or measure effectiveness. This has led to the development of various frameworks and or standards for determining 'good' aid, discussed in details in chapter 1. They also include the statutory and imposed frameworks within which NGOs and charities operate, such as the Australian Government accreditation process for NGOs in Australia (AusAID 2007). It also includes the voluntary principles and codes utilized in humanitarian and other development sectors, such as the Red Cross Code of Conduct and the SPHERE standards. There has also been considerable interest in monitoring and evaluation approaches that provide an assessment of aid effectiveness. Official aid donors have tended to rely on linear models of performance assessment such as Results Based Management. However as aid effectiveness is being understood as a more complex concept, this simplistic measurement tool is being challenged (Wallace & Chapman, 2003; Brehm, 2004; Eyben, 2005). The interest is in developing more sophisticated models which take account of complexity and interrelationships in assessment of aid and development. One example has been the various explorations of impact in recent years. The 'impact' discussion has suggested that perhaps aid agencies should be assessing what changes have occurred in people's lives rather than the activities undertaken by those agencies (Hofmann et al, 2004; Woodhill & Pabari, 2006) (see more details in Chapter 1). That is, that aid effectiveness is related to its relevance and significance for people within their context and their own definition of their needs, rather than being something which can be assessed by an external and supposedly objective measure.

The Evidence Base

Finally the broader debates seem to suggest that there still is not a lot of evidence on which to base the pursuit of more effective aid. Despite many years of discussions and focus on aid effectiveness which have resulted in many ideas and ideological approaches to aid effectiveness, there is limited applied research and valid evidence about what does lead to effective aid. This is true for donors and official aid providers as much as the NGOs (Radelet, 2006).

New NGO Developments

Since the initial development of the NGO Effectiveness Framework, Australian NGOs have been further engaged in consideration of this notion of effectiveness. Considerable resources have been dedicated in some organisations to operationalising the Effectiveness Framework and the ideas described above are obviously providing a further influence on some of the new developments. There are now several examples within the Australian NGO sector where there are new organizational forms or different ways of 'doing' development. For example, Save the Children Australia is experimenting with using multiple frameworks to assess their effectiveness, trying to approach the issue from many directions to understand the difference they are making. They have developed a Program Quality Framework that considers their work from the perspectives of strategic relevance, sector standards (including the original NGO Effectiveness Framework) and rights based approaches, gender, sustainability and risk assessment frameworks and impact assessment.

As another example, Oxfam Australia have worked extensively on developing their 'one-program' approach to development intervention, which brings together the elements of development, advocacy and humanitarian work across local, national and international locations to suggest that effective change needs to be understood as action across all these dimensions. So effectiveness has many aspects, interrelated and complex, takes time to achieve and is located across multiple settings. The emerging debates in the industry have also challenged and changed the way aid and development work is practiced. Some newly emerging NGOs have chosen to focus their planning and management around the notion of impact. The International Youth Parliament, a developing youth focused network concerned with giving voice to young people in order to promote their engagement in effective development, has started with impact as the core driver for the organization and is developing systems and activities from that base. Rather than start with what they can do or what development agencies typically do, they are starting from a vision of effective change and working backwards to development strategies and interventions that will lead them in that direction.

As people have explored the idea of relationships being central to effective development new organizational forms are being developed. The new Rwanda Australia Association, developed as a non-NGO development agency, focuses its work not around controlling the flow of resources and capacities from Australian to Rwanda, but rather in enabling and connecting people in relationship between the two countries to allow both to work for change according to agreed principles in each country. Caritas Australia is undertaking a similar experiment in developing a new program area which is fundamentally focused on building relationships between actors from Australia and PNG, for them to develop relationships and ways of working together. The anticipated outcomes are still emerging, but the expectation is that both sides of the partnership will change and develop through the process.

Some organizations have become concerned with wider assessment of their effectiveness. The Anglican Board of Mission in Australia (ABM) has focused on the challenge of coherence around values and practice. ABM has been establishing methods to have others assess their values and the degree to which this is reflected in their capacity and actions as an organization. Oxfam Australia has recently begun to try to assess their work from the perspective of bottom-up accountability. Do the intended beneficiaries consider that the interventions have been effective? Likewise Caritas Australia is in the process of redeveloping its entire program management system in order that it reflects their partner reality and ways of operating, rather than the donor expectations and needs for accountability. So partners will determine how projects and programs will be designed and managed and people will make the assessments about the outcomes and impact of those interventions.

THE NEXT CHALLENGES

Australian NGOs have been engaged for some years in this examination and practice of more effective development and recent practice examples mentioned above suggest that they have continued to respond to emerging challenges, developing new practices and new organisational forms. Some key challenges remain however. While there is some experimentation with bottom up accountability among NGOs, much still remains to be explored to understand effectiveness from the perspective of those intended as the beneficiaries of the interventions (Chambers, 2005; Shivji, 2006).

Alternative organisational forms are emerging among some NGOs; however recent assessments suggest that they still have a long way to go in moving outside the well known aid and development 'box' (Sorgenfrei & Wrigley, 2005). Indeed as NGOs are increasingly being 'contracted' by donor governments, and thereby forced into conventional approaches to aid delivery, there is some danger that the room they have to experiment with more effective forms of aid is being limited (Wallace, 2005; Chambers, 2005). Australian NGOs need to find ways to promote their difference and to engage with donors while also challenging those organizations around their aid approaches.

Finally and perhaps most urgently, monitoring and evaluation processes need to be focused towards more useful and comprehensive assessment of aid effectiveness. While ideological debates will continue about definitions and approaches to effective delivery, the answers are only likely to emerge from research and evidence based examples. Such evidence relies on appropriate and relevant systems of performance assessment for aid interventions. The tools and approaches need to be in place so that the debates can continue from a position of information and knowledge. NGOs need to invest in researching their approaches to aid delivery and need to increase their monitoring of outcomes and their impact for people (Hofmann, et al, 2004).

So, while Australian NGOs have been responding to the challenge of effective aid and have much to demonstrate to the wider sector, they need to maintain their journey and experimentation. The invitation needs to be extended to partners and community people as well as donors and multilateral organisations, to be part of that journey. Australian NGOs need to find ways to lead and also to listen.

REFERENCES

Acharya, S. & Thomas, L. (1999), "Finding a pathway: understanding the Work and Performance of NGOs in Ahmedabad, India", *Occasional Papers series*, No. 22, INTRAC, Oxford.

ACFOA (2002) "Research report for the ACFOA strategy on quality", NGO Effectiveness Conference, July, Australian Council for Overseas Aid, Canberra.

ACFOA (2003), "Communiqué from the ACFOA Conference on promoting NGO Effectiveness", Australian Council for Overseas Aid, Canberra

Adong, R. (2005), "The current procedures and policies dominating the disbursement of aid: are they building strong relationships and enabling NGOs to meet their stated aims?" research report funded by ESCOR and DIFD, United Kingdom.

AusAID (1995) *Review of the Effectiveness of NGO Programs*, Goanna Print, Canberra.

AusAID (2002) *Rapid Review of NGO Project Quality Work-in –Progress Report* No 5, Quality Assurance Group Program Evaluation Section, Office of Review and Evaluation, Goanna Print, Canberra.

AusAID (2007) "Accreditation for Non-Government Organizations", Canberra. *http://www.ausaid.gov.au/ngos/accreditation.cfm*

Australian National Audit Office (1996) Accounting for Aid – the Management of Funding to Non-Government Organizations, Australian Agency for International Development Audit Report, Canberra.

BOND (2006), "A BOND *Approach to Quality in Non-Governmental Organizations: Putting Beneficiaries First"*, August, United Kingdom.

Brehm, V., (2004), "Autonomy or Dependence? North-South NGO Partnerships", *INTRAC briefing Paper No. 6,* Oxford.

Carlson, C. de Lamalle, J.P., Fustukian, S., Newell-Jones, K (2005) "Improving the delivery of health and education services in difficult environments: lesson from case studies", International Development Health Systems Resource centre, DFID, United Kingdom.

Chambers, R. (2005) "Aid and Administrative Capacity", in *Ideas for Development*, Earthscan, Oxford.

Crooke, M. (1996), "NGOs and Official Development Assistance", in P. Kilby (ed) *Australia's Aid Program: Mixed Messages and Conflicting Agendas*, Monash Asia Institute and Community Aid Abroad, Melbourne.

DFID (2003) "Better government for poverty reduction: More effective partnership for change", Consultation document, Department for International Development, United Kingdom.

Eyben, R. (2005), "Donors' Learning Difficulties: Results, Relationships and Responsibilities", *IDS Bulletin Vol 36 No 3* September, Institute of Development Studies, United Kingdom.

Fielding, D., McGillivray, M. & Torres, S. (2006) "A Wider Approach to Aid Effectiveness", UNU-WIDER, Research paper No. 2006/23, February, United Nations University - WIDER, Helsinki.

Fowler, A. (1997) *Striking a Balance*, Earthscan/INTRAC, London.

Helms, B. & Latortue, A. (2004), , *Aid Effectiveness Initiative,* CGAP, Washington. "Elements of Donor Effectiveness in Microfinance: Policy implications"

Hoffmann, C., Roberts, L., Shoham, J & Harvey, P. (2004) "*Measuring the Impact of humanitarian aid",* Humanitarian Policy Group, ODI, United Kingdom.

Interaction (2006) "NGO Impact Initiative", *Synthesis Report,* October, United States.

Kelly, L. & Chapman, R. (2003) "*Australian NGOs and AusAID – partnerships for quality assurance and improving effectiveness",* Presentation to the joint French and DAC Working Party on Evaluation, Workshop on Partners in Development Evaluation – Learning and Accountability 25 – 26 March, OECD, Paris.

Kilby, P. (2006) "Accountability for Empowerment: Dilemmas Facing Non-Governmental Organizations", *World Development* Vol. 34, No. 6, 951-963.

Lehtinrn, T. (2002) "*Measuring the performance of EC development cooperation: lessons from the experiences of international development agencies",* DFID, United Kingdom.

Madon, S. (2000) "International NGO: Networking, Information Flows and Learning", London School of Economic and Political Science, *Development Information Working Paper Series, Working Paper No. 8,* London.

Masud, N. & Yontcheva, B. (2005), "Does Foreign Aid Reduce Poverty?" IMF Working *Paper*, May, Washington.

Moore, M. H., Brown, L. D., & Honan, J. P. (2001) "Towards a Public Value Framework for Accountability and Performance Management for International Non-Governmental Organizations" paper presented at the Hauser Center/ Keio University Workshop on 'Accountability for International Nongovernmental Organizations', November, Harvard University.

Nancy, G & Yontcheva, B. (2006) "Does NGO Aid Go to the Poor?", *IMF Working Paper*, February, Washington.

Oakley, P. (1999) Danish NGO Impact Study: A Review of Danish NGO Activities in Developing Countries – *Synthesis Report*, INTRAC/BECH Distribution, Oxford/Copenhagen.

Radelet, S. (2006), "The Role of the World Bank in Low-Income Countries." In Nancy Birdsall (ed.) *Rescuing the World Bank, Center for Global Development*, Washington.

Roche, C. (1999) *Impact Assessment for Development Agencies,* Oxfam. Oxford.

Saltmarshe, D., Ireland, M. & McGregor, J. A. (2003) "The Performance Framework: A Systems Approach to Understanding Performance Management", *Public Administration Development*, 23, 445-456.

Scott, A. (2004) "Assessing Multilateral Effectiveness", International Division, Department of International Development, United Kingdom.

Schacter, M. (2001) "The Heart of the Matter: Donors, Development Assistance, and Public Sector Reform", *Policy Brief No. 10,* February, Institute on Governance, Canada.

Shivji, I. (2006), "The Silences in the NGO Discourse", *Pambazuka Special report 14*, Fahuma, Oxford.

Smillie, I & Hailey, J (2001) *Managing for Change: Leadership, Strategy and Management in Asian NGOs*, Earthscan, London.

Sorgenfrei, M & Wrigley, R. (2005) "Building Analytical and Adaptive Capacities for Organizational Effectiveness", *Praxis Paper No.7*, INTRAC, Oxford.

Stewart, F. (2003) "Evaluating Evaluation in a World of Multiple Goals, Interests and Models", Paper presented at the fifth Biennial World Bank Conference on Evaluation and Development "Evaluating Development Effectiveness: Challenge and Ways Forward" July, Washington.

UNDP (2003), *Development Effectiveness Report*, UNDP, New York.

Wallace, T. (2005) "NGO Dilemmas: Trojan horses for global neoliberalism", from Socialist Register, *www.yorku.ca/socreg*

Wallace, T. & Chapman, J. (2003) "Is the way aid is disbursed through NGOs promoting a development practice that addresses chronic poverty well? An overview of an on-going research project." Presentation at STAYING POOR: CHRONIC POVERTY AND DEVELOPMENT POLICY, International Conference, IDPM, University of Manchester, 7 to 9 April 2003. *http://idpm.man.ac.uk/cprc/Conference/conferencepapers.htm*

Woodhill, J. & Pabari, M. (2006) "The managing for Impact Approach", Practice report, Capacity org. *http://www.capacity.org/en/layout/set/print/content/view/full/1935*

World Bank (2003) "Multi-partner Evaluation of the Comprehensive development framework", *Report 25882,* May 16, World Bank, Washington.

World Bank (2005), "Paris Declaration On Aid Effectiveness: Ownership, Harmonization, Alignment, Results And Mutual Accountability", *Board Report,* April, World Bank, Washington.

In: Australia: Economics, Political and Social Issues
Editors: Lachlan J. Williams and Ethan N. Lee
ISBN: 978-1-60456-856-1

Chapter 9

AUSTRALIA: BACKGROUND AND U.S. RELATIONS

Bruce Vaughn
Specialist in Asian Affairs Foreign Affairs, Defense, and Trade

SUMMARY

The Commonwealth of Australia and the United States are very close allies. Australia shares similar cultural traditions and values with the United States and has been a treaty ally since the signing of the Australia-New Zealand-United States (ANZUS) Treaty in 1951. Australia made major contributions to the allied cause in both the first and second World Wars and has been a staunch ally of Britain and the United States in their conflicts.

Under the former Liberal government of John Howard, Australia invoked the ANZUS treaty to offer assistance to the United States after the attacks of September 11, 2001, in which 22 Australians died. Australia was one of the first countries to commit troops to U.S. military operations in Afghanistan and Iraq. In October 2002, a terrorist attack on Western tourists in Bali, Indonesia, killed more than 200 persons, including 88 Australians and seven Americans. A second terrorist bombing, which killed 23, including four Australians, was carried out in Bali in October 2005. The Australian Embassy in Jakarta, Indonesia, was also bombed by members of Jemaah Islamiya (JI) in September 2004.

Kevin Rudd, of the Labor Party, was elected prime minister on November 24, 2007. While Rudd has fulfilled an election promise to draw down Australian military forces in Iraq and has reversed Australia's position on climate change — by signing the Kyoto protocols — relations with the United States remain very close. Rudd has initiated a review of Australia's defense policy that is expected to reaffirm Australia's traditional view that the United States is a key source of stability in the Asia-Pacific region.

The previous Howard Government and the U.S. signed a bilateral Free Trade Agreement (FTA) and negotiated a Treaty on Defense Trade Cooperation that would require Senate ratification to come into force. Despite the strong strategic ties between the United States and Australia, there have been some signs that the growing economic importance of China to Australia may influence Australia's external posture on issues such as Taiwan. It is likely that Australia would not support a policy of containment of China if the United States sought this.

Australia plays a key role in promoting regional stability in Southeast Asia and the Southwest Pacific. Australia has led peace-keeping efforts in the Asia-Pacific region, including East Timor and the Solomon Islands, and has supported U.S. efforts and worked closely with key regional states in the war against terrorism in Southeast Asia. These actions demonstrate Australia's resolve to promote stability in Southeast Asia and the South Pacific. Australia has also worked closely with Indonesia to counter terrorism in Southeast Asia.

RECENT DEVELOPMENTS

The Rudd Government

In November 2007, Kevin Rudd was elected prime minister, ending former Prime Minister John Howard's term in office that began in March 1996. Prime Minister Rudd has reaffirmed Australia's and the Labor Party's commitment to its alliance relationship with the United States even as he has differed with the United States on Iraq and climate change. Rudd has moved to draw down Australian military forces in Iraq while Australian troops remain in Afghanistan. The Australian left has grown increasingly disillusioned with the war in Iraq and views U.S. foreign policy as increasingly unilateralist. U.S. policies on Iraq, Guantanamo Bay, and Abu Ghraib appear to have negatively affected the Australian public's perceptions of American power. Despite this, support for the ANZUS alliance with the United States remains strong among most Australians.

Minister for Defence Joel Fitzgibbon announced the commissioning of a new Defence White Paper for Australia on February 22, 2008. The white paper process will include a set of accompanying reviews and a community consultative process to underpin the white paper. The white paper is not expected until some time in the first half of 2009. Such a review could have significant implications for Australia's defense policy and procurement in the future.[1]

The fact that Rudd chose to visit the U.S. on his first visit abroad as the opposition leader, prior to becoming prime minister, signaled that, despite potential differences on Iraq and climate change, he views the U.S. strategic alliance to be of central importance to Australia. Rudd is generally viewed as part of the moderate element within the Labor party.[2] Rudd may take a very active role in foreign policy given his former career in the Department of Foreign Affairs and Trade. Rudd may also place relatively more emphasis on the United Nations than Howard did.

Australia's External Posture

During the 2007 election campaign, Rudd identified maintaining a strong alliance with the United States, engaging more fully with Asia, and seeking to play a more active role in

[1] Cynthis Banham, "Rudd to Shake Up National Security," *The Sydney Morning Herald,* January 19, 2008.
[2] Greg Sheridan, "Alliance Safe with Labor," *The Australian*, April 21, 2007.
policy.

the United Nations as the three pillars of Australian foreign policy.[3] Australia's Defence Update 2007, prepared under the previous government, appears to have changed Australia's policy emphasis on China's military buildup by identifying it as potentially leading to "misunderstanding and instability" in the region.[4] Some observers of Australian foreign policy have speculated that Australia increasingly will have a difficult time developing a robust trade relationship with China while at the same time continuing its close strategic and defense relationship with the United States. Former Australian Defence Minister Brendan Nelson traveled to Beijing in July 2007 to explain to the Chinese that the Defence Update, as well as growing trilateral ties between Australia, Japan, and the United States, did not mean that Australia in any way supports a policy of containment of China. Australia and Japan signed a Joint Declaration on Security Cooperation in March 2007. [5]

Subtle shifts in Australia's position relative to China may emerge under Rudd. He is expected to take a direct interest in Australia's foreign policy toward China. As a Mandarin speaker Rudd is well informed on China policy but will be conscious of not wishing to be perceived as too close to the Chinese by Australian voters or the United States. Rudd was posted to Beijing as a diplomat and worked as a consultant on China in the private sector. According to some observers, Rudd is seeking a balance through strong ties with both the United States and China.[6]

Defense Policy

Minister for Defence Joel Fitzgibbon announced in February 2008 that the Rudd government would fulfill an election promise and initiate a new Defence White Paper. Initiating such a review is not surprising given the turnover of government from the Liberal Party to the Labor Party. A Ministerial Advisory Panel has been formed to provide external advice consisting of Professor Ross Babbage, Major General Peter Abigail (ret.), and Dr. Mark Thompson.[7]

There has been a long standing debate in Australian defense planning circles over the relative emphasis on continental defense of Australia and the need to configure Australian forces to integrate with key allies in expeditionary operations — traditionally with Great Britain and, since the end of World War Two, the United States. Despite this debate, there has been much continuity in practice, especially with regard to support for Australia's commitments to the Australia-New Zealand-United States (ANZUS) alliance.

Key analysts have speculated that the new Defense White Paper will emphasize the defense of Australia and the ability to lead regional operations. Other issues to be addressed may include contributions to coalition operations with the United States, particularly in the Asia-Pacific, and related interoperability issues. Efforts to curb terrorism and the evolving

---

[3] Russell Trood, "Rudd Needs a Clearer Idea to Stem Growing Disarray," *The Australian*, July 4, 2008.

[4] W. Chong, "Aussie Warning on China's Military Growth," *Straits Times*, July 6, 2007.

[5] Department of Foreign Affairs and Trade, Australia-Japan Joint Declaration on Security Cooperation, March 13, 2007.

[6] Dennis Shanahan, "One Man Band Rudd Risky as China's Mate," [http://www.theaustralian.news.com.au].

[7] The Hon. Joel Fitzgibbon, MP and Minister for Defence, "New Defence White Paper," February 22, 2008.

geopolitics of Northeast Asia will also likely receive emphasis in the document.[8]

Fitzgibbon has committed the government to maintain an annual real three percent increase in defense funding through 2018.[9] It is estimated that this increase will bring Australian defense expenditure up from 2% of GDP to 2.6%.[10] Fitzgibbon has reportedly stated that he believes Australia will go ahead with the $16 billion purchase of the Joint Strike Fighter built by Lockheed Martin in Fort Worth, Texas.[11]

Bilateral Developments with the United States

Secretary of State Rice reaffirmed the close relationship between the United States and Australia during her July 2008 visit to Perth, Australia, where she noted that Australian military contributions in Afghanistan are "tremendously appreciated" and stated "there is no better friend for the United States than Australia."[12] The close relationship with the Rudd government was similarly reaffirmed by Defense Secretary Gates during his February 2008 visit to Australia when he stated, "The bonds of unity that grew from our common heritage and have been strengthened on battlefields around the world are every bit as strong as they have ever been."[13]

The United States and Australia signed a Treaty on Defense Trade Cooperation in September 2007. This treaty is proposed at a time when the United States has found few friends willing to work as closely with it in its efforts to contain militant anti-Western Islamists as Australia has proven to be. The treaty with Australia would need to be ratified by the U. S. Senate to come into force.[14]

Australia and the Environment

Drought in some areas and flooding in other parts of Australia have brought increased focus on the environment by the Australian electorate. The Australian Commonwealth Scientific and Industrial Research Organization (CSIRO) has predicted that new weather patterns will mean that parts of eastern Australia, where most Australians live, will receive only 40% of their past average annual rainfall by 2070.[15] Labor's more proactive stance on environmental issues may have helped Rudd win the last election. One of Rudd's first actions as Prime Minister was to sign the Kyoto Protocol.

Australian Minister for Climate Change and Water, Senator Penny Wong, released the

---

[8] Richard Brabin Smith and Paul Dibb, "Now is the Time for Strategic Priorities," *TheAustralian,* June 7, 2008. For more detailed discussion of the White Paper see Hugh White, "The New Defence White Paper: Why We Need It and What It Needs to Do," *Lowy Institute*, Sydney, April 2008.

[9] "Fitzgibbon Says Hes Committed to Defence Funding," *Australian Associated Press,* July 8, 2008.

[10] J. Irvine, "Treasury Warns on Military Spending," *The Sydney Morning Herald,* July 7,008.

[11] "Fitzgibbon Says JSF Most Likely the Fighter for Australia," *Australian Associated Press,* July 11, 2008.

[12] U.S. State Department, "Rice with Aust. Foreign Minister Smith," July 25, 2008.

[13] States News Service, "Joint Press Conference with Secretary of Defense Robert Gates, Australian Minister of Foreign Affairs Stephen Smith, and Australian Defense Minister Joel Fitzgibbon, States News Service, February 23, 2008.

[14] For more information see CRS Report RS22772, *The U.S.-Australia Treaty on Defense Trade Cooperation,* by Bruce Vaughn.

[15] John Vidal, "Australia Suffers Worst Drought in 1,000 Years," *The Guardian,* November 8, 2006.

Australian Government's Green Paper on a Carbon Pollution Reduction Scheme on July 16, 2008. In releasing the paper, Minister Wong pointed out that Australia is one of the world's hottest and driest places and that Australian agriculture and water supplies are threatened by climate change. The scheme involves emissions trading with government-set limits on how much carbon pollution industry can produce. The government intends on implementing the scheme in 2010.[16]

A key challenge for Australia in implementing the scheme will be addressing Australia's use of coal. Australia has extensive reserves of coal and is thought to have a 200-year supply. Approximately 83% of Australian power comes from coal. This dependence has made Australians some of the highest emitters of carbon on a per capita basis. Australian coal exports are expected to increase by a third over the next five years. This has led some to view Australia as exporting its problem even if it achieves its goal of reducing its own emissions by 60% from 2000 levels.[17]

Soon after taking office the Rudd government indicated that it was considering using naval vessels to track Japanese whaling vessels near Australian waters in order to collect evidence possibly to make a case against Japan's whaling in the International Court of Justice. The Japanese whaling fleet reportedly intended on killing some 1,000 whales, including 50 humpback whales.[18] This pressure on whaling issues with Japan was a departure from the policy orientation of the previous Howard Government that signed a security agreement with Japan in 2007. Developing positive relations with Japan is a priority of the Rudd government despite differences over whaling.

BACKGROUND ON AUSTRALIA

Australia was first inhabited from 40,000 to 60,000 years ago. The Aboriginal people of Australia are the world's oldest continuous culture. Today, they account for only about 1% of Australia's total population. While the Aboriginal population was hunter-gatherers, they developed a complex "dream time" culture, a spiritual culture focusing on connections to ancestors and the Australian landscape. Captain James Cook claimed Australia for Britain in 1770, and in 1788 the first European settlement, largely made up of convicts, was established at Sydney, New South Wales. Australia evolved into a pastoral settler society based on sheep and wool with the increasing importance of minerals following the gold rush beginning in 1851.

While the majority of Australians have British or Irish ancestry, Australia's immigrants also came from elsewhere in Europe particularly after World War II.[19] Today, Australian immigration is increasingly from Asia, with Asians accounting for approximately 7% of the population. Despite the centrality of the "bush" or the "outback" to the national myth, Australia has evolved into a very urbanized society with only 15% living in rural areas.

---

[16] Senator Penny Wong, Minister for Climate Change and Water, Green Paper on Cardon Pollution Reduction Scheme Released, July 16, 2008.

[17] "Greens and the Black Stuff," *The Economist,* July 26, 2008.

[18] Ross Peake. "Cabinet to Focus on Military, Whaling," *The Canberra Times,* December 17, 2007.

[19] In 1947, 89.7% of Australia's population was Anglo-Celtic. By 1988 this had dropped to 74.6%. Department of Immigration and Citizenship, "National Agenda for a Multi-cultural Australia," [http://www.immi.gov]

Australia made major contributions to the allied cause in both the first and second World Wars and has been a staunch ally of Britain and the United States in their conflicts abroad.

Australia at a Glance

Government: Parliamentary democracy and federal state system
Leadership: Prime Minister Kevin Rudd
Head of State: Queen Elizabeth II, who appoints a Governor-General.
Political Parties: Labor, Liberal, National, Greens, Democrats.
Area: About the size of the lower 48 U.S. states
Capital: Canberra, population 323,000
Population: 21 million
Population growth rate: 0.824%
Ethnic groups: Caucasian 92%, Asian 7%, aboriginal and other 1%
Foreign-born population: 23.6%
GDP growth: 4.1% (2007 est.)
GDP per capita ppp: $33,300
Inflation: 2.4%
Unemployment: 4.9%

Sources: CIA *World Factbook*, State Department Background Notes, Economist Intelligence Unit

Australia is slightly smaller than the contiguous lower 48 United States and has a population of some 21 million. Australia's main export partners are China, Japan, South Korea, the United States, and New Zealand. Australia's main exports are coal, iron ore, gold, crude petroleum, and bovine meat. While some 72% of GDP is derived from the services sector, 52% of exports come from mining and agriculture, which together account for 8% of GDP. [20]

Australia is an independent nation within the British Commonwealth. The Head of State is Queen Elizabeth, who is represented by the Governor General, Major General (ret.) Michael Jeffery. In practice, power is held by the Prime Minister and Cabinet, who are elected members of Parliament. Australia has a bicameral parliament composed of a House of Representatives, with 150 members elected by popular preferential ballot, and a Senate, with 76 members. Twelve Senators from each of the six states are elected for six year terms of office. The two territories have two senators each who are elected for three year terms. Parliamentary elections are called by the government but must be held at least once every three years. Voting is mandatory in Australia.[21] The Liberal-National Party coalition and the Labor Party are the two main political forces in Australia.[22] There is a growing Republican movement in Australia that supports breaking with the crown.

Australia has for some time been undergoing a national identity debate related to its relationships with Asia, in which it is geographically situated, and with Britain, the United

[20] "Background Note: Australia," Bureau of East Asian and Pacific Affairs, Department of State, July 2007.
[21] "Background Note: Australia," Bureau of East Asian and Pacific Affairs, Department of State, July 2007.
[22] U.S. Department of State, "Background Note: Australia," December, 2004, and Central Intelligence Agency, "World Factbook, Australia," June, 2005.

States, and Europe, with which it has deep cultural and historical linkages. Australian trade interests are increasingly focused on Asia, and in particular China, while its key strategic relationship is with the United States.[23]

Domestic Political Context

Labor Party leader Kevin Rudd's November 24, 2007 electoral victory over former Prime Minister John Howard, who lost his own parliamentary seat representing Bennelong, marks a significant shift away from the Liberal Party-dominated government that has ruled Australia since 1996. Former Defence Minister Brendan Nelson replaced Howard as leader of the Liberal-National Party Coalition. As Opposition Leader, Nelson has not presented a strong challenge to Rudd. According to a recent poll, only 13% of Australians favor Nelson, as opposed to 68% who favor Rudd. The next federal elections do not have to be held until 2010.[24] The most dramatic political decision brought about by the election thus far is Australia's policy reversal on climate change. Rudd has signed the Kyoto Protocol on Climate Change and stated that he wants Australia to be a leader on climate change policy.[25] Rudd is also expected to change labor policies brought into force by the previous Howard government.

Relations with the United States

Bilateral Ties

The Commonwealth of Australia and the United States are very close allies. Australia shares similar cultural traditions and values with the United States and has been a treaty ally of the United States since the signing of the Australia-New Zealand-United States (ANZUS) Treaty in 1951. Australia has been a strong partner in the global war against terror and its citizens have been the victims of several terrorist attacks. Australia invoked the ANZUS treaty to offer assistance to the United States after the attacks of September 11, 2001, in which 22 Australians were among the dead. Australia was one of the first countries to commit troops to U.S. military operations in Afghanistan and Iraq.

Under former Prime Minister John Howard, the Australian government demonstrated a strong commitment to its alliance with the United States through its contribution of combat troops, including special forces, to Afghanistan and Iraq. Under the leadership of Howard and President Bush, the United States and Australia strengthened at the government-to-government level an already very close relationship between two long-term allies. Shared perspectives on the war against militant Islamists also enhanced this close relationship.

Public attitudes in Australia diverged from the close government-to-government relations under the former Prime Minister. Australians' negative perceptions of President Bush and his policies have adversely affected Australia's perception of the United States. That said, these

[23] For a history of the evolution of Australia's external relations see David Lee, *Australia and the World in the Twentieth Century* (Melbourne: Circa Publishers, 2006).
[24] "Country Report Australia," *The Economist Intelligence Unit*, July 2008.
[25] "Australia to be 'Climate Bridge'," *BBC News*, December 6, 2007.

negative impressions have yet to harm Australians' positive perceptions of their bilateral alliance with the United States.[26] Prime Minister Rudd's government has clearly articulated that it wishes to maintain strong ties with the United States and that it views American engagement in the Asia-Pacific as key to maintaining regional security.[27]

The United States continues to view the bilateral relationship with Australia as one of its closest relationships. Vice President Cheney stated during his February 2007 visit to Australia that "Australians and Americans ... respect and like each other ... never before has our alliance been stronger."[28] Rudd has declared his "passionate" and "rock solid" support of the alliance.[29] President Bush also reaffirmed the strength of the alliance when in Sydney in September 2007.[30]

Bilateral relations across the political spectrum have not always been close. The former leader of the opposition Labor Party, Mark Latham, was criticized by the former Howard Government in the lead-up to the 2004 election for describing President Bush in unfavorable terms and for his intent to withdraw Australian troops from Iraq if elected. In response to Latham's proposed policy, President Bush stated that it would be a "disastrous decision" that would "dispirit those who love freedom in Iraq and embolden the enemies who believe they can shake our will."[31] Many on the left of the Labor party also opposed a free trade agreement (FTA) with the United States.[32] The exchange between Latham and Bush made the ANZUS alliance an election issue in Australia in 2004. Former Deputy Secretary of State Richard Armitage's criticism of Labor's earlier policy on Iraq led former Labor Prime Minister Paul Keating to urge the United States to stay out of Australian elections.

Trilateral Ties

The United States, Japan, and Australia initiated a trilateral security dialogue in 2002. China, the Korean Peninsula, and the war against terror all provide an impetus for security collaboration between these three partners.[33] In May 2005, Secretary of State Rice stated that the dialogue would "intensify" and be elevated to the Ministerial level and would discuss a broad range of regional and global security issues.[34] The announcement came a short time after a series of anti-Japanese demonstrations in China marked a deterioration in the bilateral relationship between Japan and China. The announcement also came soon after Australia had sent a contingent of 450 soldiers to Iraq to protect a group of Japanese engineers based in southern Iraq. Then-Prime Minister Howard stated that "working alongside and in partnership

---

[26] Tim Johnson, "Australians are Split Over the U.S. Poll Finds Many Worried by America's Political Direction," *The New York Times,* December 10, 2007.

[27] "Redrawing the US Alliance, The Rudd Government will Maintain Strong Ties," *Canberra Times,* December 8, 2007.

[28] "Vice President's Remarks with Australian Prime Minister John Howard," Sydney, U.S. Department of State, February 24, 2007.

[29] Ralph Cossa, "U.S. - Australia Still Mates," *PacNet,* December 17, 2008.

[30] President Bush and Australian Prime Minister Howard Discuss U.S.-Australia Defense Trade Cooperation Treaty in Joint Press Availability, Office of the Press Secretary, The White House, September 4, 2007.

[31] "Australia: Friendly Fire," *Far Eastern Economic Review*, July 15, 2004.

[32] Mark Davis, "Latham Faces Party Showdown on FTA," *Financial Review,* July 21, 2005.

[33] A. Searle and I. Kamae, "Anchoring Trilateralism: Can Australia-Japan-US Security Relations Work," *Australian Journal of International Affairs,* December, 2004.

[34] "US Security Talks with Australia, Japan to Intensify," *US Fed News,* May 4, 2005.

with a close regional ally and partner such as Japan is very important from Australia's point of view."[35]Commentary speculated that the deployment had as much to do with bolstering ties with Japan as it did with Iraq.[36] Australia's 2007 Defence Update described Japan as Australia's closest ally in the region.[37]

At the time of the announcement of the elevated trilateral security dialogue there was much speculation that China was to be the central focus of the dialogue. It was reported that "a resurgent China and recalcitrant North Korea" were key issues to be discussed.[38] Nuclear weapons proliferation is also thought to be part of the group's agenda.[39] It was also reported that the move could "revive Chinese concerns about containment by potential strategic competitors." Australia, the United States, Japan, and India formed a core group during the relief effort in the wake of the December 2004 tsunami. One interpretation of the reason Australia and Japan would wish to upgrade the trilateral security dialogue is that there is uncertainty over whether China's rise will generate a more prosperous and stable East Asia or whether China will seek to use East Asian regionalism to exclude the United States, which neither Australia nor Japan would wish to see.[40]

Dr. Rice stated in the lead-up to a 2006 meeting with Australian counterparts that, "I think all of us in the region, particularly those who are longstanding allies, have a joint responsibility and obligation to try and produce conditions in which the rise of China will be a positive force in international politics, not a negative force." Some Australian strategic commentators were concerned that statements by the Secretary of State that portrayed the Trilateral Security Dialogue as directed at containing China may provoke China into a more aggressive posture.[41] Many in Australia value Australia's lucrative trade relationship with China even as they look to the United States as Australia's overwhelmingly most important strategic ally.

Defense

Australia did much to augment its defense capabilities under Howard's leadership, including a 47% real increase in defense spending under his watch.[42] The 2007 defense budget represents a 10.6% increase over 2006. Howard committed his government to a 3% annual real increase in defense spending out to the year 2016. Prime Minister Rudd has similarly pledged support for robust defense expenditures. Keeping the United States engaged in Asia has been a key foreign policy objective of Australia and one that continues to enjoy broad political support.

The annual trilateral ANZUS meeting has been replaced by the Australian-U.S. Ministerial consultations (AUSMIN). The AUSMIN consultations are a key aspect of the now

---

[35] Prime Minister Howard as quoted in "Australia Commits More Troops in Iraq to Safeguard Japanese Forces," *Radio Australia* transcript, February 22, 2005.

[36] Dan Blumenthal, "Strengthening the U.S.-Australian Alliance: Progress and Pitfalls," American Enterprise Institute, April/May, 2005.

[37] W. Chong, "Aussie Warning on China's Military Growth," *Straits Times*, July 6, 2007.

[38] Geoff Elliott, "China and North Korea Focus of New US Security Talks," *The Australian,* May 6, 2005.

[39] "Rice Downer Agree on trilateral Strategic Talks with Japan," *Asian Political News,* May 9, 2005.

[40] "Three Against One," *South China Morning Post*, May 11, 2005.

[41] "Rice to Make First Visit as Secretary of State," *Australian Associated Press,* March 14, 2006.

[42] The Honorable Brendan Nelson, Minister for Defense, "Defence Update 2007 - Protecting Our People, Interests, and Values," July 5, 2007.

defacto bilateral alliance relationship under what was a trilateral Australia-New Zealand-United States (ANZUS) alliance. Differences over New Zealand's nuclear policies in the mid 1980s led New Zealand to be de facto excluded from the alliance. The 2008 AUSMIN meeting focused on issues such as the need to work together to promote regional prosperity and security, to increase broad-based engagement with Indonesia, and to encourage China to adopt a transparent approach to its military modernization. The meeting also noted the further deepening of bilateral defense cooperation through the earlier signing of the U.S.-Australia Treaty on Defense Trade Cooperation.[43] The two countries cooperate extensively in the area of intelligence and operate early warning and intelligence joint facilities at Pine Gap and Nurrungar.[44] The decision to work with the U.S. on missile defense is part of a larger decision by Australia to continue a close connection with U.S. military strategy and operations.

In recent years, defense policy makers in Australia have asked if the traditional underpinnings of Australian defense planning and capability development — defense of Australia, operations in the region and coalition warfare — "still provide a sufficiently firm but flexible foundation for planning and capability development, particularly when addressing today's threats."[45] Australia has sought to configure its defense force for both continental defense and maneuver warfare.[46] Australia's evolving strategy increasingly takes a global as well as regional view of threats to Australia. As a result, Australia is placing increasing importance on forces that are suitable for joint operations and expeditionary warfare at locations distant from Australia, such as Iraq and Afghanistan, as well as regional deployments in East Timor and the Solomon Islands. Australia has a close arms procurement relationship with the United States.[47]

Counterterror Cooperation

Australia was the first country to offer its armed services to the International Coalition Against Terrorism (ICAT) and has sent rotations of special forces troops plus regular troops to Afghanistan. The former Howard government supported the United States in Iraq by sending about 2,000 defense personnel, F/A-18, P-3 and C-130 aircraft, two ANZAC Frigates, and a special forces task group.[48] Australia has also joined the U.S.-sponsored Proliferation Security Initiative (PSI). The PSI's aim is to interdict aircraft and ships that could be carrying weapons of mass destruction, missiles, or drugs. This staunch support stems from Australia's desire to support its treaty ally and from a shared perspective on Islamist extremist violence.

On October 12, 2002, two bombs decimated two crowded nightclubs full of foreign tourists in Bali, Indonesia, killing more than 200 foreigners and Indonesians and injuring over

---

[43] "Australia-United States Ministerial Consultations, 2008 Joint Communique," [http://www.dfat.gov.au].

[44] For a more detailed discussion of the Australia-U.S. defense relationship see Thomas Durrell-Young, "The Nuanced Australia-U.S. Defense Relationship," Woodrow Wilson International Center for Scholars, Asia Program, June 1, 2005.

[45] Ministry of Defense, *Australia's National Security: A Defense Update* (Canberra: Commonwealth of Australia, 2003).

[46] Paul Monk, "Revolution in Defence," *The Financial Review*, July 8, 2005.

[47] "US Calls on Canberra to Play Role Outside Asia-Pacific," *Australia Radio,* Australian Broadcasting Corporation, February 7, 2006.

[48] "Operation Falconer,"Australian Department of Defense, [http://www.defence.gov.au].

300. There were 88 Australians among the dead and seven Americans. Indonesian officials attributed the bombing to the militant Islamic network Jemaah Islamiya (JI), which has links to Al Qaeda. JI also carried out an attack against the Australian Embassy in Jakarta in September 2004 and a second attack in Bali in October 2005. Some within JI have reportedly set as their goal the establishment of an Islamic state that encompasses Indonesia, Malaysia, the Southern Philippines, and Northern Australia. Australian and Indonesian counterterror cooperation has improved as a result of cooperation on the investigation into the Bali blasts. Australia has signed anti-terrorism pacts with a number of its Southeast Asian neighbors. It also provides counterterror support to the Pacific Island Forum Secretariat.[49] (For further discussion of Australia's role in the war against terror, see CRS Report RL31672, Terrorism in Southeast Asia, coordinated by Bruce Vaughn.)

Afghanistan

The new Labor government's Defence Minister Joel Fitzgibbon has stated that "we are winning the battles and not the war" in Afghanistan. Australia has indicated that new tactics are needed to bring stability and has called on NATO countries to increase their commitment to Afghanistan. Australia has approximately 1,000 troops stationed in Afghanistan, mostly in Oruzgan Province.[50]

Iraq

Prime Minister Rudd has long stated that he intends to draw down Australian combat troops in Iraq.[51] Although Australia has provided combat support to U.S. operations in Iraq and Afghanistan since the beginning of U.S. involvement in these conflicts, it is now shifting emphasis away from Iraq. Australian Defence Minister Fitzgibbon recently explained Australia's decision to reduce its military commitment to Iraq by stating that its obligations had

> ... left us with insufficient ability to deal with contingencies in our own immediate region, where we need to be constantly in readiness to deal with issues which may arise among the fragile states of the South Pacific — the so called arc of instability.[52]

Although Australia will leave P-3 Orion aircraft and an Australian frigate in the Persian Gulf, the drawdown of its military commitment marks a shift in policy emphasis away from Iraq.

Economic and Trade Issues

According to some observers, Australia's economic strategy can be described as a mix of both Asian regionalism, in which China is increasingly assuming a prominent role, and globalism.[53] Australia has prospered in recent years due to a significant extent on exports of

---

[49] Minister for Foreign Affairs Downer, "Counter-Terrorism Package," March 7, 2003.

[50] Patrick Walters, "We're Losing the War in Afghanistan," *The Australian,* December 17, 2007.

[51] "Australia Warns of NATO Failure in Afghanistan," *Voice of America,* December 17, 2007.

[52] "Troops Needed in Our Region," *Sydney Morning Herald,* July 16, 2008.

[53] Michael Evans, "US-Australia Relations in Asia," Woodrow Wilson Center Asia Seminar, June 1, 2005.

commodities to Asia. An estimated 52% of Australian exports are derived from agriculture and mining.[54] This is particularly so in the state of Western Australia because of the mining industry. The national economy is now slowing from an estimated GDP growth rate of 4.3% in 2007 to a projected 2.7% in 2008. The Australian dollar — which was close to a 24-year high in June 2008 — is expected to decrease in value as higher interest rates and increasing fuel costs are undermining consumer confidence.[55] As of 2006, Australia's key export partners were Japan (19.6%), China (12.3%), South Korea (7.5%), the United States (6.2%), New Zealand (5.5%), and the United Kingdom (5%).[56] The Australia-United States Free Trade Agreement (AUSFTA) came into force on January 1, 2005. The United States is Australia's major economic partner with overall trade in goods and services reaching approximately $47 billion in 2007.[57]

While Australia's economy is dominated by its services sector, the agricultural, mining, and energy sectors account for the bulk of its exports. Among its largest export items are coal, gold, iron ore, aluminum, mineral fuels, meat, and wheat. The Australian economy and balance of trade are strongly influenced by world prices for primary products. In recent decades Australia has been progressively opening up its economy. Infrastructure development and climate change are viewed as two key issues of importance to continued economic growth. Australian droughts have worsened in recent years and are predicted to continue to get worse in years ahead. The Australian economy experienced real growth of 2.6% in 2006 and an estimated 4.1% in 2007. The newly elected Rudd government has pledged to restore some labor union rights to collective bargaining for workers. China's rapid growth and steady demand in Japan are expected to provide a favorable external trade environment for Australia.[58]

Australia is also seeking an FTA with China. It is estimated that an FTA with China would significantly increase Australia's GDP. Chinese Premier Wen Jiabao stated that an FTA was expected in two years during his April 2006 visit to Australia.[59] Australia and China signed an agreement on the export of uranium from Australia to China in April 2006.[60] The pace of negotiations reportedly has been slow. China and Australia held their 11th round of negotiations in June 2008.[61]

ASIA-PACIFIC AFFAIRS

Australia's Identity and Asia

Australia's identity as a nation is intertwined with its ongoing debate over how it should

[54] Bureau of East Asian and Pacific Affairs, Department of State, "Background Note: Australia," February 2008.
[55] "Country Report Australia," *The Economist Intelligence Unit*, July 2008.
[56] "Australia," *CIA World Factbook*, July 15, 2008.
[57] Australian Minister for Trade, The Hon. Simon Crean MP, "Australia-U.S. Ministerial Trade Talks," June 3, 2008.
[58] "Australia: Country Report," *The Economist Intelligence Unit,* December 2007.
[59] "China, Australia Make Significant Free Trade Progress," *Mineweb,* April 7, 2006.
[60] Geoff Hiscock, "Australia, China Sign Uranium Deal," *CNN,* April 3, 2006.
[61] Department of Foreign Affairs and Trade, Government of Australia, "Australia-China FTA Negotiations," June, 2008.

engage Asia. Former Prime Minister Howard approached the debate by making the point that Australia need not choose between its history, which is grounded in the West, and its geography, which locates Australia on the periphery of the Asia-Pacific region. Former Labor Prime Minister Paul Keating (1991-1996) moved enthusiastically to engage Asia, building on his predecessor Bob Hawke's (1983-1991) efforts that included the formation of the Asia Pacific Economic Cooperation (APEC) forum in 1989. Many in Australia viewed Keating's initiatives as going too far, reflecting the fact that many Australians' sense of identity was not grounded in an "Asian" identity.

These debates over identity are real to Australians. Although Australia is a large continent, its population of only 21 million people is located relatively close to key population centers of Asia, including Indonesia, China, and India. Australia's isolation from its key cultural partners and strategic allies in the West has led traditionally to an existential fear of being overwhelmed by Asia. This has given way in recent years to increasing interest in Asia as it is viewed as a source of prosperity and no longer only as a potential threat. The Rudd government's decision to extend an apology to the Aboriginal population of Australia demonstrates that the dominant Anglo-Celtic identity is increasingly prepared to accommodate non-white Australian identities. Increasing Asian immigration is also changing the face of Australia. Australia's shifting trade patterns have drawn it to Asia even as it has not reconciled itself with what this means for its identity.

The evolving regional and global strategic landscape has led many in Australia to begin to re-conceptualize the role of geography in Australian external and security relations. While it remains to be seen how Kevin Rudd's leadership will shape Australia's engagement with Asia, the Howard Administration consistently took the position that Australia does not have to choose between its history and its geography, meaning that it can engage Asia while maintaining close ties to Western liberal democracies with similar values.[62] Australia has in the past relied on concepts such as the defense of Australia, self-reliance within an alliance framework, forward defense, and forward engagement, all of which relied to a large extent on Australia's geography and/or its historical ties to great and powerful friends and allies.

Australia is now adapting these concepts to integrate a regional Asia-Pacific outlook and a global perspective in an effort to maximize its national interests. This evolving posture is largely the outcome of a number of key recent events that have shaped how Australia perceives the external environment, the most significant of which are: the rise of China; the Asian financial crisis of 1997 and its political impact on the region; Australia's East Timor intervention of 1999 and increasing instability in Southeast Asia and the Southwest Pacific; the war against terror and deployments to Afghanistan and Iraq; and the Bali bombings of 2002 and 2005 and the bombing of the Australian Embassy in Jakarta in 2004. Many of these events had significant global as well as regional dimensions.[63]

The former Howard government's central foreign policy tenet, that Australia does not have to choose between its history and geography, is now viewed by many as undergoing a

[62] For a recent discussion of Australian foreign policy see Alexander Downer, "Securing Australia's Interests Australian Foreign Policy Priorities," *Australian Journal of International Affairs*, March, 2005.

[63] See Michael Evans, "US-Australia Relations in Asia," Woodrow Wilson Center Asia Seminar, June 1, 2005, and Allan Gyngell, "Australia's Emerging Global Role," *Current History,* March, 2005, for excellent discussions of these events and their impact on Australian strategic thought.

significant test as Australia's strategic relations may increasingly be at odds with Australia's trade interests. Southeast Asian terrorism, with its linkages to global terrorism, and the potential disintegration of unstable states to the north of Australia, such as the Solomon Islands, East Timor, and Papua New Guinea, are key security interests for Australia that compel Australia to play an active role in promoting regional security in tandem with American regional interests. Although Australia does not see conflict between the United States and China as inevitable, such a conflict would make Australia's position with China more difficult.

Australia's Asian Engagement

Although Australia has increasingly recognized the need for close relations with Asia, it has tried not to emphasize these ties at the expense of its Western roots and democratic values. Australian governments have traditionally sought to keep the United States closely involved in East Asia and the Pacific. Some Asian countries have welcomed the strengthened U.S.-Australian defense relationship, but others, notably China, have been less supportive. Beijing strategists are thought by some to be concerned that strengthening of the U.S. alliances with Australia and Japan may be aimed at "containing" China. Some have argued that greater Australian support of the United States may undermine Australia's efforts to engage Asia at a deeper level.[64]

Rudd's Asia-Pacific Community Concept

In June 2008, Prime Minister Rudd put forward an inclusive vision for an Asia-Pacific Community that would include the United States, China, Japan, India, and Indonesia as well as other regional states as a way of shaping the evolving regional architecture of Asia. The group would discuss political and security issues as well as economic issues.[65] Rudd's initiative has been criticized by some for not consulting with regional leaders before it was announced.[66] The proposal was not overly well received in Southeast Asia and Malaysia came out against the concept.[67] It appeared that India gave Rudd cautious support for the concept.[68] Rudd's proposal now joins other proposed Asian architectures including the East Asia Summit, APEC, Association of Southeast Asian Nations (ASEAN) plus three, and the ASEAN Regional Forum. Rudd's concept differs from these most significantly in that it includes the United States and India and would address political and security issues as well as economic issues.[69]

---

[64] Derek McDougall, "Australia and Asia-Pacific Security Regionalism: From Hawke and Keating to Howard," *Contemporary Southeast Asia* (Singapore), April, 2001.

[65] Stephen Loosely, "Pacific Allies Must Foster an Asian Regional Dialogue," *The Australian,* June 20, 2008.

[66] David McLennan, "Rudd Plan for Asian Community Written Off," *Canberra Times*, July 4, 2008.

[67] "History Repeats as Malaysia Cool to Aust Asia-Pacific Idea," *Australian Associated Press,* July 11, 2008.

[68] "FM Mukherjee Supports Australian Proposal to Form Asia-Pacific Community," *The Times of India*, June 8, 2008.

[69] Rory Medcalf, "Rudd's Asian Aria Sounds Familiar," *Australian Financial Review*, June 10, 2008.

Indonesia

Indonesia's geographic proximity and size make good relations with Jakarta a key foreign policy priority for Australia. While Australia's relationship with Indonesia has at times been troubled, as was the case as a result of Indonesians' displeasure over Australia's role in East Timor's independence, relations are at present positive. The strategic aspect of the relationship is defined by the 2006 Lombok Treaty as well as a recently renewed Memorandum of Understanding on Combating International Terrorism.[70] Many Australians were killed in the 2002 Bali bombing carried out by the Jemaah Islamiya terrorist group. The Australian Embassy in Jakarta was also bombed in 2004 and a second terrorist attack struck Bali in 2005. Australia will provide Indonesia with an estimated AD $462 million in official development assistance in 2008-2009.[71]

Australia and Indonesia have experienced difficulties, as well as successes, in their bilateral relationship in recent years. Tensions over temporary asylum granted by Australia to a number of West Papuans have been of particular concern to Indonesia. An April 2006 poll in Australia found 75% of Australians favoring self-determination for West Papua.[72] Such tensions have occurred even as bilateral cooperation on counterterrorism and security has improved.[73] Indonesian fears over Australia's role in the Indonesian provinces on the western half of the island of Papua New Guinea can be better understood in context of the recent independence of East Timor, which was formerly an Indonesian province. Australia, under the United Nations, played a key role in assisting East Timor to become an independent nation. The East Timor intervention was viewed negatively in Indonesia and led to the end of the previous Agreement on Mutual Security between Canberra and Jakarta.[74] Australia and Indonesia resumed joint military exercises with an air force exercise held in April 2005.[75]

In November 2007, the Indonesian Peoples Representatives Council ratified a security treaty, previously ratified by the Australian parliament, which was signed in Lombok, West Nusa Tenggara, by former Foreign Minister Alexander Downer and Foreign Minister Hassan Wirajuda. The treaty recognizes Indonesian sovereignty over West Papua.[76] In December 2004, Australia announced a decision to provide AD$20 million to Indonesia for counterterror assistance over the next five years.[77] Australia's generous post-2004 tsunami assistance also improved relations between Australia and Indonesia.

China

Prime Minister Rudd will likely continue to develop Australia's trade and political relations with China. Australia and China commenced a bilateral Strategic Dialogue in February 2008. Rudd, a former diplomat who speaks Mandarin, is likely to carefully balance his approach to China with Australian values. Rudd reportedly took up the issue of Tibet

---

[70] Hon Stephen Smith MP, Minister for Foreign Affairs, "Launch of Australian Strategic Policy Institute Strategy Report on Indonesia," May 27, 2008 Parliament House, Canberra.

[71] Department of Foreign Affairs and Trade, "Indonesia Country Brief," June 2008. In August 2008, the Australian dollar was worth approximately 87 U.S. cents.

[72] "Howard Rejects Papua Poll," *Canberra Times,* April 20, 2006.

[73] "Indonesia's Rift with Australia," *Sydney Morning Herald,* April 21, 2006.

[74] Richard Woolcott, "Foreign policy priorities for the Howard Government's Fourth Term," *Australian Journal of International Affairs,* June, 2005.

[75] "Australia and Indonesia Hold First Military Exercise for Six Years," *Oster Dow Jones,* April 12, 2005.

[76] "Indonesian Parliament Approves Papua Sovereignty Treaty with Australia," *BBC News,* November 29, 2007.

[77] Adianto Simamora, "Terrorism Bolsters Australia's Ties with Indonesia," *The Jakarta Post,* December 28, 2005.

during his April 2008 visit to China.[78] Rudd prefers a "practical" approach to China that will not alarm Beijing as was reportedly the case with an earlier proposal to develop a quadrilateral security architecture consisting of the United States, Japan, Australia, and India in 2007. In this way, some in Asia view Australia under Rudd as more independent of the United States than it was under Howard.[79]

One of the most significant changes in Australia's external relations, and one with potential implications for the bilateral relationship with the United States, is Australia's growing relationship with China. Australia's trade with China has more than tripled over the past decade.[80] There is a debate in Australia on whether Australia's growing trade ties with China will lead Australia to have to choose between economic engagement with China and its close strategic relationship with the United States. Australia has taken the position that China's rise has come with "a growing understanding that its continued development and future prosperity depends on maintaining a stable regional and international environment."[81] In 2006, Australia-China merchandise trade was $34.6 billion while Australia-U.S. trade was $26.1 billion.[82] There is little enthusiasm in Australia for what is perceived as an increasingly tough policy stance on China by some in Washington.[83]

While it remains to be seen where Rudd will take Australia's China policy, it may have much continuity with the previous government's approach. The government of former Prime Minister Howard favored a policy of engagement with China. His Foreign Minister Alexander Downer stated that "a policy of containment of China would be a very big mistake." This view reflects concern in Australia that more hawkish elements of the U.S. security community may seek a shift of U.S. policy away from "pragmatic constructive engagement to a more confrontational position" toward China.[84] Other areas of policy departure with the United States include Australia's April 2006 agreement to sell uranium to China and Canberra's reluctance to condemn the European Union's move to lift its arms embargo of China in 2005.[85] Australia has 40% of the world's known uranium reserves.[86]

In August of 2004, Foreign Minister Downer, in response to a question on whether the ANZUS alliance applied to a potential conflict with China over Taiwan, stated that the treaty would not automatically be invoked.[87] Some have described the Downer statement on Taiwan as a "radical restatement of Australian policy while others have passed it off as gaffe."[88] Former Prime Minster Howard warned against taking the pessimistic view that conflict between America and China is inevitable and has stated that "we see ourselves as having a role in continually identifying, and advocating to each, the shared strategic interests these great powers (the United States and China) have in regional peace and prosperity." [89]

---

[78] Michael Fullilove, "Rudd Steps Out Into the World with Elan," *Sydney Morning Herald,* July 14, 2008.
[79] P.S. Suryanarayana, "Australia: A Free Thinking Ally of the U.S.," *The Hindu,* June 16, 2008.
[80] Janaki Kremmer, "How Trade May Corral Australia's Sheriff," *Christian Science Monitor,* June 8, 2005.
[81] Minister for Foreign Affairs, Alexander Downer, "Australia and China's Shared Interests -Security and Strategic Dimensions," August 13, 2004.
[82] "Australia Trade Data," *World Trade Atlas,* 2006.
[83] Tony Pratt, "Caught in the Middle," *Financial Review,* May 6, 2005.
[84] Patrick Walters, "Containing China a Big Mistake," *The Australian,* March 16, 2006.
[85] Brendan Nicholson and Orietta Guerrera, "Embrace China, Downer Tells U.S." *The Age,*March 16, 2006.
[86] Barry Hing, "China's Pacific Power Play," *The Straits Times,* April 6, 2006.
[87] Peter Jennings, "Australia's Regional Diplomacy Challenge," *Financial Review*, April 30, 2005.
[88] Greg Sheridan, "Chinese Human Rights Abuse a No-go Zone," *The Australian*, June 25, 2005.
[89] Hugh White, "US May Play Hardball with Australia Over China Ties," *The Straits Times,*April 16, 2005 and Hugh White, "Howard's Asian Balancing Act," *The Age*, April 13, 2005.

Japan

Under Howard, the Canberra-Tokyo relationship was taken to a new degree of closeness through the Japan-Australia Joint Declaration on Security Cooperation. This reinforced security ties already established through the Trilateral Security Dialogue among the United States, Japan, and Australia. Australian Minister of Foreign Affairs Stephen Smith claimed recently that Japan has been Australia's "closest and most consistent friend in our region for many years."[90] Some in Japan are reportedly concerned that Rudd's government will place Australia's relationship with China ahead of its relationship with Japan.[91] Australian exports to Japan fell 2.5% from 2006 to 2007. Despite this, Japan remained Australia's largest export market.[92]

Relations initially were not as close as they were under Howard as the Rudd government pressed Japan to curb its whaling in the Southern Ocean. Despite a rough start, relations have improved in recent months. Rudd has sought to portray tensions over Japan's whaling as "disagreement between friends" that was not likely to "undermine in any way the strong and positive nature of our bilateral relationship." [93]During Prime Minister Rudd's June 2008 visit to Japan, he and Prime Minister Yasuo Fukuda issued a Joint Statement on Comprehensive Strategic, Security, and Economic Partnership which signaled the intention of the two governments to continue cooperation in a broad range of policy areas. [94]

India

Minister for Foreign Affairs Stephen Smith has stated that "While many commentators have been focusing on the rise of China, not enough attention has been paid to the rise of India.... As the world sees the potential of an Asian/Pacific century unfold, Australia sees India at the heart of this historic shift in political and economic influence." At the core of Australia's relationship with India is expanding trade. Australian trade with India has been expanding by 30% per year over the past five years. India and Australia have initiated a Free Trade Agreement feasability study. The Rudd government believes India should have a permanent seat on the United Nations Security Council.[95] Australian Defence Minister Joel Fitzgibbon has stated that maritime security and counterterror cooperation are potential areas for cooperation between India and Australia.[96] Foreign Minister Smith has reiterated the Rudd government's position that it will not lift a ban on uranium sales to India.[97] The Rudd government reversed the former Howard government's decision to sell uranium to India because India is not a signatory to the Nuclear Non-Proliferation Treaty.[98]

---

[90] Stephen Smith, MP, Minister for Foreign Affairs, "A Modern Australia for a New Era," Sydney April 9, 2008.

[91] Daniel Flitton and K. Murphy, "Rudd's Arrival at G8 to renew Japanese Ties," *The Age,* July 8, 2008.

[92] Department of Foreign Affairs and Trade, Government of Australia, "Japan Country Brief," July 2008.

[93] "Australia's PM Visit to Japan and Indonesia Reaffirms Bilateral Relationships," *Global Insight*, June 13, 2008.

[94] Department of Foreign Affairs and Trade, Government of Australia, "Japan Country Brief," July 2008.

[95] The Hon. Stephen Smith MP, Minister for Foreign Affairs, "India: A New Relationship for a New Century," Department of Foreign Affairs and Trade, [http://www.foreignminister. gov.au]

[96] P.S. Suryanarana, "Australia for Practical Military Cooperation with India," *The Hindu,* June 3, 2008.

[97] "No Uranium But Australia Wants Strong Ties with India," *Indo-Asian News Service,* June 20, 2008.

[98] "Rann Refuses to Back Sale of Uranium to India," *ABC News*, June 11, 2008.

Regional Dynamics in the Southwest Pacific

Kevin Rudd has made it clear that he wishes to place relatively more emphasis on Australia's relationship with the Southwest Pacific, a region in Australia's immediate neighborhood. Australia has led peace-keeping efforts in the region, including East Timor and the Solomon Islands. These actions demonstrate Australia's resolve to promote stability in the South Pacific. Rudd has already sought to improve relations with Papua New Guinea and has traveled to East Timor, where he promised that Australian troops will remain through 2008 to help maintain security.[99]

East Timor

Australia's commitment to regional security and humanitarian concerns in the Asia-Pacific region was demonstrated by its involvement in East Timor. The former Portuguese colony was occupied by Indonesia from 1975 to 1999. In 1998, diplomatic intervention by Prime Minister Howard prompted the dialogue between Indonesian officials and East Timorese nationalists that resulted in an agreement to hold U.N.-supervised elections in 1999. On August 30, 1999, nearly 80% of East Timor's electorate voted to separate from Indonesia. Following the announcement of the result, anti-independence militias launched a campaign of violence. On September 15, 1999, the U.N. Security Council authorized the International Force East Timor (INTERFET) to restore peace and security and protect and support the U.N. mission personnel in East Timor. INTERFET operated under a unified command structure headed initially by Australia. East Timor became independent in 2002.[100]

Australia and East Timor have reached an agreement for the exploitation of energy resources beneath the Timor Sea. It has been estimated that East Timor will receive up to $15 billion in revenue over the next 40 years in oil and gas royalties.[101] In 2004 and 2005 some Members of the U.S. Congress expressed concern over Australia's position on negotiating its maritime boundary with East Timor and arrangements for joint exploitation of energy resources in the Timor Sea. Australia had previously negotiated a delineation of the border with Indonesia that was more favorable to Australia. Australia and East Timor have agreed to postpone final demarcation of their maritime boundary.

The Solomon Islands

Australia's Regional Assistance Mission to the Solomon Islands demonstrates Australia's resolve to reassert its influence and promote stability in the South Pacific. Australia headed a multinational force to restore order in the Solomons in 2003. In April 2006 it once again sent a quick reaction force to the Solomons to quell rioting and violence following the election of Prime Minister Snyder Rini.[102] These interventions, when taken in the context of Australia's involvement in East Timor and ongoing efforts to promote peace and good governance in Papua New Guinea, demonstrate Australia's commitment to promote stability in the region in order to prevent countries from slipping into anarchy. Australia has also proposed that the smaller of the South Pacific microstates pool their resources for their common good.

---

[99] Michelle Grattan, "Troops Will Stay, PM Promises," *The Age,* December 15, 2007.

[100] "Australian PM Hints at Long-term Military Presence in East Timor," *BBC Monitoring Service*, June 19, 2003.

[101] "Turning Timor Oil Into Prosperity," *The Sydney Morning Herald*, July 11, 2005 and "East Timor PM Says Gas Deal with Australia is Fair," *BBC News*, July 8, 2005.

[102] John Kerin, "Flying Squad to Quell Solomons Riots," *Financial Review,* April 20, 2006.

Treaty of Amity and Cooperation and East Asian Summit

Australia, which has in the past been viewed by some as America's "Deputy Sheriff" in the region, signed the Treaty of Amity and Cooperation, which enabled it to participate in the East Asian Summit (EAS) in Malaysia in December 2005. The EAS is a grouping that includes the 10 ASEAN states plus China, Japan, and South Korea (known as the "plus three" states) and Australia, New Zealand, and India. When a similar grouping, without Australia or New Zealand, was previously proposed as the East Asian Economic Caucus (EAEC) by former Malaysian Prime Minister Mahathir, the United States was reportedly able to thwart the concept and instead champion the Asia Pacific Economic Cooperation (APEC) grouping with Australia.

Previously, the Howard Government had opposed signing the Treaty of Amity and Cooperation but reportedly signed the treaty to be included in the regional grouping. Australia had not wanted to sign the treaty, which binds members to a policy of non-interference and non-aggression, because of concerns that it might interfere with Australia's ANZUS commitments or Australia's policy of preemption against terrorist attack.[103] The Howard Government supported the U.S. policy of preemption and since the Bali bombing has reserved the right to act preemptively to neutralize terrorist threats to Australia.[104] The inclusion of Australia, New Zealand, and India appears to have been the result of some ASEAN states' preference for more expansive membership to balance the influence of China.

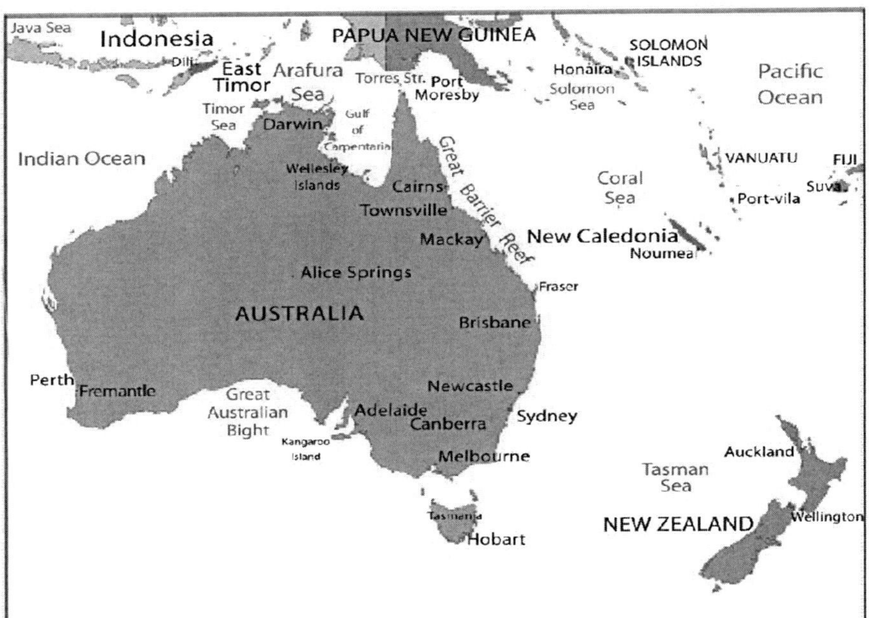

Figure 1. Map of Australia

Source: Map Resources. Adapted by CRS.

[103] Tim Johnson, "Ultimatum to Australia Over Summit," *Financial Times,* April 13, 2005 and Marian Wilkinson, "Invitation off Limits Until Howard Comes to the Party on Treaty," *Sydney Morning Herald,* April 9, 2005.

[104] Anthony Smith, "Still Great Mates: Australia and the United States," *Asian Affairs*, Summer, 2003.

INDEX

A

B

C

D

F

G

H

I

J

N

Q

R

S

T

U

V